Scots Law
for
Journalists

FIFTH EDITION

ERIC M. CLIVE, M.A., LL.B., LL.M., S.J.D.,
Member of the Scottish Law Commission,
formerly Professor of Scots Law at the University of Edinburgh

GEORGE A. WATT, M.B.E.,
Former Court of Session Correspondent
of the *Glasgow Herald*

and

BRUCE McKAIN, LL.B.,
Law Correspondent of the *Glasgow Herald*

EDINBURGH
W. GREEN & SON LTD.
ST. GILES STREET
1988

First Published March 1965
Second Edition 1969
Third Edition 1976
Fourth Edition 1984
Fifth Edition 1988

© Eric M. Clive, George A. Watt
and Bruce McKain

ISBN 0 414 00814 6

Computerset by
Promenade Graphics Limited, Cheltenham
Printed in Great Britain by
Martin's of Berwick

FOREWORD
by
The Right Hon. The Lord Emslie, M.B.E.
Lord President of the Court of Session and
Lord Justice-General of Scotland

I AM delighted to be allowed to write a brief Foreword to the fifth edition of *Scots Law for Journalists*. This is a work of considerable importance and the authors are to be congratulated on maintaining the high quality attained in the fourth and earlier editions. It reads easily and clearly and affords to journalists generally, and to court reporters in particular, the background knowledge of the legal system of Scotland which they ought to possess, and sound advice, based on long experience, on how best to fulfil their role without hindrance to the ends of justice.

As I said in my Foreword to the fourth edition, it is in the best interests of the courts that what they do, and how they do it, should be as widely known as possible. If the public is to retain confidence in the judicial process it must be kept constantly aware of the problems which the judges are called upon to resolve and, perhaps more importantly, the reasons for decisions affecting the lives, liberty and rights of the people in this country which they are bound to take in compliance with the judicial oath. Few members of the public are able to attend trials and other proceedings in court to see for themselves and we, in the Judiciary, have come to rely upon court reporters to provide what I regard as a vital link between the courts and the people whom they exist to serve. The task of the journalists is not an easy one. Not only must they be informed observers of the events which they record for publication, they must in all they do be accurate, balanced and sensitive. This, the fifth edition of *Scots Law for Journalists*, is bound to simplify their task, and I would expect it to be required reading for reporters and editors generally. I would also commend the book to the legal profession, because it is important that all of us should understand clearly the objectives of the good court reporter and the problems which he faces in achieving them.

Edinburgh   EMSLIE
December 15, 1987

PREFACE TO THE FIFTH EDITION

This book, which originated under the aegis of the National Council for the Training of Journalists, combines two aims—to provide an introductory guide to the Scottish legal system and Scottish law as it affects the media, primarily for the use of trainee journalists and to give an outline of essential law and practice required by those engaged in court reporting and investigative journalism in Scotland. The work thus serves the dual purpose of a textbook for those studying for the examinations preliminary to the NCTJ proficiency test and a standard reference book for working journalists. Subjects are indexed by paragraph numbers.

This edition, besides bringing up to date many matters of detail across the ever-expanding range of aspects of the law which concern journalists and publishers, introduces a number of new subjects brought into prominence by recent developments in Parliament and the courts. These include a consideration of the law as it applies to leaked information, new judicial support for the media's right to quote from documents not read out in court, improved access to local authority meetings, the impact on journalists of the Data Protection Act 1986, the rapid growth of judicial review in Scotland, the workings of the European Court of Justice and the European Court of Human Rights, and a discussion of the new phenomenon of "adjectival racism" in the context of some recent adjudications of the Press Council.

The convenient, sometimes misused, term "media", where it appears, is intended here to cover all forms of mass information dissemination. References to the High Court relate to the High Court of Justiciary, the English High Court of Justice being given its full designation, to avoid confusion.

The law is stated as at November 25, 1987.

CONTENTS

Part I

THE LEGAL FRAMEWORK

Part II

THE COURT REPORTER

Part III

DEFAMATION

PART IV

COPYRIGHT

PART V

THE PUBLIC AND THE PRIVATE

PART VI

MISCELLANEOUS STATUTORY PROVISIONS

Part I

THE LEGAL FRAMEWORK

CHAPTER 1

INTRODUCTION

1. It must be emphasised at the outset that Scots law is a distinct system. It is based largely on Roman law while English law, on the other hand, is essentially a home-grown product. This difference was preserved by the Act of Union of 1707 which provided that no alteration was to be made in Scottish private law "except for the evident utility of the subjects within Scotland."

2. Today, however, the laws of the two countries are much more similar than they were in 1707. There is a constant tendency towards assimilation. Much legislation applies to the whole United Kingdom and great stretches of the law, particularly in the fields of taxation and commerce, are the same on both sides of the Border. An important development in the collaborative reform of the two systems began with the setting up in 1965 of the Scottish Law Commission and the Law Commission for England and Wales. The Scottish Law Commission, under section 3(1) of the Law Commissions Act 1965, has the formidable duty of taking and keeping under review all the law of Scotland "with a view to its systematic development and reform." It has a full-time chairman, who is one of the Senators of the College of Justice seconded for a term of five years, and two full-time and two part-time commissioners. In pursuit of its law reform projects it issues consultative documents exploring areas of possible reform, seeks reactions from parties with specialised knowledge as well as from the general public and, where possible and appropriate, prepares draft Bills for submission to Parliament.

3. A new vitality has energised Scots law in recent years which has removed much of the doubt about its ability to survive as a separate entity. In several important respects, indeed, it has led the way both in development of the common law and by statutory example. This revival has been accompanied by growing support for the publication of

Scottish law books, affording Scots lawyers better access to the sources they require for practice, research and teaching. Scotland since 1971 has pioneered and developed the modern shift in the approach to children in trouble, from punishment towards care and protection. The passing of legislation to combat alcohol abuse and crowd violence at sports meetings originated here—as did, centuries earlier, the system of independent local prosecutors under the Crown now emulated in England and Wales. England's abandonment of its insistence upon the unanimous jury verdict goes part-way at least towards acceptance of what has been the position north of the Border for centuries. A central element (so far as the media are concerned) in recent reforms of the law of contempt of court, which permits proper publicity of crime while affording accused persons due protection from unfairness—now enshrined in United Kingdom law—had its origin in a judgment of the High Court of Justiciary. Scotland meanwhile has followed England's example in simplification of divorce procedures, and the constant labours of the two Law Commissions continue the process of cross-fertilisation to the benefit of both systems; but Scots have much less cause than a decade or two ago to fear the assimilation of their legal system into the English. It is clearly able to hold its own and demonstrably to contribute to the improvement of other systems.

4. Whatever lies in the distant future, the present position is that the journalist working in Scotland is governed by Scots law, but may well require to know something of English law as well, particularly where a Scottish publication crosses the Border into the jurisdiction of the English and Welsh courts. The plan adopted in this book is to set out the Scottish position, and to mention the main differences in England where appropriate.

Sources of law

5. There are four main sources of legal rules—legislation, precedents, writers and custom.

6. *Legislation or enacted law* is the first and most important. This includes Acts of Parliament and subordinate legislation made under powers conferred by Parliament. Acts of Parliament may apply to the whole of the United Kingdom or to part of it. Many apply to Scotland alone. Others, such as the Defamation Act, have certain provisions which apply exclusively to Scotland. Subordinate legislation may take the form of Orders in Council (made in theory by the Queen in Council; in fact by the Government), regulations made by Government

Ministers, or rules of procedure made by courts. The term "statutory instruments" is used to describe most such legislation. In Scotland the rules made by the Court of Session to regulate procedure in civil cases are known as "Acts of Sederunt," while the rules made by the High Court of Justiciary for regulating procedure in criminal cases are known as "Acts of Adjournal." Subordinate legislation also includes the bye-laws of local authorities and other bodies.

7. It is important to remember that all legislation must derive its authority, directly or indirectly, from Parliament. There is one exception. In cases of national emergency the Crown can still legislate to some extent by Royal Proclamation.

8. *Precedent or case law* is the second source of legal rules. Any body having to make decisions over a period of time tends to seek consistency. Courts of law are no exception. The decisions and opinions of judges in important cases are recorded in law reports and constitute "precedents" if a similar case arises again.

9. The general rule is that a court is bound to follow a previous decision of itself and any higher court in the same hierarchy. However, the House of Lords, the highest court in a Scottish civil case, does not now regard itself as absolutely bound by its own previous decisions. Within the Court of Session there is a very convenient procedure, not found in England, whereby a case can be referred to a larger court when it is desired to overrule an awkward precedent.

10. Not everything said in a case is equally authoritative. A judge may make incidental comments which are not necessary for the decision of the case before him. Statements made "by the way" in this manner are known as *obiter dicta* and are not binding on other judges.

11. *Writers* are the third source of legal rules. Their authority varies. Some, such as Stair (seventeenth century) and Erskine (eighteenth century), are known as "institutional writers" and enjoy a very high authority in Scotland. English law too has its great writers, such as the eighteenth century Blackstone, but they carry less weight than their Scottish counterparts.

12. *Custom* is a subsidiary source of law. The Scottish institutional writers took customary rules and amalgamated them with Roman law to form a coherent system. Custom thus played an important part in the development of Scots law. In comparatively rare cases custom may still be recognised as a source of law, provided it is certain, fair and not contrary to a definite legal principle. The courts, for example, have applied a custom of the Stock Exchange and a local custom of Caithness regulating the rights of tenants against their landlords.

3

Two meanings of "common law"

13. Common law can mean all law other than enacted law. Thus rules derived solely from custom, precedents and the institutional writers, are rules of common law.

14. Secondly, common law is often used in the sense of "English common law." A common law system is one, like that of Australia, deriving its inspiration from the English common law.

Two meanings of "civil law"

15. Civil law sometimes means Roman law. Thus a civil law system is one, like that of France or, to a lesser degree, Scotland, deriving its inspiration from Roman law. In this sense, civil law is contrasted with the second meaning of common law given above.

16. The term civil law is also, and more frequently, used in contradistinction to criminal law. The civil law is concerned with such matters as divorce, contract, property and actions for damages. The criminal law deals with wrongful acts which are harmful to the community as a whole and which are punished by the State. The same act, for example, careless driving, may give rise to both a criminal prosecution and a civil law claim for damages.

17. In Scotland a distinction is sometimes drawn between crimes and offences, crimes being the more serious, but this distinction is of no real importance. In England crimes are divided into arrestable offences (in relation to which there is power to arrest without warrant) and other offences. The former distinction between felonies and misdemeanours was abolished in 1967.

Private and public law

18. We have already had occasion to use the term private law in quoting from the Act of Union. Broadly speaking private law regulates relations between subject and subject while public law regulates relations between State and subject. The law of divorce is a branch of private law. Criminal law is part of public law.

CHAPTER 2

THE LEGAL PROFESSION

19. We shall deal with judges later, in the context of the courts over which they preside. At sub-judicial level the legal profession, in Scotland, is divided into solicitors and advocates.

20. *Solicitors* deal directly with clients and handle all sorts of legal business. They cannot plead on behalf of a client in the Court of Session except on motion roll during the Vacation or High Court of Justiciary. The privilege of appearing in these and a few other courts is reserved for members of the Faculty of Advocates. Solicitors can, however, appear in the lower courts such as the sheriff court.

21. The solicitor intending to practise must have completed the three or four year university LL.B. course or passed the professional examinations set by the Law Society of Scotland, and also undergone a postgraduate course for one year and passed examinations to enable him to qualify for the Diploma of Legal Practice. The diploma course supplements the degree studies with emphasis on the practical day-to-day aspects of legal practice. This is followed by two years of practical training in a law office. Practising certificates are issued by the Society, the governing body of Scottish solicitors.

22. There are various societies of solicitors whose names may cause confusion. Writers to the Signet (W.S.s) and Solicitors in the Supreme Courts (S.S.C.s) are based in Edinburgh and at one time had special privileges with regard to Court of Session work. Other local societies include the Royal Faculty of Procurators in Glasgow and, particularly confusing, the Society of Advocates in Aberdeen. In spite of the diverse names, members of these societies are simply solicitors. The advantages of membership include widows' pensions and library facilities.

23. Many solicitors are also notaries public (N.P.s). This privilege, obtained by presenting a petition to the Court of Session, enables the solicitor to authenticate certain deeds of a formal nature. The notary public acts as an official witness to important deeds.

24. *Advocates*, also referred to as counsel, are not allowed to deal directly with clients and must, as a rule, rely on solicitors for their cases. The solicitor takes the litigant's instructions, interviews witnesses and does all the background work in the case. The advocate may advise on points of law and frame some of the documents involved but his main function is to plead in court.

25. To be admitted as an advocate an intrant must have passed, or gained exemption from, certain examinations. He must also have completed a period of professional training in a solicitor's office, and a period as a "devil" or, more accurately, pupil to a practising advocate.

26. If the advocate builds up a successful practice he may, after some years, apply to become a Queen's Counsel (Q.C.). This is known as taking silk. He is then a senior counsel and will, as a general rule, appear only in cases where a junior appears with him. He will tend to be engaged in fewer, but more difficult and more rewarding, cases.

27. Advocates are called barristers in England. Their training is in some respects more colourful than that of their northern brethren. They must join one of four Inns of Court and eat a prescribed number of dinners each term for three years—a system surviving from the days when the main part of the barrister's training consisted of discussion with his peers and superiors at table. Nowadays this, valuable as it may be, is supplemented by more formal instruction, culminating in the sitting of the Bar examinations. The traditional monopoly enjoyed by barristers of audience before the English High Court of Justice was for the first time broken when, on May 14, 1986, Mr Leo Abse, M.P., made a brief appearance before Mr Justice Caulfield in London. He read an agreed statement in settlement of a libel action which he and 24 other M.P.s brought against Mr Cyril Smith, M.P., for an alleged statement by him during the Falkland Islands conflict accusing them of treason in opposing the Government. It remains debatable whether Mr Abse was making a significant inroad into the barristers' exclusive right, since he was not actually pleading any cause.

28. Barristers tend to specialise much more than advocates and several of those specialising in a particular field often share one set of chambers and one clerk. In Scotland the system is different. Counsel's chambers are generally in their own houses in Edinburgh. They are not, as in England, in the nature of "offices" shared by a group. In Scotland clerical and secretarial services are provided centrally at Parliament House, Edinburgh (where the Court of Session sits), by a small number of advocates' clerks and by an organisation called Faculty Services Ltd.

6

CHAPTER 3

CRIMINAL COURTS AND PROCEDURE

SCOTTISH CRIMINAL COURTS

Jurisdiction

29. In dealing with courts the word jurisdiction constantly recurs. Its main meaning is simply a power to hear and decide. A court has appellate jurisdiction if it has power to hear and decide appeals, original jurisdiction if it has power to hear and decide cases coming before it directly, at first instance, and not on appeal from another court.

Summary and solemn jurisdiction

30. Courts of summary jurisdiction deal with the less serious crimes. Proceedings begin with a complaint and there is no jury. The punishment which can be awarded is limited. The courts of summary jurisdiction in Scotland are the sheriff courts and district courts.
31. Courts of solemn jurisdiction deal with the more serious crimes. Proceedings take place on an indictment and there is always a jury of 15. The sheriff courts and the High Court of Justiciary are the only courts of solemn jurisdiction in Scotland. It will be observed that the sheriff court has both summary and solemn jurisdiction, the sheriff sitting alone in summary cases and with a jury in solemn cases.

District courts

32. District courts sit in each local government district or islands area unless the Secretary of State directs, in view of the likely lack of business for such a court, that no district court shall be established for a particular district. They replaced, as from May 16, 1975, the former justice of the peace courts, burgh courts and police courts. The judges are either lay justices of the peace or legally qualified stipendiary magistrates. Most justices of the peace are appointed by the Secretary of State for Scotland but, in addition, each local authority can nominate up to one quarter of its members to serve as *ex officio* justices for its area. Justices are not paid a salary or fee for their judicial duties, but they are entitled to prescribed payments to cover their travel and subsistence costs and loss of earnings. A stipendiary magistrate is appointed by the local authority. He must have been an advocate or a solicitor for at least five years. Only a few district courts have stipendiary magistrates. The majority consist of justices of the peace. Normally the court consists of one or two justices.

33. The district courts have jurisdiction over a wide range of minor offences, such as breach of the peace and many offences under local authority bye-laws. Except where particular statutes provide otherwise, their powers of punishment are limited to a fine of up to £1,000, or 60 days' imprisonment or both. A district court when constituted by a stipendiary magistrate has, in addition to the above jurisdiction and powers, the summary criminal jurisdiction and powers of a sheriff.

34. Prosecutions are conducted by district prosecutors who must comply with directions given by the Lord Advocate regarding prosecutions in the district court and must report to the Lord Advocate, if called upon to do so, on matters concerning the discharge of their functions. The clerical work of the court is the responsibility of the clerk of the district court, who is appointed and employed by the local authority, who may be full-time or part-time, and who must be an advocate or a solicitor. The clerk also acts as legal assessor in the court, advising the justices as to the law.

35. The procedure and rights of appeal in district courts are similar to those in summary procedure in the sheriff courts and will be considered later.

36. It has been said that justices need to be "fatherly rather than grandfatherly." For this reason, justices over the age of 70 are put on a supplemental list and cannot perform judicial functions. The Secretary of State has power to place justices under the age of 70 on the supplemental list in certain circumstances—for example, if they decline or neglect to take a proper part in the exercise of their judicial or other functions or to attend suitable courses of instruction.

Children's hearings

37. Children's hearings are not really courts at all, but as they in fact deal with most offences committed by children it is appropriate to consider them here. (See also Chapter 12.) "Children" for this purpose means children under the age of 16 and certain children over that age who are already subject to a supervision requirement or who have been referred to the hearing from another part of the United Kingdom. The policy behind the Social Work (Scotland) Act 1968, which introduced children's hearings, is based on therapy rather than punishment. In certain circumstances children may be "in need of compulsory measures of care." These circumstances include cases where the child is beyond the control of his parent; or where through lack of parental care he is falling into bad associations or is exposed to moral danger; or where he has been the victim of certain offences (such as cruelty to children); or where he has failed to attend school regularly without reasonable excuse. The circumstances also include the commission of an offence and in fact a large proportion of the cases brought before children's hearings are brought on the offence ground. The hearing does not, however, conduct trials. If the grounds of referral are accepted by the child and his parent the hearing proceeds to decide what course would be in the best interests of the child; it may, for example, decide to place him under the supervision of a local authority social work department, or it may decide to send him to a residential establishment. But if the grounds are not accepted—as would be the case if the referral was on an offence ground and the child denied committing the offence—the children's hearing does *not* proceed to a trial. Instead it must either discharge the referral or have the case referred to the sheriff for a finding as to whether the grounds are established. The same result follows if the hearing considers that the grounds have not been understood by the child. If the ground is an offence ground, the sheriff must apply to the evidence the standard of proof required in criminal procedure. If he finds the ground established the case goes back to a children's hearing for the appropriate measures to be taken. Hearings also have power to deal with cases referred under the Solvent Abuse (Scotland) Act 1983.

38. The people who sit on children's hearings are lay volunteers drawn from carefully selected children's panels. The organisation of hearings and the referral of cases to them are the responsibility of an officer called (rather confusingly) "the reporter" who is appointed and paid by the local authority. Procedure at the hearings is quite informal. The public is not admitted, but *bona fide* press representatives may attend. There is a stringent prohibition on the publication of identifying particulars of any child in any way concerned in a hearing. This is dealt with in more detail in Chapter 12.

39. Appeal from any decision of the children's hearing lies to the sheriff. Appeal from any decision of the sheriff in relation to the children's hearing lies to the Court of Session by way of stated case (explained later) on a point of law or in respect of any irregularity on the conduct of the case.

9

Sheriff courts

40. The sheriff courts deal with most criminal cases in Scotland. The judge is either the sheriff or the sheriff principal. Both are appointed by the Crown on the recommendation of the Secretary of State for Scotland who in turn acts on the advice of the Lord Advocate. Both must be advocates or solicitors of at least 10 years' standing. Both are full-time appointments. There are six sheriffdoms in Scotland—Grampian, Highland and Islands; Tayside, Central and Fife; Lothian and Borders; Glasgow and Strathkelvin; North Strathclyde; and South Strathclyde, Dumfries and Galloway. Each is headed by a sheriff principal who, in addition to his judicial functions, has a general duty to secure the speedy and efficient disposal of business in the sheriff courts of his sheriffdom and who has correspondingly wide administrative functions.

41. The sheriff courts have a very wide criminal jurisdiction, both solemn and summary. There are three limitations. Firstly, the jurisdiction is limited territorially. As a general rule a sheriff can deal only with crimes committed within his sheriffdom. Secondly, the jurisdiction does not extend to certain crimes, of which the most important are treason, murder, attempt to murder and rape. Thirdly, the sheriff's powers of punishment are limited to three months' imprisonment in most summary cases and two years' imprisonment in solemn cases.

42. The prosecutor in the sheriff court is the procurator-fiscal or his depute. The administrative work is done by the sheriff-clerk and his deputes.

High Court of Justiciary

43. The judges of the High Court of Justiciary are the Lord Justice-General (who is the same person as the Lord President of the Court of Session), the Lord Justice-Clerk and 22 Lords Commissioners of Justiciary. All are also judges of the Court of Session, or, more sonorously, Senators of the College of Justice. They are appointed by the Crown on the advice of the Lord Advocate and can be removed from office only for gross misconduct.

44. The seat of the High Court is at Parliament House in Edinburgh, but it also goes on circuit to other towns. All of the judges do not, of course, sit in each case. Normally there is only one but difficult cases can be heard by two or more.

45. The High Court deals with the graver crimes and is the *only* court which can try treason, murder, attempt to murder or rape. Prosecutions are conducted by the Lord Advocate, the Solicitor-General, or an advocate-depute.

46. The High Court also has jurisdiction to hear appeals from and review the decisions of cases heard on summary procedure. When sitting for this purpose it consists of at least three judges and is sometimes known as the Appeal Court of the High Court of Justiciary. It has an important paramount authority to review proceedings in all inferior criminal courts with a view to seeing that justice is done.

Court of Criminal Appeal

47. Strictly speaking, there is no such court in Scotland. However, the "Scottish Court of Criminal Appeal" is a convenient term frequently used instead of the more correct but more cumbersome "High Court of Justiciary sitting as a Court of Criminal Appeal." The court hears appeals against conviction or sentence in trials heard on solemn procedure. It is the highest Scottish criminal court. There is no appeal to the House of Lords. Three judges form a quorum but in difficult cases more may sit.

SCOTTISH CRIMINAL PROCEDURE

48. Although the details of criminal procedure can be left to the lawyer, the journalist must know the steps in outline so that he can tell what is happening and what is about to happen. In this field the laws of Scotland and England are very different. To take only one example, private prosecutions are common in England but very rare in Scotland. An outstanding case occurred in 1982 when, after the Crown had decided not to prosecute three youths following a particularly vicious attack upon a woman in Glasgow, the High Court granted her authority to bring a private prosecution (by the old process of issuing criminal letters), which went to trial and resulted in convictions for rape against one youth and for indecent assault against two others. It was the first private prosecution to have been allowed and to have succeeded under this procedure in Scotland since 1909. The three judges who allowed criminal letters to the victim described the case as strange and unique, the Crown having earlier dropped proceedings against the youths on a psychiatric report that the risk of damage to her health if she appeared in court made it inadvisable that she be called as a witness. The court's decision to have the case revived at her instance was reached after the judges were satisfied she would after all be able to appear and give evidence, without which originally it was thought a prosecution could not succeed. The court ruled there was no doubt the woman had the necessary title and interest to prosecute privately, and this course was not opposed by the Lord Advocate.

49. The Lord Advocate, assisted by the Solicitor-General for Scotland, is responsible for the investigation and prosecution of crime in Scotland. Both are appointed by the Crown. It is usual, but not always possible, for at least one of them to have a seat in Parliament. In practice the Lord-Advocate delegates most of his responsibility in criminal matters to advocates-depute who work, along with a staff of officials, at the Crown Office in Edinburgh. The procurators-fiscal investigate crime at the local level under the general supervision of the Crown Office. In the case of minor offences the procurator-fiscal has a discretion whether or not to prosecute, or to issue a formal warning, with the implied sanction of a prosecution if the warning is not heeded. He reports more serious crimes to the Crown Office which decides whether to prosecute and, if so, in which court.

50. Two general principles should be noted at this stage. The first is that everyone is innocent until he is proved guilty (and in Scotland the proof must normally be by the evidence of two witnesses, except in regard to certain minor road traffic offences punishable by fixed penalty). The second is a principle of great importance to journalists which will be dealt with in more detail later. It is that there must be no publicity which may seriously prejudice a person's trial. (See Chapter 9.)

51. There are two types of criminal procedure—summary and solemn. Different rules apply but the preliminary steps are the same. The first stage is generally the police investigation under the authority of the procurator-fiscal. Newspapers have sometimes played an active part in the exposure of crime. This will be referred to later. It is important to note that there is a grave risk of contempt of court if anything is published after arrest has been made or a warrant granted for arrest in connection with an alleged offence which creates a substantial risk of seriously prejudicing or impeding the course of justice. The police may, of course, and often do, enlist the help of the media in their inquiries and there is normally no danger in assisting as requested. In certain cases, however, it may be wise to check that the request has been cleared by the procurator-fiscal. This would seem to be advisable, for example, if the request is to publish a photograph of a wanted man in a case where the question of identification could arise.

52. The investigations may culminate in an arrest. Normally a warrant is required but some statutes allow arrest without warrant. A policeman can arrest without warrant when he finds a person committing or attempting to commit a serious crime or when he is told by the victim or a credible eye-witness that this has just occurred. He can also arrest without warrant in cases of breach of the peace or threatened violence or in certain circumstances when he finds a person in possession of stolen goods and unable to give a satisfactory explanation.

Summary procedure

53. Where the accused has not been arrested, but has simply been cited to appear, he may plead in person, through a solicitor or by letter. If he pleads guilty in his absence, he may, subject to certain safeguards, be sentenced there and then. If he pleads not guilty a date will be fixed for a trial.

54. The procedure at the trial is straightforward. The prosecutor calls his first witness and examines him. The defence can cross-examine, after which the prosecution has a limited right to re-examine. After all the evidence for the prosecution has been led, the evidence for the defence is led. Then the prosecutor addresses the court, followed by the accused or his agent and the judge pronounces his finding. This may be either guilty, not guilty or not proven. A finding of not proven has the same effect as a finding of not guilty. It is used where the court is not satisfied that the man is innocent but the prosecution has failed to discharge its burden of proving that he is guilty. If the accused is found guilty he is allowed to address the court before sentence is pronounced.

Criminal Justice (Scotland) Act 1980

55. Criminal procedure is comprehensively consolidated in the Criminal Procedure (Scotland) Act 1975, amended in a number of important respects by the Criminal Justice (Scotland) Act 1980. The latter measure introduced several novelties into the criminal law with which journalists should be familiar. The most important of these are noted in summary here. Provision made under s.22 of the 1980 Act for anonymity of children in criminal cases is dealt with in Chapter 12.

56. The Act gives police powers (ss.2 and 3) to detain a suspect for up to six hours while they make investigations to enable them to decide whether there is sufficient ground to arrest him. It should be noted that the strict liability rule under the contempt of court law (outlined in Chapter 9) does not come into operation until the arrest stage is reached or a warrant is granted.

13

57. There are safeguards for the detainee; he is not obliged to answer any questions other than those intended to ascertain his name and address; he has to be told the nature of the suspected offence; he is entitled to have his detention intimated to a solicitor and one other person of his choice; and if not arrested at the end of six hours' detention he must be released and cannot again be detained on the same grounds. If he is arrested he is entitled to have this fact intimated to a person named by him without unnecessary delay. There are special safeguards for children.

58. Under s.4 a constable may search a person without warrant if he has reasonable grounds for suspecting he carries an offensive weapon, and can arrest anyone who obstructs the search or conceals such a weapon. By s.5 a constable with power to arrest without warrant, who suspects a person is drunk, may take him to a place designated for drunken persons which has been selected for the purpose by the Scottish Secretary. The person is not liable to be detained there but may be charged with an offence.

59. The Act, by s.10, gives an accused the right to petition the sheriff to have an identification parade held where the prosecutor has not already made arrangements for one and the sheriff considers it reasonable.

60. In summary cases a person charged must not be detained for more than 40 days after being charged in court, unless his trial commences within that period, and the court has power to grant an extension for reasons similar to those provided under solemn procedure (referred to below), and subject to a right of appeal by either side.

61. District courts have power, under s.7, to try certain classes of motoring offences, including endorsable offences but not those which involve automatic disqualification, and a range of other offences including theft or reset, falsehood, fraud or wilful imposition, breach of trust or embezzlement involving an amount not exceeding £1,000.

Solemn procedure

62. In solemn procedure the accused's first appearance in court is on petition in chambers before a sheriff, and all that can be published about the proceedings at this stage, besides the identity of the accused (unless he is a child, in which event he must not be identified: see Chapter 12), is a general indication of the nature of the charges, supplied usually by the procurator-fiscal. It is important to remember that the fiscal may later proceed on an amended charge, or charges, or even drop proceedings altogether, although this is unusual.

14

63. Under s.12 the first pleading diet, called 10 days before trial, is no longer mandatory. If the accused is pleading not guilty he must give notice of any special defences such as alibi, self-defence, incrimination (accusing someone else of the crime charged) or insanity at the time of the act.

64. Section 6 revives judicial examination as a method of ascertaining, at a hearing in chambers before a sheriff, what explanation the suspect may have to give or comment he may have to make on any incriminating statement he is alleged to have made. He is questioned by the fiscal under the control of the sheriff who must ensure questioning is fair. The accused has a right to be represented by a solicitor and to consult him before answering any question, and the solicitor may ask him questions to clear up any ambiguity. The accused may decline to answer any question, but if he does so this may be commented on at a subsequent trial by the judge, prosecutor or any co-accused. A shorthand record is kept of the examination and a copy of the transcript must be made available to the accused. The record, or any part of it, may be used in evidence.

65. The Act (s.14) requires that a trial under solemn procedure must be commenced within 12 months of the accused's first appearance on petition; otherwise he must be discharged and cannot be charged again with the same offence—unless delay has been caused by his failure to appear or an extension has been granted by the court. The section also requires that an accused must not be detained for more than 80 days before being served with the indictment, and the trial must commence within 110 days of his being detained. (A trial begins when the jury takes the oath.) Provision is made for extension of these periods if the court is satisfied (in regard to the 110–day rule) that this is justified because of illness of the accused or a judge, absence or illness of a necessary witness, or other "sufficient cause." The grant or refusal of an extension is subject to appeal.

66. If during the trial the court decides that, because of the accused's misconduct, a proper trial cannot take place unless he is removed, it may order that the hearing proceed in his absence, but he must be legally represented (s.21).

67. In court the accused is called "the panel." The trial diet is before a judge (or judges in difficult High Court cases) and a jury of 15. Section 23 reduces from five to three the number of peremptory challenges of jurors allowed to each side without giving any reason. Any additional objections must be supported by a reason related to the particular juror. The clerk of court informs the jury of the charge and

15

administers the oath. Evidence is led for the prosecution, followed by evidence for the defence. Then the prosecution and the defence address the jury in turn and the judge charges the jury. The general principle is that the jury are masters of the facts and the judge master of the law. His main duty in charging the jury is therefore to set out the law applicable to the case but he may also make fair and impartial comments on the evidence. After the charge the jury may either pronounce their verdict at once or retire to consider it. The verdict may be by a majority and is "Guilty, " "Not Guilty" or "Not Proven." In the rare case where the panel is found to have been insane at the time of the alleged crime, he will be found not guilty on the ground of insanity.

68. If the verdict is "Guilty" then, after the prosecutor has moved for sentence and any previous convictions have been admitted or proved, the panel or his counsel or solicitor may make a plea in mitigation of sentence. The judge will then pronounce sentence, but if the trial has been in the sheriff court and the sheriff thinks the panel merits a heavier sentence than he can impose, he can remit to the High Court for sentence.

69. Brief mention may be made of accelerated trial procedure. This is a method of speeding up procedure where the accused gives notice that he intends to plead guilty and wants his case to be disposed of at once. He gets a shortened form of indictment and is cited to a diet in the sheriff court where he can be sentenced at once or remitted to the High Court for sentence.

70. The only sentence for murder is life imprisonment except where the person convicted is under 18, the sentence in this case being detention without limit of time in a place and under conditions to be directed by the Scottish Secretary, or if he is over 18 but under 21, when the sentence is detention for life at first in a young offenders' institution (s.43) and thereafter in prison (the person being liable to be detained for life). Detention during Her Majesty's pleasure is abolished. Where the sentence passed is for life the judge may recommend the minimum term to be served and must give his reasons if he does so; a recommendation is appealable as part of the sentence.

71. No prison sentence may be imposed on a person over 21 who has not previously been so sentenced to detention, unless the court thinks no other course is appropriate (s.42). No one under 21 may be sent to prison, and borstal training is abolished, being replaced by detention in a young offenders' institution (s.45).

72. Section 32 gives the High Court and sheriff courts power to authorise evidence of any witness for either side who is unable to attend a trial to be taken on commission, provided his evidence is necessary and its submission to the court in transcript will cause no unfairness to the other party.

73. At the close of the prosecution evidence in either solemn or summary procedure the accused is entitled (in solemn procedure in the absence of the jury) to submit a plea that there is no case to answer (s.19). If the plea is sustained the accused is acquitted, if refused the trial proceeds to defence evidence. Any report of submissions made on such a plea can be safely published only after the proceedings have ceased to be "active" (see Chapter 9, "Contempt of Court").

74. The Act (s.78) creates the new category of offence known as vandalism, which it defines as wilfully or recklessly destroying or damaging anyone else's property without reasonable excuse.

75. By s.80 it is no longer an offence for consenting parties over 21 to perform a homosexual act in private provided no more than two persons are present and it does not take place in a public lavatory.

76. Offenders can be ordered, under s.58, to pay compensation to their victims, either instead of or in addition to any other method the court may select for dealing with them, for personal injury, loss or damage caused by their offences. The provisions do not apply to loss resulting from death or from a road accident unless caused by the convicted person. There is no limit to compensation under solemn procedure, but in summary cases the limits are set by statute. Where the convicted person's means are insufficient to meet a fine besides compensation, priority is given to the latter. A compensation order is treated as a sentence for appeal purposes.

77. Sections 68–76 are designed to control violence at or in connection with sporting events by making it illegal to carry alcohol on public service vehicles, or other vehicles adapted to carry more than eight passengers, taking spectators to or from games held at grounds designated by the Scottish Secretary, to be in possession of alcohol when entering such a ground or have any firework, flare or smoke bomb or container for liquid which could be used as a missile, or to be drunk at the ground or when entering it.

78. The main differences between summary and solemn procedure can be summed up thus. In summary procedure there is no petition for committal. Proceedings begin with the complaint. In solemn procedure there is usually a petition for committal and proceedings are on indictment. Cases on summary procedure are heard in the sheriff courts or district courts. There is no jury. Cases on solemn procedure are heard in the sheriff or High Court and there is a jury. Appeal in summary

17

procedure is by stated case or bill of suspension to three judges sitting in the High Court. Appeal in solemn procedure is to at least three judges of the High Court sitting as a Court of Criminal Appeal.

Appeals

79. The 1980 Act made some important changes to the procedure for appeals in summary cases. The initial step is an application for a stated case, note of appeal (against sentence only) or bill of suspension, which must take place within one week of the decision under appeal (the stage at which the proceedings again become active under the Contempt of Court Act 1981: see Chapter 9).

80. The draft stated case prepared by the sheriff or justice is subject to adjustments proposed by either side if they are agreed at a hearing arranged for this purpose. The judge stating a case for appeal must give his reasons if he refuses any adjustments, and these may be taken into account by the appeal court, which also has power to hear additional evidence or order that this be heard by a person it appoints for the purpose. The appeal court may also appoint an assessor with expert knowledge to assist in deciding an appeal.

81. There is also a right of appeal against conviction by way of bill of suspension where the stated case procedure would not be appropriate or competent. The prosecutor may appeal against acquittal or sentence on grounds, in either case, of alleged miscarriage of justice. The court may remit a case back with directions to affirm the verdict, quash the verdict and authorise a new prosecution (to be begun within two months) on the same or similar charges as before. Where an appeal against acquittal is sustained the court may convict and sentence the respondent, remit the case back to the court below with instructions to do so, or remit back for the lower court's opinion.

82. Where the appeal court in solemn procedure has allowed an appeal against conviction on the ground that there has been a miscarriage of justice (Sched. 2, para. 19), a new prosecution may be brought within two months charging the accused with the same or any similar offence arising out of the same facts, but no sentence may be passed which could not have been passed in the original proceedings. In the first case to be brought under this provision, a man convicted of culpable homicide in the High Court at Inverness, who had been charged in 1982 with the murder of his wife's lover, appealed successfully on the ground that there was a substantial miscarriage of justice resulting from prejudice he suffered by a misdirection of the jury by the presiding judge. Under the former procedure the appellant would have been disharged, but in this case the Lord Advocate, under the 1980 Act, was granted authority by the appeal court to bring a fresh prosecution, but on this occasion charged the man with culpable homicide. The new trial took place at Edinburgh to avoid the risk of prejudice from local knowledge in Inverness of the original trial and conviction. In the event the charge was found not proven and the accused was released. Evidence at the two trials was for the most part identical. While in theory there is no limit to the number of retrials in any case, in practice more than one is unlikely. The new trial procedure is used only where a conviction at the first trial is quashed on what amounts to a technicality. The procedure, therefore, is rather exceptional, compared to practice in England where retrials are relatively common; but the 1980 Act has brought to an end the fundamental rule in Scotland that an accused could not be tried more than once on the same charge. In such a case the proceedings remain active for purposes of the strict liability rule (see Contempt of Court Act 1981, Sched. 1, para. 16, and Chapter 9) from the time authority for a new prosecution is granted by the court until a new trial is concluded or a decision is taken to drop further proceedings.

83. An accused may appeal against conviction, sentence, or both, on grounds of alleged miscarriage of justice, and formal notice has to be lodged at the Justiciary Office in Edinburgh within two weeks. This latter fact has special significance when the question of publicity arises after the end of a trial (see Chapter 9). The appeal court may uphold the verdict, quash the conviction, substitute an amended verdict of guilty (and pass a different sentence from that already passed), or set aside the verdict and grant authority for a new prosecution. Where the appeal is against sentence the court has power not only to reduce but also to increase that already passed.

84. A point of law arising where an accused has been acquitted may be referred by the Lord Advocate to the High Court for its opinion, but the result does not affect the acquittal (s.37). At the hearing of the referral the acquitted person need not be present, but counsel is appointed to attend to assist the court. If the acquitted person chooses, he may engage counsel to appear at public expense.

85. In both solemn and summary appeals there is provision for the hearing of additional evidence not available at the trial, and in either situation the Crown may appeal by bill of advocation (s.35). The High Court also has power under s.252 of the Criminal Procedure (Scotland) Act 1975 to allow the hearing of new evidence of any witnesses whether or not they were called at the trial. On the first occasion this procedure was invoked, in 1983, two Ayrshire youths convicted of rape were acquitted after the appeal court considered fresh evidence of a psychiatrist who deponed that the supposed victim had a history of sexual fantasies and was prone to making unwarranted accusations of rape and sexual interference. The Crown had reportedly been unaware of this condition of the alleged victim at the time of the trial. The appeal court held there had been a miscarriage of justice and the appellants were released. The effect upon publicity of the law of contempt in such a situation does not appear to be specifically provided for in the rules governing active proceedings in the Contempt of Court Act, but where a hearing of new evidence is allowed, it is safe to assume the case is in the same position as that where the appeal court "remits the case to the court below" (Sched. 1, para. 16(*a*)), and thus remains active from conclusion of the appellate proceedings until and including the hearing of the new evidence, and until disposal of the case.

Bail

86. A man is presumed innocent until he is proved guilty. A corollary of this is that an accused should not, unless for some good reason, be deprived of his liberty before conviction. It is reasonable, however, that if he goes free he should be required to give some security that he will appear at later stages in the proceedings. Bail is a means to this end.

87. Until the passing of the Bail etc.(Scotland) Act 1980, the normal security took the form of a payment of money under a bail bond, but the Act effectively abolished money bail except in special circumstances. Bail is now granted subject to conditions, laid down by the court or the Lord Advocate, to which the bail applicant must subscribe. These will, for example, be that he will appear at a court diet when required, does not commit an offence while on bail or interfere with witnesses or obstruct the course of justice in any other way. He may also be required to make himself available to enable inquiries to be made or a report prepared to assist the court, or be required to report regularly at a police station, or stay away from his wife or family or other person(s) specified in the conditions attached to his bail. In special circumstances either the accused or someone on his behalf may be required to lodge monetary surety for his attendance at court, which is liable to forfeiture in the event of his non-compliance.

88. Liberation on bail may also be granted by the police after arrest on a summary charge, and if the accused is refused bail at this stage he may apply to the court for bail. Because the conditions of bail are contained in a document, a copy of which the accused must receive, and which must show also his domicile of citation (his normal place of residence), access to the addresses of accused persons is more readily available to the media under the terms of the Bail Act than before it, when the accused was frequently cited at the sheriff-clerk's office.

89.   In deciding whether or not to grant bail the court may take into account the type of crime charged—whether, for example, it involves alleged interference with witnesses—or whether the applicant has a criminal record, and if so what bearing that may have upon the possibility of his being in breach of conditions attached to bail. In each case the court has to balance the right of the untried person to the presumption of innocence against the risk of justice being frustrated by the applicant's failure to keep his part of the bargain.

90.   For breach of his undertaking the person granted bail may be fined up to £400 and jailed for a maximum of three months in a summary case in the sheriff court or a similar sum and 60 days in the district court. If he is charged on indictment, he is liable to a fine (with no maximum laid down) and imprisonment up to two years. Any penalty imposed may be in addition to the sentence passed by the court in respect of the original offence.

91.   The only crimes not bailable are murder and treason, except by the authority of the Lord Advocate or the High Court.

92.   In addition to the provisions for pre-trial bail, a person convicted and sentenced to jail or detention may be granted bail pending disposal of an appeal.

93.   There is a right of appeal against refusal, or against the conditions attached to the granting, of bail. The Crown may appeal against the granting of bail. In either case the appeal is normally heard by a High Court judge in chambers. The proceedings are kept private to protect the accused from possible prejudice arising from publicity of statements made as a necessary part of information required by the judge in relation to the accused's record or disclosure of other matters likely to influence the minds of potential jurors or witnesses at a subsequent trial. Reporters, however, have a right of access to the decision, and this information is usually supplied by the Justiciary Office.

DIFFERENCES IN ENGLAND

The criminal courts

94.   *Magistrates' courts* in England consist of local justices or stipendiaries. Two justices normally form a quorum. They deal with offences

21

punishable on summary conviction and sit without a jury. In composition they resemble Scottish district courts, but their jurisdiction is much wider and embraces many cases which in Scotland would be tried by a sheriff without a jury. They deal with a very large number of motoring offences and other minor statutory offences. It follows that much of the criminal trial work done in Scotland by professional judges is done in England by lay magistrates. Appeal from the magistrates' court is to the Crown Court, where there is in effect a re-trial and from there, on a point of law, by way of "case stated" to a divisional court of the Queen's Bench Division. Appeals on a point of law can also be taken by case stated direct from the magistrates to the divisional court.

95. *Juvenile courts* are magistrates' courts which deal with offences (excluding homicide) committed by children and young persons, and certain other matters requiring special measures to be taken for the care or control of children and young persons. A child, for this purpose, is a person under the age of 14, and a young person is a person who has attained the age of 14 and is under the age of 17. The jurisdiction of juvenile courts in England corresponds roughly with that of children's hearings in Scotland and there are similar restrictions on publicity. The juvenile courts are, however, much more like ordinary courts than are children's hearings in Scotland. They consist of justices, although these are drawn from a special panel. They can make a finding that a child or young person has committed an offence; and for this purpose the ordinary rules of evidence and the ordinary onus of proof in criminal proceedings apply. Appeal lies to the Crown Court. In Scotland, as we have seen, the children's hearing does not in any sense try offences: if an offence ground for compulsory measures of care is denied, the hearing will have the case referred to the sheriff court for a finding as to whether the ground is established.

96. *The Crown Court* has exclusive jurisdiction over all trials on indictment in England and Wales. Trial is by judge, or judges, and jury. The Crown Court deals with all the more serious offences, some of which would be dealt with, in Scotland, by a sheriff and jury and some by the High Court of Justiciary with a jury. Crown Court business can be conducted at any place in England and Wales and, in practice, Crown Courts are established in all the larger centres. The judges may be (a) High Court judges, who deal with the more serious indictable offences, (b) circuit judges, who are legally qualified, full-time judges or (c) recorders, who are legally qualified, part-time judges, appointed on a temporary basis. For the hearing of appeals of cases remitted from the magistrates' court for sentence, the judge in the Crown Court must sit with from two to four justices of the peace. In other cases the judge may sit with up to four justices. Appeal is to the criminal division of the Court of Appeal.

97. *The Central Criminal Court* is the name given to the Crown Court sitting at the "Old Bailey" in London. The name was preserved for traditional reasons and there are certain other minor traditional peculiarities about this court, but legally it is simply the Crown Court sitting in London.

98. *Divisional Court of the Queen's Bench* consists normally of three judges of the Queen's Bench Division of the English High Court. It hears appeals on points of law by "case stated" from the magistrates' courts or from decisions of the Crown Court in appeals from the magistrates' courts. A "case stated," as might be assumed, corresponds to a stated case in Scotland.

99. It is also possible for a person convicted by the magistrates, or, on appeal by the Crown Court, to apply to the divisional court for order of *certiorari*. This is an appeal to the general supervisory jurisdiction of the court which it can exercise if, for example, the proceedings have been contrary to natural justice.

100. *The Court of Appeal* consists of a number of high-ranking *ex officio* and ordinary judges. Its criminal division hears appeals from convictions on indictment and certain appeals against sentence. The quorum is three but more may sit. There is always an uneven number of judges. As in the case of the Scottish Court of Criminal Appeal there is appeal to the court without leave on a point of law but in other cases either a certificate from the trial judge that the case is fit for appeal or the leave of the Court of Appeal must be obtained. There can be appeal against sentence only with the leave of the Court of Appeal.

101. In English, but not Scottish (except for decisions of the Courts-Martial Appeal Court in a Scottish case) criminal cases, there may in some circumstances be an ultimate appeal to the *House of Lords*. It is necessary:

- (*a*) that the court from which the appeal is brought should grant a certificate that a point of law of general public importance is involved and
- (*b*) that either that court or the House of Lords should certify that the point is one which ought to be considered by the House of Lords. On these conditions there is appeal from the Divisional

23

Court of the Queen's Bench Division, from the Court of Appeal or from the Courts-Martial Appeal Court.

102. *The House of Lords* as a court differs from the House of Lords as a legislative body. As a court it consists of at least three and usually five of the nine Lords of Appeal. These Lords of Appeal are salaried judges, appointed from among the most eminent lawyers in the United Kingdom and awarded life peerages. Two of them are usually Scots lawyers. Other peers who hold, or have held, high judicial office, may also sit. (In 1975 the Lord Justice-Clerk, Lord Wheatley, who was made a life peer in 1970, sat with the two Scottish and two English Lords of Appeal to hear an English case.)

Criminal procedure

103. In 1986 English criminal procedure took an important step towards the Scottish model by transferring the conduct of prosecutions from the police to a network of centrally-funded Crown prosecutors in each of 31 areas of England and Wales, under the authority of the Director of Public Prosecutions, who reports to the Attorney-General and who deals with difficult cases or sensitive cases involving a political element. The initial decision whether proceedings will be brought (unlike the position in Scotland) remains, however, with the police. In Crown Courts the prosecution is handled by barristers in private practice briefed by Crown Prosecution Service solicitors or barristers directly employed by the Service.

104. Criminal offences in England are either summary or indictable. Some offences are triable either summarily or on indictment: these are known colloquially as "hybrid offences." As a general rule summary offences are tried in the magistrates' courts without a jury and indictable offences are tried in the Crown Court with a jury. The division, however, is not watertight because (*a*) a person charged with certain indictable offences can consent to be tried summarily, (*b*) hybrid offences, although "indictable" in the sense that they *can* be tried on indictment, may also be tried summarily and (*c*) with some exceptions, a person charged before a magistrates' court with a summary offence can elect to be tried by jury if his offence can lead to more than three months' imprisonment and if he appears in court in person. It will be seen that the defendant in England has more control over the mode of trial than the accused in Scotland: in Scotland the mode of trial, in so far as the law allows a choice, is within the discretion of the prosecution, the only minor exception being the accelerated trial procedure noted above.

105. The following are other important respects in which English criminal procedure differs from Scottish. There is a preliminary inquiry by the justices into indictable offences to see whether or not a person should stand trial. This inquiry is generally in public. However, in many cases the defendant does not lead evidence and the only evidence for the prosecution consists of written statements. In such cases, if the defendant is legally represented and raises no objection, the justices may commit for trial without any consideration of the strength of the prosecution evidence. In other cases there will be a preliminary hearing, and witnesses may give evidence orally. There are, however, restrictions on publicity, designed to avoid the risk of prejudice to the defendant. These are dealt with in detail later (see Chapter 31) but the general principle is that the evidence called by either side cannot be published until after the trial, if the defendant is committed for trial, or until after the committal proceedings, if he is not. If the justices do decide to commit the defendant for trial they will specify the location of the Crown Court where the trial is to take place. Certain serious offences, such as murder, must be sent to a place where a High Court judge visits the Crown Court.

106. A criminal jury in England consists of 12 and not, as in Scotland, 15 jurors. The verdict is either "Guilty" or "Not Guilty." English law regards a unanimous verdict as normal and desirable, but since 1967 has made provision for a majority verdict. However, this is hedged about with conditions which have no counterpart in Scots law. A majority verdict must be supported by at least 10 jurors (or nine if the number of the jury has been reduced to 10 by death, illness or other cause). The Crown Court cannot accept a majority verdict unless it appears to the court that the jury have had a reasonable time for deliberation. The time can vary according to the nature and complexity of the case, but in any event must be at least two hours. In England there is no verdict of "Not Proven." The illogical verdict of "Guilty but Insane, " which never found a place in Scotland, has now been abolished in England.

107. With regard to the procedure at the actual trial an important difference is that in England the prosecutor begins by making an opening speech instead of, as in Scotland, simply leading his evidence. Although useful for the media, this practice has been criticised on the ground that counsel may make allegations which are not borne out by the subsequent evidence but which may yet make a profound impression on the minds of the jury, who at this stage of the proceedings are likely to be particularly attentive and receptive.

108. Another difference used to be that, while in Scotland the accused has always had the right to make the final closing speech, in England the prosecution often had this privilege. By the Criminal Procedure (Right of Reply) Act 1964, however, the position in England was changed and the general rule now is that the defence has the right to the last word. Again the prosecution in England may be allowed to lead evidence to rebut any new matter introduced in the evidence for the defence.

109. Finally, in England applications for bail are often dealt with *in public* by the justices conducting the preliminary inquiry into indictable offences. In Scotland privacy is the general rule.

CHAPTER 4

CIVIL COURTS AND PROCEDURE

Sheriff court

110. The sheriff court has a very wide civil jurisdiction extending to almost all types of action. Exceptions are actions of reduction of deeds and actions to prove the tenor of lost documents. Legislation introduced in 1982 gave sheriffs jurisdiction to deal with divorce actions (see Chapter 11). They already had power to handle actions for judicial separation, separation and aliment, or affiliation and aliment. Actions involving amounts under £1,000 must be brought in the sheriff court. They cannot be heard by the Court of Session. There is no upper limit to the value of cases which can be dealt with in the sheriff court. Civil jury trial in the sheriff court was abolished in 1980.

111. An important part of the sheriff court's work is its commissary jurisdiction. This is concerned with such questions as the appointment and confirmation of executors to administer the estates of deceased persons. Only when he has obtained confirmation is an executor entitled to uplift and administer the estate.

112. Procedure in civil cases in the sheriff court has been modified by the Sheriff Courts (Scotland) Act 1971. Certain cases, including all actions for payment of money not exceeding £1,000 in amount (exclusive of interest and expenses), are known as summary causes. They are begun by filling in a printed form of summons. Evidence is not recorded. Appeal lies from a final judgment of the sheriff to the sheriff principal on any point of law, and then from the sheriff principal to the Inner House of the Court of Session if the sheriff principal certifies the case as suitable for such an appeal. The procedure in ordinary causes, including actions for amounts over £1,000, is more formal and follows the lines of Court of Session procedure, with some modifications noted later. Appeal is either to the sheriff principal and from him to the Inner House of the Court of Session, or else direct to the Inner House of the Court of Session.

The Court of Session

113. The Court of Session sits in Edinburgh and consists of the Lord President, Lord Justice-Clerk and a maximum of 22 other judges. As we have seen, the personnel is the same as that of the High Court of Justiciary.

114. The court is divided into an Inner House which is largely an appeal court and an Outer House which deals with cases at first instance. The Court of Session remains one court however. The division between Inner and Outer House is not a strict one. Judges from the Inner House may sit as single judges in the Outer House to help with pressure of work and, on occasion, judges from the Outer House may be brought in to make up an additional appellate bench, known as the Extra Division (Administration of Justice (Scotland) Act 1933, s.2). In theory, the court could still sit as a whole court to hear cases of particular difficulty but the raising of the number of judges and limitations of space have made this impracticable.

115. The Inner House is in turn divided into two divisions of equal status, the First Division and the Second Division. The First Division consists of the Lord President and three judges. The Second Division consists of the Lord Justice-Clerk and three judges. The Outer House consists of judges who sit singly and are known as Lords Ordinary. The reason for this peculiar name is that at one time there were two types of judges in the Court of Session, Ordinary Lords and Extraordinary Lords, the latter being nominees of the King who required no legal qualifications. The power of appointing Extraordinary Lords was lost in 1723.

116. The Inner House is mainly an appeal court, hearing appeals from the sheriff courts and from the Outer House as well as from various other special courts and tribunals. It also has an original jurisdiction in certain types of petition including many petitions to the *nobile officium* (see paras. 598–600). The judges of the Outer House have an original jurisdiction in most actions involving more than £500.

117. The Court of Session has a general power to review the judgments of inferior courts and tribunals on the ground that they have exceeded their jurisdiction or have failed to observe fundamental rules of justice, such as the rule that both parties must be heard before a decision is given.

The House of Lords

118. There is appeal from the Court of Session to the House of Lords. An appeal must be lodged within three months of the judgment appealed from.

119. What follows is once again a mere outline designed to give a general picture of the steps involved in getting a case into court. The person who brings an ordinary civil action is called the pursuer, the person against whom it is brought, the defender.

120. In the case of ordinary actions in the Court of Session the first step is for the pursuer's solicitor or counsel to prepare a *summons*. This is, in essence, a document summoning the defender to appear at court, setting forth the pursuer's claim and asking the court to give judgment in his favour. A copy of the summons is served on the defender, usually by recorded delivery or registered post. There is then a period of grace, known as the *induciae*, designed to give the defender time to take legal advice and decide on his course of action.

121. On the expiry of this period, the pursuer's solicitor lodges in the court offices a *process* which consists of the summons and various other documents which will be needed later in the proceedings.

122. The next stage is that the case appears in the *calling list* of the Court of Session. This is the first public announcement of the action. The only details given are the names and addresses of the parties and the names of the pursuer's counsel and solicitors.

123. If the defender does not defend, the court will give judgment for the pursuer—a decree in absence. In divorce and other actions affecting status, however, decree will not be given until the grounds of action have been proved by sufficient evidence. If the defender does wish to defend, he must enter appearance and lodge *defences* containing his answers to the pursuer's allegations.

124. In an action for divorce or separation, however, there is no open record; the parties merely note their adjustments on the summons and defences.

125. After the parties have completed their adjustments, the court makes an order closing the record. A *closed record* is then printed and added to the process.

126. The next steps in the procedure vary. There may be a preliminary dispute about further procedure and this may have to be decided by a judge. In the normal course of events, the case will eventually be heard by a judge alone or by a judge and jury. An action for damages which involves difficult questions of mixed fact and law may be regarded as unsuitable for a jury. In civil cases, the jury numbers 12 and may return a majority verdict. The procedure in court is dealt with later in the section on court reporting (see Chapter 13).

127. To recapitulate, the procedure in an ordinary civil action in the Court of Session is, in rough outline, summons—lodging of process—case in calling list—appearance—defences—open record—closed record—proof or jury trial.

128. The procedure in an ordinary civil action in the sheriff court is broadly similar. The pursuer's solicitor draws up an *initial writ* instead of a summons and a copy is served on the defender. There is no calling list as such and the defender must, if he wishes to defend, enter appearance *within* the *induciae*. Thereafter he must lodge defences. There is no printed open record. Adjustments are simply made on the initial writ and defences. When adjustments are complete the sheriff closes the record and the case will proceed to debate or proof.

Optional procedure

129. Following criticisms of delays in personal injury cases, a committee chaired by Lord Kincraig recommended reforms aimed at simplifying procedure and giving the court more control over the conduct of cases. The result was the introduction in the Court of Session in 1986 of an optional procedure in such cases. The written pleadings are in a short, simplified form and a closed record is not obligatory. At an early stage the case is sent to a diet roll where a judge decides what course it will take. For example, he may order a hearing on the amount of damages alone, or, if the law is not in dispute, an inquiry only into the facts of the case.

130. There are, of course, special procedures in special types of case. The points of most interest to journalists are dealt with later in the section on court reporting. For the present we may merely note that the procedure with regard to petitions differs from that outlined above. The person presenting the petition is called the petitioner and the person opposing it is known as the respondent.

Magistrates' courts

131. The magistrates' courts in England have a varied civil jurisdiction, the most important aspect of which is jurisdiction in matrimonial proceedings and certain other family law matters. They deal with very large numbers of applications by wives for maintenance for themselves and their children. They also deal with adoption orders and affiliation proceedings. Many family law matters which are dealt with in Scotland by professional judges in accordance with one set of legal rules are thus dealt with in England by lay magistrates in courts which are associated by the public with minor criminal offences and according to laws which differ from those applying in the High Court. Appeals from matrimonial orders lie to the divisional court of the Family Division, and from there with leave to the Court of Appeal and House of Lords. Other aspects of the magistrates' civil jurisdiction include actions for the recovery of rates, income tax and unpaid gas, water and electricity bills as well as certain licensing matters. Appeal on such matters lies to the Crown Court.

Crown Court

132. The Crown Court has a limited civil jurisdiction, which consists mainly of the hearing of certain appeals from civil cases and licensing decisions in the magistrates' courts.

County courts

133. County courts correspond roughly to sheriff courts in their civil capacity. The name is misleading. There is not in fact one court for each county. The judge is a circuit judge (who, as we have seen in relation to the Crown Court, is a legally qualified, full-time professional judge). He usually sits alone although in rare cases there may be a jury of eight.

134. Each court also has a legally qualified registrar who performs the functions of the clerk of court but also has minor judicial functions. Subject to certain safeguards, he can hear cases where the amount in dispute is small (the limit being varied from time to time) and can deal with cases where the person sued does not appear or where he appears and admits the claim.

135. The jurisdiction of the county court is wide. However, unlike the civil jurisdiction of the sheriff court it is subject to upper financial limits, which are changed from time to time to keep pace with inflation. Subject to these limits the county court can deal with actions founded on contract or tort, with actions for recovery of land, with proceedings relating to the administration of trusts and the estates of deceased persons and with various other types of proceedings.

136. There is a right of appeal on points of law and in many cases also on the facts from the county court to the Court of Appeal.

31

High Court of Justice

137. The High Court of Justice is divided into three divisions—the Queen's Bench Division, the Chancery Division and the Family Division. Sittings of the High Court may be conducted at any place in England and Wales. In practice it sits in London and in certain designated provincial centres.

138. *The Queen's Bench Division* is presided over by the Lord Chief Justice and deals mainly with the normal civil actions arising out of contract or tort. The Queen's Bench Division also includes a Commercial Court, which deals with such matters as insurance, banking and commercial agency, and an Admiralty Court, which deals with such matters as claims for damages arising out of a collision between ships. The procedure in these commercial and admiralty matters differs in some respects from the normal procedure.

139. The divisional court of the Queen's Bench Division has a minor appellate jurisdiction in civil cases, hearing certain appeals by case stated. It also has a supervisory jurisdiction which extends not only to the quashing of the orders of inferior courts or officials by the order of *certiorari* but also to the granting of the writ of *habeas corpus*, to secure the release of someone unlawfully detained, the order of *mandamus* or of *prohibition* to direct or prohibit something to be done, and the writ of attachment to secure the arrest of someone for contempt of court or disobedience of a court order.

140. *The Chancery Division* is presided over in theory by the Lord Chancellor. It deals with a variety of matters, often having an element of accounting or finance about them, and including the administration of estates, probate cases where the validity of the will is disputed, partnership actions, trusts, winding up of companies, taxation, patents, trade marks and copyright, bankruptcy and various conveyancing matters.

141. *The Family Division* consists of a President and other High Court judges. It deals mainly with defended matrimonial causes, including proceedings for divorce, nullity of marriage, judicial separation and the wardship and guardianship of children. It also, as we have seen, hears appeals by way of case stated from decisions of magistrates' courts in matrimonial and similar proceedings.

The Court of Appeal

142. The Court of Appeal has a civil division as well as the criminal division considered above. In practice the court consists of the Master

of the Rolls and the Lords Justices of Appeal, although such high rank-
ing judges as the Lords of Appeal of the House of Lords, the Lord
Chancellor, the Lord Chief Justice and the President of the Family
Division are *ex officio* members. The court hears appeals in civil cases
from the county courts, the High Court and various special courts and
tribunals.

Supreme Court of Judicature

143. This is the name given to the Court of Appeal, the High Court
and the Crown Court taken together.

House of Lords

144. There is appeal from the Court of Appeal to the House of Lords
if either court grants leave to appeal.

In addition there is a "leap-frog" procedure whereby an appeal can
be made direct from the High Court to the House of Lords, without
intervening proceedings in the Court of Appeal. This procedure is
available only if (a) the trial judge grants a certificate and (b) the
House of Lords grants leave. The trial judge will grant a certificate only
if all the parties consent, and a sufficient case is made out for use of the
leap-frog procedure, and a point of law of general public importance
(turning on the construction of an enactment or statutory instrument or
on a binding decision of the Court of Appeal or House of Lords) is
involved. There is no such procedure in relation to Scottish appeals to
the House of Lords.

Judicial Committee of the Privy Council

145. A body of distinguished lawyers, including senior judges and
former judges, acting as a court of appeal from the supreme courts of
Commonwealth countries. It was formerly the final court of appeal in
the British Empire, and still decides appeals from certain members of
the Commonwealth—although with changes in the latter's structure
their numbers have dwindled—and from the Channel Islands and the
Isle of Man. In theory its decision is merely advice to the Crown on
whether to allow or refuse the appeal. Within the United Kingdom, the
Judicial Committee hears appeals from the decisions of English ecclesiastical courts and various professional disciplinary bodies such as the
Disciplinary Committee of the General Medical Council. (See
paras. 210–211.)

European Court of Justice

146. The court's powers are laid down in the European Economic Community Treaty, and one of the consequences of the accession of the United Kingdom to the Community in 1972 was that the court assumed jurisdiction to give preliminary rulings on any question raised before any court or tribunal of a member state, criminal or civil. Such courts and tribunals (a category widely interpreted by the European Court, but understood to embrace any body with power to decide a point of law), including those in Scotland may in certain circumstances request it to give such a ruling. The criteria are contained in Article 177 of the Treaty of Accession. The national court must be satisfied that a decision by the European Court is necessary to enable it to give a judgment in the case before it. Where interpretation of statutes of bodies set up by an Act of the Council of Europe arises before a Scottish court or tribunal it may request the European Court to give a preliminary ruling on any question where the Scottish court or tribunal considers this necessary to enable a judgment to be reached. The national court or tribunal may take this course either at the instance of any party in the case or on its own initiative. Once the ruling has been given the case returns to the court or tribunal where it began. The procedure is likely to be adopted in situations where the national law may appear to be incompatible with Community law and an interpretation of the latter is necessary to enable the case to be decided in light of the European Court's interpretation. The proceedings before the originating court are meantime stayed. Normally the hearing of oral submissions before the Court and its judgment are in public.

147. The first case referred from a Scottish court under this procedure was a claim for a student's grant made by a Frenchman which had been refused by the Scottish Education Department. A question requiring an interpretation of Community law was referred to the European Court in June 1986 by Lord Clyde sitting in the Outer House of the Court of Session. The applicant, born in France of an English father and a French mother, claimed he was entitled to a grant in light of certain provisions of EEC law.

European Court of Human Rights

148. Not to be confused with the European Court of Justice, which deliberates in Luxembourg, is the European Court of Human Rights which sits in Strasbourg. Whereas the Court of Justice is concerned with the interpretation of European Community rules, often of a highly technical nature, the Court of Human Rights handles a broad range of cases frequently of great constitutional significance. A list of some of the cases referred from the United Kingdom confirms this. The court has been asked to rule on issues such as corporal punishment in schools, the closed shop, pensioners' rights, contempt of court, the use of "plastic bullets" and telephone tapping.

149. The court is part of the machinery set up under the European Convention on Human Rights in 1950. Where a breach of human rights is alleged a state or an individual can make a complaint to the European Commission of Human Rights in Strasbourg. This can be done only after all remedies in the applicant's own country have been exhausted. The commission investigates the circumstances and may refer the case to the Court of Human Rights.

150. The commission comprises a member from each of the states which signed the convention, the members being elected by the Committee of Ministers of the Council of Europe; the court consists of judges elected by the Consultative Assembly of the Council of Europe.

151. If a case goes to the court there will normally be a public hearing in Strasbourg to elaborate on written submissions. The court's final judgment is delivered in public, usually by the reading of a summary of the decision. A full text of the judgment is made available outside the court. (See also paras. 420–422, 435–436).

SOME PROCEDURAL DIFFERENCES IN ENGLAND

152. The procedure in England differs in many respects from that in Scotland. The details are not likely to concern the Scottish journalist. It should be noted, however, that the pursuer is called "the plaintiff" in England and the defender "the defendant." It should also be noted that in England divorce proceedings take place on a petition. In Scotland one talks of the pursuer and the defender in an action of divorce. In England one talks of the petitioner and the respondent in a petition for divorce. This difference of terminology is frequently a source of error. Another difference which sometimes gives rise to confusion relates to the form of divorce decrees. In England the court granting a divorce pronounces first a *decree nisi*. This is a provisional decree which does not dissolve the marriage and does not allow the parties to remarry. Only after the lapse of a certain time (currently six weeks) can the decree be converted into a *decree absolute*. In Scotland a decree of divorce takes effect immediately, and there is nothing comparable to a *decree nisi*.

Chapter 5

MISCELLANEOUS SPECIAL COURTS

The Lands Valuation Appeal Court

153. If a ratepayer is dissatisfied with the valuation of his property for rating purposes, he can appeal to the valuation appeal committee of the area. From there he has a further right of appeal on a point of law by way of stated case to the Lands Valuation Appeal Court or to the Lands Tribunal for Scotland. In England appeal against assessments is to a local valuation court and from there to the Lands Tribunal.

Restrictive Practices Court

154. All restrictive agreements between manufacturers or traders must be registered with an official known as the Registrar of Restrictive Trading Agreements. If he thinks they are not in the public interest he may bring them before the Restrictive Practices Court. The burden is then on the parties to the agreements to show that they are in the public interest.

155. When sitting in Scotland the Restrictive Practices Court usually consists of one judge of the Court of Session and at least two lay members qualified by experience in, or knowledge of, industry, commerce or public affairs. There is appeal to the Court of Session on points of law by way of a stated case.

156. When sitting in other parts of the United Kingdom the court is similarly composed of a judge and two or more laymen. There is appeal on a point of law to the Court of Appeal or the Court of Appeal of Northern Ireland.

Election courts

157. The function of these courts is to hear petitions, rare now, but at one time common, complaining against irregularities in the conduct of elections. In Scotland the Election Court in the case of a parliamentary election consists of two judges of the Court of Session. In the case of a local government election, it consists of the sheriff principal of the sheriffdom in which the election took place.

158. Election courts can try prosecutions for corrupt and illegal practices. The law on this point has often a curiously archaic ring. Corrupt practices are the more serious and include bribery and treating, that is, treating people to "meat, drink or entertainment" in order to influence votes. One glass of beer may not justify the charge but a large number may, and "giving drink to women that they may influence the votes of their fathers, brothers or sweethearts" has been held to be treating (*Encyclopaedia of The Laws of Scotland,* vol. 7, p. 306). It is also a corrupt practice to exert undue influence on voters—by force or threats of force or by threats of temporal or spiritual injury. Illegal practices include such offences as paying or receiving money for the conveyance of electors to or from the poll, voting when disqualified or inducing a disqualified person to vote.

159. In England election courts consist, in the case of a parliamentary election, of two High Court judges and, in the case of a local election, of a senior barrister.

Registration Appeal Court

160. Appeals regarding the registration of voters can be taken in the first instance to the sheriff and from there to a special Registration Appeal Court consisting of three judges of the Court of Session. The type of case which the court deals with can be illustrated by its decision in 1955 that a minister of the Church of Scotland who had been summoned to the General Assembly and who would accordingly be unable to vote at the polling station allotted to him, was entitled to be registered as an absent voter. In England appeals regarding registration of voters are made to the county court and then to the Court of Appeal.

The Scottish Land Court

161. The Scottish Land Court consists of a legally qualified chairman who enjoys the same rank and tenure of office as a judge of the Court of Session, and up to six other members of whom one must speak Gaelic. It decides various questions under the Acts relating to agriculture in Scotland. Its approval is often necessary, for example, before a landlord can serve an effective notice to quit on a farm tenant. The Land Court also deals with certain matters which in England are dealt with by bodies known as agricultural land tribunals and which relate to the exercise by the Secretary of State for Scotland or the Minister of Agriculture in England of their powers under the Agriculture Acts. If a person is aggrieved by a proposed exercise of these powers by the Secretary of State for Scotland he may require the matter to be referred to the Land Court. There is a right of appeal to the Inner

House of the Court of Session by way of stated case and only on a point of law.

The Lyon Court

162. The Lyon Court is a court held by the Lord Lyon King-of-Arms to deal with questions of heraldry and the right to bear arms in Scotland. There is appeal to the Inner House of the Court of Session and from there to the House of Lords.

Licensing boards

163. Licensing boards sit quarterly and comprise members of the district or islands council. Their functions include making decisions (after considering objections) on applications for certificates for the retail sale of excisable liquor, and on complaints, as well as imposing and revoking sanctions, giving consent to and ordering alterations to licensed premises. Certificates normally last three years. There is a right of appeal to the sheriff by either an applicant or objector or by a licence holder or a complainer, and a right of appeal to the Court of Session against the sheriff's decision. A new structure setting up these procedures and clarifying the functions of local licensing authorities, thus replacing licensing courts with licensing boards, was brought about by Part II of the Licensing (Scotland) Act 1976, which came into effect on July 1, 1977. In England liquor licences are issued by the licensing justices for the particular area.

Church courts

164. The Courts of the Church of Scotland have a statutory jurisdiction going back to 1592 and extending over the whole range of church matters, including discipline. The power to discipline officers and adherents of the church "is to be administered in faithfulness, meekness, love and tenderness" (Cox, *Practice and Procedure in the Church of Scotland,* 3rd ed., p. 380): a precept which has not always been followed. So long as matters are within the jurisdiction of the church courts, the civil courts cannot interfere.

165. The Courts of the Church of Scotland are the Kirk Session consisting of the minister and elders of a particular church, the Presbytery consisting of the ministers and representative elders from the parishes within its bounds, the Synod consisting of the members of the several Presbyteries within its bounds and finally the General Assembly with representatives from the whole church. Certain appeals in relation to

38

character and conduct are heard by a Judicial Commission of the General Assembly, which can decide at any stage of the proceedings whether they will be heard in public.

166. The courts of other churches in Scotland, including the Episcopal Church, have no statutory powers, their jurisdiction, like that of a club committee, depending on agreement between the members. The civil courts can intervene if there is a breach of this agreement affecting property interests just as in any other case of breach of contract. The courts can intervene also where there has been a denial of natural justice within the courts of a church in dealing with a complaint against a minister or a member or where those courts have exceeded their powers. Such a case occurred in 1986 when the Second Division of the Court of Session ruled that the Synod of the Free Presbyterian Church of Scotland had erred in suspending two ministers for life on grounds of contumacy (wilful disobedience). In his judgment in favour of the ministers, Lord Ross, Lord Justice-Clerk, said that the court had a limited jurisdiction to interfere with decisions of the governing body of a church. There could be no question of the court reviewing the merits of the synod's decision, but it would entertain an action where a religious body had acted clearly beyond its constitution or where procedure was grossly or fundamentally irregular. The church had failed to show that the two ministers were ever given an order they had disobeyed. They were dealt with after being found guilty of contumacy. They were also entitled to know what the case against them was; they were convicted before being given any hearing and without any charge being put to them.

167. England also has a system of ecclesiastical courts within the established church. As reorganised by the Ecclesiastical Jurisdiction Measure 1963 these are:

(a) in each diocese a bishop's court known as the Consistory Court,
(b) in each of the provinces of Canterbury and York an archbishop's court (called in Canterbury the Arches Court of Canterbury and in York the Chancery Court of York) and a Commission of Convocation,
(c) for *both* provinces (*i.e.* the whole country) a Court of Ecclesiastical Causes Reserved and a jointly chosen Commission of Convocation.

Ecclesiastical offences in England are divided into two types—those which do not involve matters of doctrine, ritual or ceremonial, and those which do. Offences of the first type include "conduct unbecom-

39

ing the office and work of a clerk in Holy Orders" and "serious, persistent or continuous neglect of duty." The Consistory Court deals with offences of this type committed by a deacon or priest. Appeal is to the Arches Court of Canterbury or the Chancery Court of York. The Commission of Convocation for the relevant province deals with offences of this first type committed by a bishop and the Commission of Convocation for *both* provinces deals with offences of this type committed by an archbishop. Appeal in each case lies to a special Commission of Review appointed by the Crown. The Court of Ecclesiastical Causes Reserved deals with offences of the second type (*i.e.* those which do involve matters of ritual, doctrine or ceremonial) and it has jurisdiction whether the offence is committed by a priest, deacon, bishop or archbishop. Appeal is to the special Commission of Review. As a rule all these English ecclesiastical courts sit in public.

Courts-martial

168. There are three types of military courts-martial—a *general court-martial* which consists of at least five officers and can try officers as well as other ranks, a *district court-martial* which consists of at least three officers and cannot try an officer or award more than two years' imprisonment and a *field general court-martial* which normally consists of at least three officers and is, in effect, an emergency general court-martial for the trial of offences committed on active service.

169. In the case of a general court-martial there must be, and in the case of other courts-martial there may be, a judge-advocate—a qualified lawyer whose function is to advise the court on the law and summarise the facts. He does not take part in the actual decision of the court.

170. Procedure at a court-martial follows that in an English criminal court, even when it sits in Scotland to try a Scottish soldier.

171. A finding of "not guilty" is final, but if the finding is "guilty" both decision and sentence are subject to confirmation by the confirming officer—usually the officer who convened the court-martial or any officer superior to him. This is no mere formality. Findings may be quashed or sentences greatly reduced. To give just one example, a Scots Guards officer was sentenced by a court-martial at Edinburgh Castle in February 1963 to be dismissed the service for fraudulently appropriating £1.30 from the sergeants' mess fund. The confirming officer commuted the sentence to a severe reprimand. Accordingly reports must always state that "findings and sentence are subject to confirmation." It should be noted too that a case remains *sub judice* until confirmed and that any comment on it before that date may amount to contempt of court.

172. The above remarks apply to military courts-martial. Air force courts-martial are very similar. Naval courts-martial consist of five to nine officers of or above the rank of lieutenant. Their findings and sentences are not subject to confirmation but take effect immediately. The authorities do, however, go over the record of the proceedings at a later date and may quash the conviction or reduce the sentence if there has been some irregularity.

173. A person who has been tried by an ordinary court is not liable to be re-tried by a court-martial. Under the Armed Forces Act 1966 a person who has been tried by a court-martial cannot be tried later by an ordinary court for the same, or substantially the same, offence.

174. Courts-martial meet at irregular intervals. The practice regarding notice varies. In some cases, the media are sent notice of pending trials but usually notice is simply posted at the service headquarters and it is necessary to keep in contact if important cases are not to be missed.

175. There is appeal from the findings of a court-martial to the Courts-Martial Appeal Court, which consists of the judges of the English Court of Appeal together with nominated judges from the English High Court, the Scottish High Court of Justiciary and the Supreme Court of Judicature of Northern Ireland. The Lord Chancellor can also appoint other persons of legal experience to be judges of the court. Three judges normally sit but there may be a larger uneven number. Five sat to hear and allow an appeal by a Colonel Osborn in December 1962 from his conviction of indecently assaulting a German boy.

176. Application for leave to appeal must first be made to the Courts-Martial Appeal Court. There is no appeal against sentence, but the court may vary the sentence incidentally if, for example, it finds that the accused was wrongfully convicted on one charge but that he was properly convicted or should have been convicted on another. Where a point of law of general public importance is at stake there can be a further appeal to the House of Lords. This is the only case where the decision of a criminal court sitting in Scotland may eventually be heard by the House of Lords.

Standing civilian courts

177. These operate outside the United Kingdom for the trial of persons employed by the armed forces or accompanying them but not subject to military law. They comprise an assistant judge-advocate-general, sometimes with two assessors, and may be compared to English magistrates' courts. A civilian convicted by such a court has a right of appeal to a court-martial or may petition a reviewing authority against conviction or sentence or both.

CHAPTER 6

OTHER BODIES

TRIBUNALS

178. There are a large number of tribunals which exercise quasi-judicial functions and which are yet not properly to be regarded as courts. They are a fairly modern phenomenon and at first were regarded by some with disfavour, on the grounds that a man should not be judged except by the ordinary courts of the land. It is now generally recognised, however, that if they are an evil, they are a necessary evil. The ordinary courts could not deal with all the questions arising under the many statutes regarding life in the welfare state and even if they could it is perhaps not desirable that they should. The courts are designed to deal with questions of law and to deal with them as correctly and justly as possible. Their high standards in these respects have been achieved at the expense of speed and cheapness. In many types of case rough justice done quickly and cheaply is better than a more perfect justice done slowly and expensively.

179. Before 1958, however, the justice done by tribunals was rougher than it needed to be. The decisions of many were final even on points of law and often decisions were handed down from the clouds without any reason being given. The Tribunals and Inquiries Act of 1958 (now replaced by the Tribunals and Inquiries Act 1971, which continues the same policies) introduced important reforms. It provided for the possibility of appeal to the courts on points of law from the most important tribunals and it stipulated that reasons should be given for decisions. A Council on Tribunals was set up to keep the position under review.

Industrial tribunals

180. These tribunals exercise jurisdiction in relation to various questions arising under the legislation on industrial training levy, redundancy payments, selective employment payments, equal pay, contracts of employment, trade unions and labour relations, and health and safety at work. In particular, they deal with complaints by employees of unfair dismissal and, if a complaint is upheld, have power to order the reinstatement of the employee or an award of compensation. The tribunals normally consist of a legally qualified chairman and two other members selected from a panel of persons with knowledge or experience of employment in industry or commerce. The Employment Protection Act 1975 provided for the setting up of a special Employment Appeal Tribunal to hear appeals on questions of law from industrial tribunals. This consists partly of nominated judges, at least one being from the Court of Session, and partly of members having special knowledge or experience of industrial relations.

National Health Service tribunals

181. The National Health Service (Scotland) Act 1947 provided for the setting up of a tribunal for the purpose of inquiring into cases where it is claimed that a doctor, dentist, pharmacist or optician should be removed from the National Health Service list. The tribunal consists of a legally qualified chairman and two other members. If it decides that the practitioner should not be removed from the list, the matter is at an end. There is no appeal. If it decides for removal, the practitioner can appeal to the Secretary of State and has also an appeal to the Court of Session on a point of law. The tribunal meets in private unless the practitioner otherwise requests but its decisions are generally made public by a communication to the media.

182. In England, the National Health Service tribunal has a corresponding jurisdiction and operates in the same way.

Transport

183. The traffic commissioners of an area (a full-time chairman and two others) deal with road *passenger* traffic. They grant road service licences and public service vehicle licences. Appeal from their decisions in these matters is to the Minister of Transport and from him on a point of law to the Court of Session or, in England, the High Court. They also deal with public service vehicle drivers' and conductors' licences. Appeal in these cases is to the sheriff or in England the magistrates' court. The traffic commissioners sit in public. The licensing authority for an area (in fact the chairman of the traffic commissioners) issues operators' and transport managers' licences in connection with the carriage of goods by road and also grants special authorisations for the use of large goods vehicles. There is appeal from its decisions to the Transport Tribunal. It is also responsible for the issuing of heavy goods vehicles drivers' licences and in this case appeal is to the sheriff or, in England, the magistrates' court.

184. The Transport Tribunal consists of a legally qualified president, and four other members experienced in finance, commerce or transport. Appeals regarding road haulage matters are heard by the Road Haulage Appeals Division of the Tribunal, which consists of the president and two of the members. The Transport Tribunal sits in public. When considering a Scottish case, it sits in Scotland. There is appeal to the Court of Session on a point of law.

Miscellaneous tribunals

185. There are various other tribunals of varying importance. The *Lands Tribunal for Scotland* deals with disputes concerning compensation for the compulsory acquisition of land, with the variation and discharge of certain obligations contained in the titles to land, and with the valuation of land for certain tax purposes. In addition parties may voluntarily refer a matter to the tribunal as an arbiter. The tribunal consists of both lawyers and valuers, with a legally qualified president. Appeal on a point of law lies to the Court of Session. The tribunal sits in public, except when it is acting as arbiter under a voluntary reference, when it may, if requested, sit in private. There is a similar *Lands Tribunal* for England, with a slightly different jurisdiction including the hearing of rating appeals. *Rent tribunals* decide disputes relating to the rents of properties falling under the Rent Acts and have a discretion whether or not to sit in public. *Supplementary benefit appeal tribunals* and *social security local tribunals* and *medical appeal tribunals* deal with disputes or appeals from local officers with regard to these respective matters. *Pensions appeal tribunals* decide appeals from decisions of the Secretary of State for Social Services on claims to pensions for war injuries and sit in public, except in certain specific circumstances. *The Patents Appeal Tribunal* consists of a judge of the High Court in England and hears appeals from decisions of the Comptroller-General of Patents, Designs and Trade Marks on such questions as whether an alleged invention is patentable. It has a discretion, rendered necessary by the sometimes secret nature of its subject-matter, whether or not to sit in public. For the purpose of certain Scottish appeals, there is a Scottish Patents Appeal Tribunal consisting of a judge of the Court of Session. *The Performing Right Tribunal* sits in public to hear disputes regarding the terms and conditions of licences to perform works protected by copyright. It has to decide, for example, what rates Scottish dance halls should pay for open licences to include copyright music in their programme. It is not to be confused with the Performing Right Society which is a private body representing the interests of copyright owners. The above is by no means an exhaustive list. There are many

45

other tribunals and there are other bodies, such as the General Commissioners for Income Tax, which are not called tribunals but which perform the same function and come under the control of the Council of Tribunals.

186. Inquiries into matters of national importance can take three forms—a tribunal of inquiry, a committee of inquiry or a royal commission.

Tribunals of inquiry

187. Tribunals of inquiry are appointed by Parliament to inquire into matters of "urgent public importance." Their findings are laid before Parliament and published by the Stationery Office. An example was the Vassall Tribunal set up in November 1962, to inquire into the circumstances surrounding Vassall's spying activities and, in particular, allegations that the presence of a spy within the Admiralty had been known to the First Lord of the Admiralty and his service chiefs for about 18 months before Vassall's arrest. Other tribunals of inquiry have been the Waters Tribunal in 1959, which inquired into allegations that John Waters, a Thurso message-boy, had been assaulted by the police, the "bank rate leak" Tribunal under Lord Parker in 1958, and the Lynskey Tribunal in 1948 which investigated stories of bribery and corruption in governmental circles.

188. Tribunals of inquiry sit in public, unless they think privacy is in the public interest in view of the subject-matter of the inquiry or the nature of the evidence to be given. They can exclude the public for part only of the proceedings. The Vassall Tribunal conducted approximately two-thirds of the hearing in private.

189. There is power to order witnesses to attend and give evidence. There is also power to refer cases of contempt of the tribunal to the High Court in England or Court of Session in Scotland for consideration and, if necessary, punishment.

190. There has been dissatisfaction with tribunals of inquiry. They are designed to ascertain facts but often succeed in imprinting rumour still more firmly in the public mind. They are equipped with the cumbrous machinery of a court of law and yet expected to deal with the volatile issues of politics. They often seem to be either unduly restricted by their terms of reference, or, as in the case of the Vassall Tribunal, embarrassed by their width. Nevertheless, tribunals of inquiry have an essential role to play and the remedy would seem to be not to change the system but to use tribunals only in cases of the *most* urgent public importance.

Committees of inquiry

191. Either House of Parliament may set up a committee of inquiry to investigate any matter of public importance. The committee may include persons who are not members of Parliament. Committees of inquiry were widely used at one time but have now been superseded in practice by tribunals of inquiry. Their main disadvantage is that it is difficult to exclude the suspicion or, indeed, the actual presence, of political bias.

Royal commissions

192. Royal commissions are often set up where the object is not so much to find out facts for their own sake as to consider a situation with a view to reform. There have been royal commissions on, among other things, the Press, capital punishment, the law of marriage and divorce and legal services in both Scotland and England and Wales. Commissioners are appointed by the Crown and given power to summon witnesses and demand information. Their report is generally published as a Command Paper.

193. In practice royal commissions often sit in public but may hear evidence in private and may receive written evidence which need not be published. The bodies submitting such evidence may send it to the Press for publication and where this is done there is no objection to publishing it.

Local inquiries

194. Local inquiries are held, generally in public, under various statutes. Planning inquiries are among the most common and deal with such questions as whether planning permission should be granted for the erection of multi-storey buildings in city centres. Local inquiries are also held when there are objections to a proposed Private Act of Parliament.

In Scotland inquiries are held by reporters who are often practising advocates. In England inquiries are carried out by inspectors. The reporter or inspector reports his findings and recommendations to the appropriate Minister who then gives his decision.

Fatal accidents and sudden deaths inquiries

195. The law on these inquiries has been consolidated and amended by the Fatal Accidents and Sudden Deaths Inquiry (Scotland) Act 1976. Public inquiries are held (a) in the case of fatal accidents at work, (b) in the case of deaths in legal custody (in, for example, a police station or prison) and (c) in any case in which it appears to the Lord Advocate to be expedient in the public interest that an inquiry should be held on the ground that the death was sudden, suspicious or unexplained, or occurred in circumstances such as to give rise to serious public concern. Even in cases (a) and (b) an inquiry will not be held if the Lord Advocate is satisfied that the circumstances of the death have been sufficiently established in criminal proceedings. The inquiry is held by the sheriff, without a jury. The fact that a person is examined as a witness at an inquiry does not prevent criminal proceedings later being taken against him but the sheriff's determination as to the cause of death and other relevant facts is not admissible in evidence in any judicial proceedings arising out of the death or accident.

196. The sheriff may prohibit the publication in any newspaper or broadcast of any identifying particulars (including a picture) of any person under 17 involved in the inquiry in any way. (See Chapter 12.)

Shipping and railway inquiries

197. There is statutory provision for inquiries into deaths at sea, shipping casualties and railway accidents. These are again in no way trials or civil actions. Their sole purpose is the ascertainment of the facts.

198. Where a death occurs on board any foreign-going British ship, an inquiry is held, generally in public, by a Department of Transport superintendent at the next port of call if in the U.K. or by a British consul if in a foreign port. If it is thought that death was caused by violence or other improper means the department can if need be "take steps for bringing the offender or offenders to justice."

199. Department of Transport shipping casualty inquiries are held when a ship is lost, abandoned or materially damaged if at the time of the casualty the ship was registered in the U.K. or was in the U.K. or its territorial waters.

200. A preliminary inquiry may be made by a person appointed by the Secretary of State for Transport. If a formal inquiry is considered desirable it is held by a court of summary jurisdiction (the sheriff court in Scotland and if in England, Wales or Northern Ireland, by a wreck commissioner) assisted in each case by one or more assessors who are experts in nautical engineering or other relevant matters. In practice shipping casualty inquiries in Scotland are held in public. The questions on which the opinion of the court is desired *must* be stated in open court. In practice the rest of the proceedings are also in public. After hearing the case the court must report to the Secretary of State for Transport. The court has power to cancel or suspend the certificate of a master, mate or engineer, if it finds that the casualty was due to his "wrongful act or default." Its decision on this matter must be announced in open court.

201. The Secretary of State for Transport has power to order inquiries into train accidents. These are held by an Inspecting Officer of Railways who has a wide discretion as to the procedure. In practice the public are admitted but may be excluded if, for example, evidence would be likely to prejudice an accused at a subsequent criminal trial.

The Ombudsman

202. On the model of the Scandinavian Ombudsman, the office of Parliamentary Commissioner for Administration was created in 1967, to investigate complaints by citizens against actions of the Executive or of bureaucratic incompetence giving rise to injustice. Appointed by Parliament, the Commissioner is independent and his duty is to act impartially between government and the individual. A separate Commissioner with particular and similar duties in relation to the administration of the National Health Service came into being in 1973. The journalist is most likely to be concerned, however, with the work of the Local Commissioners for Administration—one for England and Wales (created in 1974) and another for Scotland (1975). As in the case of the Parliamentary Commissioner, the local ombudsmen are entirely independent, their main function being to investigate complaints by members of the public who consider they have been victims of injustice as a result of maladministration by a local authority.

203. The majority of complaints are concerned with matters of housing, planning and building control, education and environmental health. The Commissioner issues an annual report, which is published, and his report on each individual complaint is also made public through the media. The identity of the complainant is not usually disclosed, but the local authority concerned is named.

204. Complaints are normally made in the first instance through a councillor, but in the event of his failure or refusal to pass it to the Commissioner, the complainant may submit his grievance direct, provided it is made in writing. The Commissioner will not usually look into any complaint where provision is already made for recourse to a court, tribunal or Minister, unless for some reason the complainant is unable to follow that course. In carrying out his inquiries, the Commissioner has the same powers to compel attendance of witnesses and insist on production of documents as has the Court of Session.

205. The procedure is informal and private, and he prepares a draft report for the chief executive of the local authority concerned, for comment. In this way any dispute on the facts is established before the formal report is prepared and published. If there is a finding of maladministration resulting in injustice the onus is on the local authority to indicate to the Commissioner what action they propose to take to rectify matters. If he is not satisfied (as happens in a small minority of cases) he presents a further report.

206. The weakness of the system is that, apart from issuing his finding and pointing the direction in which he holds the remedy lies, the Commissioner is powerless to do more. But the pressure his efforts bring to bear on defaulting authorities through the publicity his reports receive in the media should not be underestimated; and his functions are seen as concerned with settling questions of principle rather than dealing with disputes involving issues of compensation. Even without powers of enforcement, his watchdog and investigative role for the most part achieves its essential purpose in producing a solution without recourse to law.

PROFESSIONAL DISCIPLINARY BODIES

207. There are various bodies set up under statute to supervise discipline in the professions. Broadly speaking, they all have power to strike members off the respective registers if (a) they have been convicted of a criminal offence or (b) they have been guilty of "infamous or disgraceful conduct in a professional respect." In the case of doctors, it used to be said that conduct of this type was usually one of the five As—adultery, abortion, alcohol, addiction or advertising but the liberalisation of the abortion law has decreased the risk of transgressions under that heading. The details of what criminal convictions warrant removal vary strangely. Opticians, for example, can be struck off on conviction of a serious offence by a court in the United Kingdom, doctors on conviction by a court in the United Kingdom or Ireland and dentists on conviction by a court anywhere.

208. The professional disciplinary bodies dealing with doctors, dentists, opticians and pharmacists should be clearly distinguished from the National Health Service tribunals dealt with earlier. The former are concerned with discipline in the profession, the latter with breach of the terms of employment in the National Health Service. The former can remove a name from the register of members of the profession, the latter only from the list of those members of the profession employed in the National Health Service.

209. The general rule is that proceedings of these bodies take place in public, but that they may exclude the public in the interests of justice or for other special reason. Exceptions to the rule are noted below.

210. Professional disciplinary bodies fall into two classes, those from which appeal is to the Privy Council and those from which appeal is to the Court of Session. Reports must always state that the name will be removed "failing the entry of an appeal to the Privy Council within twenty-eight days" or as the case may be. Even where the name is removed it is generally possible for the person concerned to apply after a suitable period for restoration to the register.

211. Bodies from which appeal lies to the Privy Council within 28 days are the *Disciplinary Committee of the General Medical Council*, the *Disciplinary Committee of the General Dental Council*, the *Disciplinary Committee of the Council of the Royal College of Veterinary Surgeons* and the *Disciplinary Committee of the General Optical Council* all of which conform to the general rule regarding meeting in public. Under the Professions Supplementary to Medicine Act 1960, disciplinary committees were established in the case of chiropodists, dieticians, medical laboratory technicians, occupational therapists, physiotherapists, radiographers and remedial gymnasts. Meetings are held in public, generally, and there is appeal to the Privy Council within 28 days.

212. Bodies from which appeal lies to the Court of Session or the High Court in England within three months are the *Statutory Committee of the Pharmaceutical Society* which must open in public and announce its decisions in public but can if it thinks fit hold any other part of the hearing in private, and the *Disciplinary Committee of the Architects Registration Council* which appears to have discretion as to meeting in public.

213. *The Scottish Solicitors' Discipline Tribunal* can strike a solicitor off the roll, suspend him and, in cases of professional misconduct, fine him up to £4000. There is a right of appeal to the Court of Session within 21 days, in which event the hearing is in private but the judgment may be released for publication. The tribunal's deliberations are in private but orders striking a solicitor off the roll or suspending him from practice are issued to the media (unless an appeal is pending).

The tribunal is an independent body, not an offshoot of the society; there are four lay members who, like the solicitor members, are appointed by the Lord President of the Court of Session. Complaints are prosecuted by fiscals, who are private practitioners independent of the Council of the Society. Although the majority of complaints are brought by the society, private prosecutions may be taken. Caution should be exercised in drawing conclusions from a mere statement that a solicitor has been removed from the roll. He may have had his name removed at his own request if, for example, he intends to become an advocate or he may simply have allowed his membership to lapse. There is a disciplinary tribunal system in England similar to that operating in Scotland; there is a right of appeal within eight days to the Divisional Court of the Queen's Bench Division, and, with leave, from there to the Court of Appeal.

214. The Scottish tribunal exercises a discretion to decide whether to identify any solicitor in publicity it issues in connection with disciplinary measures it takes against him, and in practice it names only those found guilty of the more serious misconduct. The Court of Session may overrule the tribunal on the issue of identification. In 1986, in the case of an Edinburgh solicitor found guilty of charging a client grossly excessive fees, the First Division rejected his appeal against censure and a fine of £1000, and affirmed the tribunal's decision that he should be named.

215. Complaints procedures in the solicitors' branch of the profession in Scotland were augmented in 1976 with the appointment of a Lay Observer, an independent investigator whose function is to examine allegations made in writing by members of the public concerning the society's treatment of any complaint made to it about a solicitor or solicitor's employee, and to ensure that the society acts reasonably, impartially and efficiently in investigating complaints. While the appointment has been welcomed as an added check on the investigation of the conduct of lawyers by lawyers, it has also been criticised for its lack of power to take complaints direct to the tribunal. In practice the Lay Observer can act only after a complaint has been considered by the society and the complainant remains dissatisfied. The Lay Observer can comment on its handling of a case but the society is not bound to follow any suggestions he/she may make.

216. The Scottish Bar is a tight-knit body with high standards of conduct and a strong corporate spirit. Any disciplinary measures required would be taken in private by the Dean of the Faculty of Advocates and his Council.

Complaints about judges

217. Under s.12 of the Sheriff Courts (Scotland) Act 1971, the Lord President of the Court of Session and the Lord Justice-Clerk have power, either on their own initiative or at the request of the Secretary of State for Scotland, to carry out a joint investigation into the fitness for office of any sheriff principal or sheriff and to report to the Secretary of State if they consider that the judge is unfit for office by reason of inability, neglect of duty or misbehaviour. The Secretary of State thereafter may order the removal of the sheriff from office. Judges of the High Court and Court of Session can be removed from office only by an address to both Houses of Parliament.

218. In England, High Court judges under the Act of Settlement hold office during good behaviour, subject to removal on an address to both Houses of Parliament. The Lord Chancellor, a political appointee, is not subject to this procedure. He has authority to remove a circuit judge on grounds of incapacity or misbehaviour. In 1968 Lord Hailsham, Lord Chancellor, expressed the view that he would welcome a complaints board, with statutory procedure similar to that in force in Scotland in relation to sheriffs.

219. In 1987 the English Bar came under a new administrative and disciplinary structure—the General Council of the Bar and of the Inns of Court—comprising representatives from the six Crown Court Circuits, the specialist Bar associations, the Inns of Court, and 51 barristers elected by the general Bar. The Council replaces the Senate of the Four Inns of Court which formerly exercised disciplinary powers over barristers. Judges are now excluded from membership of the body, but may be co-opted to certain committees. The purpose of the change was mainly to give the Bar a more effective and democratic governing body and more clout on matters such as negotiating legal aid fees and exclusive rights of audience in court, and to enable it to "speak with one voice." Under the new structure complaints against barristers are investigated by a committee of the Council and there are disciplinary tribunals made up jointly of judges and barristers.

MISCELLANEOUS

220. There are multifarious bodies, from the committee of the local literary and debating club to the committee of the Stock Exchange, which exercise quasi-judicial functions. These bodies have no statutory jurisdiction and their powers stem from contract between the members. The ordinary courts will interfere with their decisions if they have

53

broken the terms of the contract, for example, by not following the procedure laid down in the rules, and if some property interest is affected. These bodies meet in private but, may, in terms of their rules, publish their decisions in various ways. They include the committees of Stock Exchanges, the "courts" of the churches in Scotland other than the Church of Scotland and the ruling bodies of various sports. Racing authorities such as the Jockey Club, the National Hunt Committee and the Steeplechase Committee have, in addition to disciplinary power over their members and officials, a power to "warn off" the courses under their jurisdiction which extends to spectators as well as those more actively engaged in the sport. The Press Council consists of a lay chairman, up to five lay members and 20 journalistic and managerial representatives. It acts as a sort of disciplinary body without teeth, having power to investigate and report on complaints against the Press but no power to take effective disciplinary action against newspapers or journalists concerned. Complaints must be lodged within three months of publication. Its address is 1 Salisbury Square, London, EC4.

221. Complaints about broadcasts by the BBC or any of the independent broadcasting companies on the ground that they are unfair or an infringement of privacy go before the Broadcasting Complaints Commission. In the case of the BBC general complaints on matters of principle are the responsibility of the Director-General (*via*, in Scotland, Broadcasting House, Queen Margaret Drive, Glasgow, G12 8DG). Unlike the BBC, whose rules are self-imposed, the independent radio and television companies, operating under the Independent Broadcasting Authority, must observe a code prohibiting the transmission of anything, whether in general or in advertisements, offending against good taste or decency or likely to lead to crime or disorder or be offensive to public feelings. There are rules governing accuracy and impartiality of news bulletins and programmes on current affairs, the portrayal of violence in television programmes and the times at which programmes may be broadcast which might be unsuitable for young viewers. Complaints against alleged breaches of the code are directed to the IBA at 70 Brompton Road, London, SW3 1EY.

Part II

THE COURT REPORTER

Chapter 7

RIGHTS AND RESPONSIBILITIES

222. The aim here is to present a guide, for quick reference, which will meet the situations most likely to cause difficulty or raise doubts in the minds of journalists concerned with court reporting in Scotland. There are judicial pronouncements bearing upon certain aspects—in some cases most important aspects—of the court reporter's work, but these are only pieces in the jig-saw puzzle. The statutory enactments and decisions of the courts leave unanswered vast areas of difficult and sometimes perilous territory for the journalist to tread when reporting court proceedings. In pointing, as best we may, a safe path through the pitfalls we must depend largely upon practical experience.

223. It is perhaps worthwhile observing early in the study of such a subject the importance of the role played by the reporter who, though he enjoys no rights within the courts other than those accorded to other members of the public, bears the responsibility of presenting a picture for the public of the process of our law. At best, only a very small proportion of the members of the public are able, or sufficiently interested, to attend and witness for themselves the doing of justice. In the civil courts in particular—and here one thinks especially of the Court of Session, the supreme civil court in the land—the public (apart from the media) are often entirely absent. The desire of our judges to ensure that justice is not only done, but is also seen to be done, can hardly be fully realised if the only persons present to observe whether it is done are counsel and solicitors for the parties and the judges themselves. The intention must be to ensure that the safeguard of justice visibly done is in practice more than just a pious aim, and to this end the presence in court of representatives of the public ensures the survival of our most valued principles. This, however, is only one of the responsibilities borne by the court reporter. Others will emerge in the course of the pages that follow.

224. Attention will be concentrated upon the rules, written or under-

55

stood, to which the reporter operating in the law courts in Scotland must pay heed. For a comprehensive review of the law affecting journalists, the reader is referred to other sections of this book.

225. Scotland by the Act of Union has preserved its own independent system of law. This is a matter for pride in the minds of most Scots, but it creates certain problems for those with a predisposition to think of the law of the United Kingdom as a unit. No doubt broadcasting and the wide circulation in Scotland of English newspapers or Scottish editions of them are largely responsible for the widespread tendency among Scots to see the law through English eyes and even to use English legal terms with reference to Scottish cases. To take a small example, "co-respondent" has a special meaning which has become fixed in the minds of most people who read newspapers or are receptive to other modern methods of mass communication. How often one sees the term used in relation to Scottish divorce proceedings: yet, in Scotland the term is co-defender, and "co-respondent" here is non-existent. This is more than a mere puristic quibble, for if there are different and distinct terms in Scotland and England, why should we in Scotland use the English one with reference to Scottish cases?

226. It is the practice in the drafting of many United Kingdom statutes for Parliament to devote the major part of a Bill to the English law and to append, where appropriate, an "application to Scotland" section. Likewise, it is common for books dealing with the legal system, published for the guidance of the layman, to give only secondary consideration to the Scottish structure. This is inevitable owing to the much greater volume of law and the greater complexities of the English organisation. One of the purposes of this book has been to shift the emphasis, so as to give an independent guide to the complexities of the Scottish system, while not entirely ignoring the English. The latter, however, will occur largely for comparison where it seems necessary to warn against the risk of assuming that the two systems are the same.

227. It is hoped the guide will assist not only reporters working regularly in the Scottish courts, and those whose duty it is to handle the reports they hand in, but also visiting journalists from England or other countries who may be understandably unfamiliar with our native and, in some ways, peculiar judicial system.

228. It has been thought appropriate to add an index for the benefit of busy working journalists who have not the time to thumb through several textbooks and Acts of Parliament to get an answer to their queries.

229. This section falls naturally into parts dealing respectively with the end which the court reporter shall have in view and the means he must adopt in order to attain it. Before he applies his mind to the methods available to enable him to gather his material, the court reporter will be well advised to consider seriously what are his real objectives. It is better, where so much may be at stake—not only the reputations of the persons named in his reports but possibly also his own career—that he should not merely muddle along, hoping to pick up bits of advice from court officials or lawyers whom he may encounter.

230. Lawyers practising in the courts, and staff, have usually had little occasion to acquaint themselves with the special aspects of the law which are the particular concern of the court journalist. Sufficiently equipped with the essential knowledge not only of his rights in presenting reports of court proceedings for publication, but also of his obligations to keep within the law and to observe certain moral standards, the reporter may proceed with confidence, seeking only such information from official sources as he knows he is entitled to use and involving his editor as little as possible in the necessity to seek legal advice.

Accuracy and justice

231. Given the prerequisite of accuracy—and nowhere in the field of journalism is it more vital—the writer of court reports has to keep constantly in mind the fact that he must fit his activities into the existing system of justice. Not only should he feel in tune with the conception of justice which has guided our law-givers and administrators, but he has to remember that unless he develops an almost instinctive awareness of the meaning of the particular kind of justice recognised by the law of Scotland, he is liable to find himself sooner or later in conflict with the system to a more or less serious degree. There is no doubt it was failure to appreciate this basic notion underlying the safe reporting of court proceedings in Scotland which resulted in contempt complaints against newspapers, radio and television in recent years, which were dealt with by the High Court of Justiciary by way of heavy fines.

232. The meaning of justice, as applied to the functions of the court reporter, must vary from one country to another, according to the particular standards locally demanded by the law and the courts. The Scottish concept, it is worth remembering, has developed along lines which are directed distinctively towards the protection of the rights of the individual. In no country is this idea given greater emphasis in the day-to-day administration of the courts, both civil and criminal. It may be

read into many of the suggestions and recommendations in the following pages that the alternative to the course outlined would or could
amount to a denial of justice in some form or another—or could be
interpreted as such if the matter came to an issue. And we are concerned in this sphere not only with doing justice to an accused person
or to the parties to a litigation; the reporter has to be aware no less of
the need for a just treatment in his reports of other participants in the
proceedings, including witnesses, counsel, solicitors, and not least the
judge.

233. It is as well, in passing, to note that he should bear in mind also
the necessity for doing justice to himself. If he produces a report which
falls short of his capacity in some respect, he is doing himself an injustice in the eyes of his readers. In court reporting, even more than in
other branches of the profession, the writer must view his work according to the standard of his most critical reader.

234. Injustice to the judge may be one of the most dangerous
offences of all, since, in this category would fall such things as contempt of court or what was called murmuring a judge. (This was a
statutory offence in Scotland under an Act of 1540, which was repealed
by the Statute Law (Repeals) Act 1973.) Where the contempt is
patent, the court has a remedy as was demonstrated in the recent cases
in the High Court already referred to. But, it would be a mistake to
proceed on the basis that it is an injustice only if there is a "come-
back," a real risk of retribution. There are many situations in which a
newspaper may be unfair to a judge, but where the court has no remedy at all. In such cases the injustice, although not in itself punishable,
is in some regards more reprehensible because judges are usually
unable to make public statements for their own personal protection.
One instance will suffice. A man was convicted of murder and the date
for execution fixed. He appealed, which automatically caused a suspension of the execution. When his appeal failed, a new date for the
hanging had to be fixed. The wrong date was announced, but a correction made within minutes. All the members of the Press had, however,
left the court, and the clerk hurried to the Press Room and informed
the reporters of the correction. One paper made a feature of the mistake, under a streamer heading which blamed the judge for getting the
date of the hanging wrong. What, in fact, had happened, was, that the
clerk had accidentally passed the wrong date to the judge who accepted
it without question. The mistake was not the judge's, but he was publicly blamed for what looked like a rather careless slip. No journalist
with a sense of justice could claim that this was a fair report.

Balance

235. It is not enough that a story should include all the passages which make hard news as well as interesting or amusing reading; it is equally important that it should leave out nothing which is essential for the fair presentation of a balanced report, viewed from the position of the parties. Court reporting, unlike many other types of journalism, entails a degree of responsibility to publish what may sometimes be dull or uninteresting in order to preserve a safe and just balance between the opposing elements in the conflict before the court.

236. While exercising proper caution in the matter of keeping his report within the bounds of safe, fair and accurate journalism, the reporter is also entitled to keep in mind the essential difference between matter which is actionable and that which merely gives rise to annoyance or irritation. Many parties complain about Press reports of their cases who have no real ground for legal complaint. The journalist has to be prepared for, and to recognise, the groundless protest when it arises. He must retain a position of complete detachment from the viewpoint of any participant in a case, since if he falls into the trap of feeling sympathy for one side he will be in danger of causing prejudice to the other.

237. It will not always be necessary or desirable to proceed to the ultimate limits permitted by law in reporting the personal and more intimate details of certain types of cases. There is much material in matrimonial cases, for example, which is legally permissible under the terms of the Judicial Proceedings (Regulation of Reports) Act 1926, but which taste and a sense of humanity will guide one to exclude from one's report. It may, for example, be preferable to exclude the name or other means of identification of an insane or mentally defective person; and where issues of legitimacy of children have to be publicised every effort has to be made to protect the interests of the children. (Statutory restrictions in this field are dealt with in Chapter 12.) When, on the other hand, it is decided to omit from a report matter which in ordinary circumstances would be regarded as news, whether the name of a party or an allegation, the reporter should be able to supply a valid reason for his decision. Otherwise his paper may be accused of deliberate suppression without good cause or from oblique motive.

238. Any approach made to the reporter by a party or his representative (or indeed by a court official) with a view to suppressing material which he believes should be published, should be referred to his editor or his deputy, and in the meantime the report should be written up as if no such approach had been made. The duty to write the story is the reporter's, that of deciding whether to publish it is the editor's. Moreover, the reporter must treat with caution requests by interested parties to publish an explanation or correction bearing on the issues in a case before the court. Such extraneous material may suit the interests of one party but interfere with those of his opponent. The journalist's position of neutrality demands that he should be firm in rejecting such advances. The court journalist will at the same time find it necessary to cultivate good relations with court staff and practising lawyers. In certain spheres, such as the Court of Session, a harmonious liaison with the profession and court staff forms a major part of the reporter's equipment.

Closed doors

239. While for special reasons proceedings may sometimes be held behind closed doors, it is one of the fundamental principles of the Scottish system that the judicial processes are public. It is only in this way that justice may not only be done but may be seen to be done. There are still in operation, indeed, two Acts of the Scottish Parliament, 1686, c. 18, and 1693, c. 26 regulating the position. (By the Statute Law Revision (Scotland) Act 1964 these are now called respectively the Evidence Act 1686 and the Court of Session Act 1693.) The first of these lays down that there shall be "publication of the testimonies of witnesses." The second provides that "in all tyme comeing all bills, reports, debates, probations, and others relating to processes shall be considered, reasoned, advised, and voted by the Lords of Session with open doors . . . but with this restriction, that in some speciall cases the said Lords shall be allowed to cause remove all persons except the parties and their procurators."

240. The types of "speciall cases" that are in practice taken in private are few, but it is as well that the reporter should appreciate in each instance the justification for his exclusion. In the criminal department, for example, bail appeals, although they may be heard in court, (Criminal Procedure (Scotland) Act 1975, s.300(3)) are usually heard in chambers because, to enable the judge to determine whether the appellant is a person likely to fail to surrender to his bail, he is informed of any criminal record the man may have. Since such applications precede trial, it is in the interests of justice that such particulars must not be made public at this stage.

241. Cases brought in the sheriff court or Inner House of the Court of

Session under the procedure connected with the adoption of children are, with rare exceptions, (see para. 571) heard wholly in private.

242. Actions of declarator of nullity of marriage involve sometimes the leading of evidence which can only suitably be given in private, since it would often be difficult to persuade witnesses to speak freely on matters such as sexual perversion or impotency in the presence of spectators. The decision is normally given in public.

243. The doors may be closed in any case on the order of the judge for part of the hearing where it appears to him that this is necessary for the doing of justice, but it is a decision which is not reached lightly. He may decide on this course for reasons other than the particular character of the evidence; for example, where he has reason to anticipate a political demonstration in the courtroom which might disrupt the proceedings, or any conduct among members of the public which would distract the attention of the court, counsel or witnesses. It is not usual for the media, who would presumably not participate in such irregular practices, to be excluded in cases of this kind.

244. The decision to close the doors, where not provided by statute, is a matter for the discretion of the judge before whom the case is heard, and it will be found that some judges exercise it more freely than others.

245. The Press are normally admitted to sittings of the Vacation Judge of the Court of Session, which occur several times a week during vacations. These proceedings are informal, the judge and counsel do not wear wig and gown, and sometimes urgent business which cannot wait until the resumption of the session is disposed of and may produce news. On one occasion in 1960, when several applications for interim custody of children were expected to be dealt with in the Vacation Court, a large number of reporters and photographers arrived outside the courtroom. Since there was little accommodation inside, and the judge, on the advice of the clerk of court, feared that there might be difficulty in disposing of business owing to congestion, he excluded the Press altogether, not only from the hearing of the custody cases but also from the entire sitting of the Vacation Court for that day. It has been generally agreed since then that (*a*) one or two representative members of the Press should have been admitted and (*b*) it was wrong to exclude the Press from the entire sitting. To be fair to the court, however, both the judge and his clerk were aware that at that particular time much sensational treatment was being accorded in some newspapers to custody disputes which were still *sub judice*, and they were no doubt influenced by this. Since that occasion the Press have rarely been

excluded from the Vacation Court, which has from time to time produced news of considerable interest and importance, and in fact tacit
recognition of the reporter's right to be there has recently been granted
in the form of special seating accommodation previously absent. The
same discretion resides in the judge, however, to close the doors in any
case where he considers this necessary for the doing of justice.

Summary trial procedure

246. There is a kind of short-cut procedure in the Court of Session
known as summary trial provided for by s.10 of the Administration of
Justice (Scotland) Act 1933, by which parties, by agreement, may bring
their dispute before a Court of Session judge of their choice for a
speedy decision, and without right of appeal. In the great majority of
such cases the procedure, so far as reporters are concerned, does not
differ significantly from that of a proof under the ordinary procedure:
evidence and counsel's speeches are heard, and the judge delivers a
judgment (which, however, is final).

247. In 1967, however, a petition was brought before the court to
determine who was the heir male of the late Lord Sempill, and the procedure appears to have been unique in that it took place entirely in
secret. The decision of the case depended on the sex of Ewan Forbes-
Sempill, who was registered in infancy as female but underwent a
change of sex as an adult. The petition, which was brought under the
s.10 procedure, was heard by Lord Hunter in a solicitor's office, no
decision or judgment was ever issued, and no Press report of the case
was therefore possible. Following Press reactions to this unusual
method of avoiding publicity, the Lord Advocate, on being consulted,
gave it as his view that under s.10(3) of the 1933 Act the course taken
by the court was justified in view of the "purely private" nature of the
matter being dealt with. It seemed to him that somewhat similar considerations to those operating in relation to nullity cases justified the
hearing being in secret. The view of Lord Kilbrandon, then Chairman
of the Scottish Law Commission, was that s.10 was intended to provide
a species of judicial arbitration, whereby people could take their *private* disputes or queries summarily before the judge they had selected
and get a final decision. The judge's opinion need not be published,
any more than the deliverance of an arbiter. The Commission, he said,
saw no reason to amend s.10.

248. Subsection (3) of s.10 provides that the judge may, on cause
shown, hear and determine in chambers any dispute or question submitted for his decision under the section. Subsection (8) lays down,

however, that the section shall apply to any dispute or question "not affecting the status of any person . . . " In other words, actions of divorce or nullity of marriage cannot be dealt with by summary trial procedure. Perhaps the most remarkable aspect of the procedure, as applied to the Forbes-Sempill case, is that the choice (with the judge's consent) lies with the parties themselves. It is a device for maintaining secrecy in judicial proceedings which one would like to believe would be rarely if ever invoked in future, since it is so directly in conflict with the principle that justice should be seen to be done, and appears remote indeed from such judicial pronouncements as those of Lord Denning and the Privy Council in the case of McPherson referred to below or the more recent recognition by Lord Reid in the House of Lords (*Sweet* v. *Parsley* [1969] 2 W.L.R. 470) of the need for vigilance on the part of the Press (*cf.* para. 223).

249. It is useful to note what a distinguished English judge, Lord Denning, said on the subject of open court hearings when he addressed the National Association of Justices' Clerks' Assistants in 1957. He said it was fundamental that proceedings in courts of justice should be public unless there were overwhelming reasons to the contrary effect. He said a judge, when he tried a case, was himself on trial to see that he behaved properly, conducted the case properly, and that his reasons, when given, justified themselves at the Bar of public opinion. How could that be done if the case was heard in secret? This principle, he said, had been affirmed by the House of Lords and the Privy Council. He recalled a nullity case in 1913 which was heard in private. A party to the case wanted her relatives to know she was not at fault, secured a transcript of the proceedings and circulated it to her relations. She was prosecuted for publishing secret proceedings, and she was held guilty of contempt of court. But this decision was reversed by the House of Lords.

250. Lord Denning also recalled a Canadian case in 1936 (*McPherson* v. *McPherson* [1936] A.C. 177) when a judge sat in a library with "private" outside the door, but kept the door open, while he heard a divorce case in which the petitioner sought to avoid publicity. The case was heard at lunch-time and the judge issued a decree which was ostensibly in public. In fact, it was secret, since no one knew about it. The Privy Council strongly condemned this inroad on the rule of publicity and held that the decree was voidable. For technical reasons, however, it was not actually set aside in this case. These instances given by an English judge of eminence are cited here as being not entirely irrelevant in Scotland. It seems reasonable to assume that if similarly fundamental issues raised in a Scottish case were to be determined in the House of Lords, which in civil matters is the supreme court for Scotland, the House would reach the same decision as in an English case. There is this further quotation from Lord Denning made on the same occasion and with which a Scottish judge might find it hard to disagree in principle: "The great principle should always be that cases must be heard in open court when the newspaper reporters are there to represent the public and there to see everything is rightly done. They are indeed, in this respect, the watchdogs of justice, but a free press has its responsibilities. Its freedom must not be abused." It must at the same time be noticed that his Lordship recognised that in special cases there may be overwhelming reasons for hearing a case in private.

251. Occasion for excluding the general public from court occurs frequently in rape trials. The Lord Justice-General, after discussion with the other judges of the High Court of Justiciary, agreed in 1973 that where, for the protection of a witness in such a case, it was considered appropriate to "clear the court," this order would not apply to reporters covering the case on the understanding that they respected the judge's intention in excluding the public—namely, to protect the witness, the victim of the alleged rape, by refraining from disclosing her identity (see Chapter 13.)

252. Section 11 of the Contempt of Court Act 1981 gives the courts power to direct non-publication of a name "or other matter" which it already was able merely to *allow* to be withheld from the public during the hearing of a case. This extension of courts' powers is more fully dealt with in Chapter 9.

THE REPORTER'S PRIVILEGE

253. Whereas the privilege of reporting judicial proceedings in England arises from statute, the right in Scotland originated in the common law (see Contempt of Court Act 1981, s.4 (Appendix)). Lord President Inglis in the case of *Richardson* v. *Wilson* (1879) 7 R. 237, put it thus:

"The publication by a newspaper of what takes place in court at the hearing of any case is undoubtedly lawful; and if it be reported in a fair and faithful manner the publisher is not responsible though the report contains statements or details of evidence affecting the character of either of the parties or of other persons; and what takes place in open court falls under the same rule, though it may be either before or after the proper hearing of the cause. The principle on which this rule is founded seems to be that as courts of justice are open to the public, anything that takes place before a judge or judges is thereby necessarily and legitimately made public, and being once made legitimately public property may be re-published without inferring any responsibility."

254. But, as was pointed out in the case of *Macleod* v. *Lewis Justices* (1892) 20 R. 218, it is only what takes place in open court which may safely be published; examples will be given later of situations in which it is not always entirely safe even to publish everything that passes in open court. On the other hand, on the authority of the decision in the case of *Cunningham* in 1986, reporters can claim qualified privilege to publish passages from a summons founded on in open court although these have not been read out in court. Lord Clyde held that a summons founded on in this way is thus made public—a ruling of importance to court reporters, as it may be applied also to documents other than the summons, although not, as the judge observed, to court productions. An important distinction between this case and *Richardson*, quoted above, is that in the latter the action had appeared on the calling list but there had been no hearing in court. (See paras. 288–295, 399–401.)

255. Beyond his admission to the courtroom and his freedom to listen to the proceedings and take notes of what he hears, the reporter must rely upon his own understanding of the privilege which entitles him to reproduce his notes of what he hears for the public to read. The nature of this privilege, which confers a substantial protection from actions for defamation and which differs in certain important respects from that accorded the media in the English courts, is dealt with in Part III. It is sufficient here to note that the privilege enjoyed by media reports of court cases is subject to the qualification that they must be fair and accurate. If either of these conditions is not fulfilled the protection provided by privilege flies off and the report may be exposed to the same rigours of actionability as if the statements published had been made outside the courtroom.

256. The practice by which reporters retain their notes for a reasonable period for possible reference is of particular importance in relation to court cases. What is a reasonable period will vary with the circumstances, but recent experience suggests that one year would not be excessive. In the protracted Court of Session litigation over the winding up of Highland Engineering Ltd., a newspaper report appeared in which counsel was quoted as stating in court that a director of the company had been trying to sell the company's assets. Eleven months after the item appeared, a director of the company who, although he was not named in the report, apparently recognised himself as the person referred to in it, wrote to the editor of the paper, alleging he had been defamed and threatening to sue the paper for damages. Fortunately the reporter was able to find his notes, which showed that the statement complained of was indeed made by counsel in court and was accurately reported. The paper was able to repulse the threat of action and nothing more was heard of the matter.

257. In the case of *Outram* v. *Reid* (1852) 14 D. 577, it was laid down that it is the duty of the newspaper editor to take every care that the statements or news contained in the paper are accurate in everything which might by possibility touch the character or credit of others.

Fairness

258. One of the most tempting errors into which the reporter must not fall, however, is to believe that, so long as his report is accurate, it is safe, that is, protected by privilege. It must also be fair. Fairness implies not only that there should be a proper balance as between the rendering of the evidence or contentions of the one side and the other, but also that the report should be free from unfair or unjust assertions about third parties who are not present or represented in court and who consequently have no opportunity to reply. An example of the sort of statement referred to is the allegation contained in a plea in mitigation of sentence submitted by counsel on behalf of an accused person. It is sometimes necessary for counsel to present to the court submissions containing assertions he has obtained from the accused. Counsel has no opportunity himself to verify the truth of these statements, and it is part of his duty to his client and to the court to bring them out. Where they implicate a third party not represented, there is a risk of doing an injustice if such statements are published. Such statements do not usually form an essential part of the report as a piece of news, although they may contain an element of scandal which would appeal to some newspapers. Where it is decided such statements should be published this should be done in such a way as to make it clear they are allegations and not necessarily statements of fact. It is necessary to be careful, in this event, in dealing with denials made out of court by offended parties, since publication of these would not be protected by privilege.

259. In the great majority of civil litigations, the case is argued in the presence of both parties or their representatives. Consequently assertions made by one against the other may be answered and the reporter has the opportunity (which he will miss at his peril) of giving the reply where one is given. But if one side makes an allegation in the presence of the other, and the latter makes no reply, the newspaper is as free to publish the allegation as if a reply had been tendered. The point is that the object of the allegation was there and had the opportunity to reply. If he chose not to do so, or just neglected to do so, that was his responsibility. In such a situation justice would be on the side of the paper, provided, of course, that the report was fair and accurate. It may be appropriate to indicate in the report that no reply was made.

260. It is important to note that a report based upon a statement made in court which is itself privileged may lose the protection of privilege if it is not clearly attributed to the speaker. If a statement from court proceedings is quoted in a Press report without attribution, the newspaper itself will bear responsibility for the statement, and if it should prove to be actionable the defence of privilege will not be open to the paper.

261. An illustration of the point was provided by a report in the *Daily Record* of November 27, 1971, about a bigamy case in Edinburgh Sheriff Court. Under the headline "Unlucky bigamist gets nine months," the report opened with the bare statement: "Robert Hogg was unlucky in his two attempts at a happy marriage. His first wife ran off with another man—and his second had a child to another man." The statement that Mr Hogg's second wife had had a child to another man was based on a submission made in court by Mr Hogg's solicitor, but it was denied by the woman in question, who sued the *Daily Record* for £2000, alleging she had been defamed. Her complaint against the paper was that the passage in the report complained of stood by itself as a statement of fact by the paper and was not attributed to anyone taking part in the judicial proceedings. At a procedure roll debate in her action in the Court of Session, in January, 1974, the judge (Lord Brand) rejected an argument by counsel for the paper that the passage, if read by itself, did not identify the woman. In his judgment, sending the case for trial by jury, he said it was one thing for a solicitor to say in court on his client's instructions that the woman had had an illegitimate child, and it was quite another matter for a newspaper to make such an assertion on its own authority. In his view, the bald statement that the pursuer had a child to another man was *prima facie* defamatory. He accepted that the remainder of the paper's report, duly attributing to Mr Hogg's solicitor in court the statement that the pursuer had had an illegitimate child, was privileged, and said it would be for the jury to decide whether the opening passage was a fair and accurate summary of the fuller, privileged passage which followed. (The case in fact never went to trial, but Lord Brand's judgment provides a useful warning on the care to be taken in publishing statements without attribution when these may be defamatory.)

Party litigants

262. In this sphere party litigants require special care. It sometimes happens that a party suing or being sued cannot or will not be represented by counsel, and opts to conduct his own case. This is always a very difficult situation for a layman, and the judges invariably extend a great degree of indulgence to such lay pleaders. The difficulty, so far as reports are concerned, is that they tend, unlike the trained advocate, to bring in irrelevancies, statements and assertions having no direct bearing on the questions before the court. The reporter may have to exclude these from his report. For, although the party litigant enjoys a higher degree of privilege than the newspaper reporter in publishing what he says, his utterances require special care since they are more inclined to contain wild or irrelevant assertions than the submissions of the trained advocate. One will often hear lay pleaders make statements at the Bar that would be regarded as entirely improper if they came from a qualified member of the legal profession. Where these statements or allegations implicate third parties who have not the opportunity to reply, or are patently irrelevant to the issue under consideration, they will form no part of a fair and balanced report of the proceedings. This caution is given especially because party litigants, being free from the normal conventions of pleading, are liable from time to time to give utterance to what appears on the face of it to be highly newsworthy material.

263. An unusual example of the party litigant and the special indulgence our courts extend in such cases concerned a boy, aged 12, who appeared personally before Dunfermline District Court on January 21, 1986, to plead on behalf of his dog Ben which was alleged to have bitten another boy. The young master knew he could be ordered to have his pet destroyed; he told the court, "As the legal owner I will be conducting the defence myself." Court officials hurriedly put their heads together and in the event, after the boy had had half-an-hour with the duty solicitor, who in turn had discussions with the depute-fiscal in private, the charge was dropped. The boy had a good defence. He said after the hearing that his dog had a scrap with another owned by the other boy, who was bitten by his own dog when he tried to separate the animals. "I was determined Ben was not going to be destroyed for something I knew he didn't do," he said.

264. The paramount need for preserving a fair balance as between prosecution and defence in criminal cases and between the opposing sides in a civil action, is deserving of special attention in evening paper work. Where the report is incomplete in one edition and presents, of necessity, an unbalanced picture of the case, particular care must be taken to ensure that the balance is restored in later editions or in the issues of the following day. Statements rebutting earlier assertions by the other side must be scrupulously recorded.

265. The proper balance necessary between opposing sides does not necessarily require the publication of equal space to each side; for example, a lengthy argument advanced by one party may be completely demolished in a single sentence spoken in reply. The reverse may sometimes also apply.

266. The reporter who by some means has come into possession of some background knowledge of a case from an outside source will have to keep in mind the fact that such embroidery, if included in his report, will not be protected by privilege.

Interpretation

267. In pursuit of accuracy the court reporter has to be especially careful in interpreting, condensing, or translating into lay language passages from legal proceedings. It may be relatively simple to copy accurately what a speaker says and to reproduce it faithfully for publication; but—unlike much of the work which occupies journalists in general reporting—the exact reproduction of terms and expressions used in court would not always be satisfactory, especially for the readers of popular papers.

268. So, the reporter must, in putting into lay terms some passage which he believes would be incompletely understood by the man in the street, in the first instance be satisfied that he himself understands the meaning of the material he is dealing with and uses precisely the words which will convey the idea intended by the speaker. Apart from offering a kind of translation of legal jargon, the reporter will frequently find it necessary to condense the habitual wordiness of legal terminology, especially when his report is based upon written pleadings in a civil action or upon such things as wills and contracts. When the legal verbiage unnecessary for a news report has been cut away, such documents often contain material of high human interest and are well worth the special effort required to make them intelligible to the ordinary reader.

269. It will usually be found appropriate in court reports to call a "trust disposition and settlement" simply a "will." There are many other expressions, more or less baffling to the ordinary mortal, that crop up from time to time, and those of most frequent occurrence are included in the Glossary at the end of this manual.

270. Even judgments may sometimes, one would assert with all humility, be improved, for public consumption, by careful condensation. It is necessary, again, that the reporter who presumes upon so responsible a task must understand at the outset precisely what the judge meant—not only what his decision meant but also the effect of the reasoning by which he reached his conclusion. When it is remembered that judgments in the Court of Session run on the average to some 20 foolscap pages or more and may extend to 50 or, less often 100 or more pages, it becomes obvious that a great deal of the reporter's time and effort are devoted to this type of interpretative abridgment, sifting the judge's statements upon the evidence and legal arguments, studying carefully his reasoning, and grasping thoroughly the end product—the decision—so that the whole may be translated into a coherent and manageable, as well as a fair and accurate, report of the judgment.

271. Where the judge in order to produce his decision has had to wrestle with difficult legal questions, perhaps involving lengthy citation of authorities, the reporter's duty will vary according to the kind of journal for which he works. In many cases the paper will be satisfied with the bare result (see para. 648). Other newspapers believe that, if their readers are to see whether justice is done, they must be given some sort of indication of the reasoning which lies behind a decision. For the bald decision of a case may sometimes seem, on the face of it, unjust or unfair. Especially where this is so, the responsible paper has a duty to reproduce, as clearly as may be, the reasoning which led to the decision—in which event its justice, or at least its justification, will become apparent.

272. To give an illustration, the mother of a young miner who was killed in a colliery accident sued for damages in respect of his death (*Laidlaw* v. *N.C.B.*, 1957 S.C. 49). Her husband had left her many years before, and she was wholly dependent on her son for support. The First Division of the Court of Session held she had no title to sue at common law, the father being the only person entitled to raise an action so long as he survived. The decision seemed a hard one since there was reason to believe the husband had renounced his right to claim damages. The court held, however, that this fact did not transfer the right to sue to the miner's mother. A fair report of this decision would necessarily contain sufficient of the judges' reasoning to ensure that the reader understood that it was the state of the law as it then stood, and not the court, that had denied the woman her title to sue. Happily the situation which arose in that case has since been remedied by statute. The reason for its inclusion here is to demonstrate the need to avoid unfair inferences of injustices being done by a court decision when in fact the court is bound by the law which it is obliged to administer.

CHAPTER 8

ACCESS TO INFORMATION

LEGAL IMPLICATIONS OF THE LEAK

273. The proliferation of the leak, with all its attendant risks and tempting scope for a sensational scoop, requires a consideration of its legal implications. We examine these in relation to five aspects of the law—parliamentary privilege, official secrets, contempt of court, defamation and copyright.

274. In the parliamentary context the leak has in a sense become acceptable as a recognised, though often clandestine, means by which government tests public opinion through the medium of the press lobby. The leak, seen here as a legitimate function of democracy, can fairly be regarded as safe; but warning signals were sounded by two cases in 1985–86 when journalists became involved, directly or indirectly, in the elaborate and antiquated procedures of Westminster.

275. The first concerned the leaking to *The Times* in December 1985 of a Commons select committee confidential draft report on radioactive waste disposal, with a consequent referral to the Committee of Privileges of the House. The Committee recommended by 11 votes to one that Richard Evans, *The Times* political correspondent (who refused to divulge the source of the leak), should be banned from Westminster for six months for breaching the rules of the House. The editor, Charles Wilson, who admitted breach of privilege, was censured for a major share of a contempt of the House. He maintained that public interest in the report was the paramount consideration. The Commons in May 1986 rejected the recommended ban by 158 votes to 124. Sir Hugh Rossi, M.P., chairman of the select committee, proposed during the debate that Evans should not be punished, as it "went against the inherent sense of fair play, while the real villain—possibly an M.P.—escapes censure." Public concern over the episode was enhanced by the nuclear power station disaster at Chernobyl which had occurred in April.

276. The breach was more than a technicality; according to Sir Hugh Rossi, publication of the final report on nuclear waste disposal policy was considerably delayed by what the paper had done, because the disclosures had made it necessary to rewrite parts of the committee's

72

report. But, the editor told the committee, his reporter's duty was to "find scoops" and his duty was to decide whether or not to publish them. He maintained that the privilege rules, written in 1837, were out of date. The case was a stark illustration of the dangers involved in defying the rules of privilege—the powers of Parliament to punish contraventions being entirely within its own discretion. Had the committee's recommended penalty been upheld, *The Times* would have been denied the right to appoint a replacement for Evans at Westminster for the six months (see Chapter 24).

277. A leak with more far-reaching ramifications, and which raised the spectre of the Official Secrets Act, concerned the disclosure in January 1986 of part of a confidential letter written by the (English) Solicitor-General, Sir Patrick Mayhew, Q.C., to the chairman of the Westland Helicopter Company, accusing the former Defence Secretary, Mr Michael Heseltine, of "material inaccuracies" in his advocacy of a take-over of the ailing company by a European consortium in preference to rival bidders in the USA. Mr Heseltine had resigned over differences within the Cabinet regarding the competing interests of the rival bidders, and after leaving the Government maintained his support for the European consortium. The recipient of the leak—which Sir Robert Armstrong, the Cabinet Secretary, later insisted was not a leak at all but "an authorised disclosure"—was a Press Association correspondent who, but for the fact that it had been cleared by a Cabinet Minister, could have been at risk of receiving classified information under the catch-all terms of s.2 of the Official Secrets Act—the Westland company being involved in defence contracts. The leak in fact had come from Downing Street, passed by Mr Leon Brittan, then Trade and Industry Secretary, without the knowledge of the Prime Minister, Mrs Margaret Thatcher, but with her subsequent approval. The resulting government crisis led also to the resignation of Mr Brittan. The episode illustrated the importance of ensuring before publication of disclosure of matters affecting national security that necessary "cover" has been given by a minister or other person with the necessary authority under the Act (see Chapter 30).

278. An important consideration in any decision whether to publish leaked information may be knowledge of the motive which prompted the disclosure. Where this may be for personal gain or to damage another person's interests, the journalist will be well advised to examine the possible effects of publication. In the case of pending court proceedings, an interested party may attempt to harm an opponent's prospects of success by disclosing details of the case before it is in open court. The temptation to publish must be resisted where this would create a substantial risk of serious prejudice to the proceedings (see Chapter 9).

279. Similar precautions, though to avoid civil action for damages rather than prosecution, may be called for when an informant discloses the contents of a letter or other document covered by privilege. Certain communications, such as those passing between a lawyer and his client, may necessarily contain defamatory statements which are not actionable so long as they remain confidential, but this protection flies off if the contents are disclosed to a third party not protected by privilege. The risk may not always be obvious to the journalist to whom such material is volunteered, where, for example, the party affected by the damaging disclosure is a company negotiating for an important contract and whose financial interests could be damaged as a result of publication. The journalist must be particularly wary of the unsolicited tip-off prompted by malice (see Part III).

280. The dangers of publishing leaked information in breach of copyright were brought home with some effect to the *Sun* in January 1987, when it reproduced the contents of a private letter sent by the Duke of Edinburgh to the Commandant-General of the Royal Marines about Prince Edward's decision to resign his commission with the corps. An angry reaction from Buckingham Palace led to an admission of breach of copyright by the paper and an undertaking to pay an undisclosed sum of damages to an unnamed charity chosen by the Duke of Edinburgh (see Part IV).

COURT DOCUMENTS

281. In the reporting of the civil courts the most recurrent problems, and at the same time the most real, are probably those connected with access to documents. In this matter it may be taken that the practice in the sheriff courts is in general the same in principle as that operating in the Court of Session, with local variations in detail. Since relatively few civil proceedings appear to be reported in the sheriff courts (which is often a pity since this may be a rich source of news), and as the precedent set by the Court of Session may be taken as a guide in the lower courts, it is intended here to deal only with the matter from the viewpoint of proceedings in the supreme court.

282. The documents which a reporter may require to see or at least refer to in order to prepare a fair, accurate and balanced report of a case at its various stages fall chiefly into the following classes: the Calling List, Court Rolls, petitions, records and judgments. The list is not exhaustive, for there is also a wide variety of other documents which in individual cases may come, by leave of the parties' lawyers or the court authorities, into the hands of reporters—such as copies of wills, contracts, letters and minutes. In general the latter may be seen and quoted only where their contents have been read out in open court, and the reporter is concerned to see them only to check the accuracy of his notes.

Calling List

283. The Calling List is published daily during the sittings of the Court of Session and on certain statutory dates during vacations, and is an official document. It is available to subscribers (including newspapers) and a copy is displayed on the day of publication on the wall in Parliament House. It contains intimation of actions newly raised in the court, and is well worth careful daily scrutiny. Each entry contains only the names and addresses of the parties to the action, and the names of junior counsel and solicitor(s) for the pursuer.

284. The Contempt of Court Act 1981 (see Chapter 9 and Appendix) relaxed the limits on publication of reports at the Calling List stage. Under the Act civil cases do not become "active" until arrangements for a hearing are made, or, if this has not happened, until the time the hearing begins—and the hearing in this context can be on a preliminary motion or an application made in relation to the action (see Sched. 1, paras. 12 and 14). The making of arrangements for a hearing occurs (in an ordinary civil action) when the record is closed, or (in a motion or application to the court) when it is enrolled or made; or, in any other case, when the date for a hearing is fixed or a hearing allowed. It is the occurrence of the earliest of these events which brings the "active" rule under contempt law into operation. These provisions have, therefore, made it much easier to prepare a report based on information about a case intimated in the Calling List without falling foul of the contempt law.

285. At this stage of proceedings, however, it is still important to note that any publicity given to a case has to observe the law of defamation. Unlike coverage of a case being heard in open court, any report based on the product of inquiries at the stage of Calling List will lack the protection of privilege (see Part III). And, since any report at this early stage may involve access to particulars contained in the Summons, special care is needed to avoid publishing defamatory matter from that source. Journalists need not concern themselves at this stage with the "strict liability" rule (see para.382).

286. One of the principal uses of the Calling List to the reporter regularly employed in the Court of Session is as a guide to what kind of cases he may expect to be available for reporting in due course. He will, for various reasons, find it an advantage to keep himself well abreast of affairs in general in order that he may recognise the first appearance of litigations arising from disputes which have already attracted publicity elsewhere. A notable case was the first action to be raised in Scotland by the parents of a child said to be handicapped as a result of the mother having taken thalidomide during pregnancy. The key in this instance was the fact that the name of the defenders (Distillers Company (Bio-Chemicals) Ltd.) had been much in the news in connection with the drug, and that the action was by a father as "tutor and administrator-at-law" for his child. A telephone call to the parents soon confirmed that it was a thalidomide case.

Summons

287. A case will in due course pass through a series of stages of development—assuming that it is not in the meantime abandoned or settled out of court (an occurrence which need not be publicly disclosed by the parties)—and the pleadings, that is, the statement by each party of the case he intends to prove, will be incorporated in an open record.

288. It is as well here to give some attention to the position of the summons, as it affects the newspaper reporter. The summons, the first stage in proceedings, is prepared at the instigation of the pursuer and served on the defender (see Chapter 9).

289. In the case of *Richardson* v. *Wilson* (1879) 7 R. 237, the First Division held that all authority on the subject was against the proposition that once an action was on the Calling List the contents of the summons could be made public. What was published was not a report of judicial proceedings, but of the contents of a writ which were at the time unknown even to the court. In a much more recent case, where there had been a hearing in open court and the contents of the summons were known to the court (*Cunningham* v. *The Scotsman Publications Ltd.* 1987 S.L.T. 698), Lord Clyde in the Outer House of the Court of Session held that reporters could seek the protection of qualified privilege in quoting from the document on the ground that it was founded on in the case, although not read out, and this amounted to publication.

290. In the case of *Richardson* the *Edinburgh Evening News* published a passage from a summons which had been intimated on the Calling List but upon which no further step in procedure had taken place. A party mentioned in the report sued the paper for slander. The defenders argued, unsuccessfully, that the paragraph which was published, being a *bona fide* and correct report of the averments in an action then called and pending in the Court of Session, they were entitled to publish it. The pursuer in the slander proceedings, on the other hand, maintained that statements contained in the report (reproduced from the summons) were untrue and slanderous. The report was not said to be in any way unfair as a representation of the statements in the summons.

291.   Lord Craighill said the principle, stated generally, was that what might be seen and heard (in court) might be published. The courts were open and accessible to all. It did not follow from this that every step of process in a cause from the calling to the final judgment was an occasion on which everything which could be discovered by an examination of the process might be published to the world. Were this so, the world would get to know the contents of writs and productions before the court. The public, he said, had no right and no interest to know more than could be learnt by attendance in court. The public could not demand to know, and newspaper reporters who catered for the public could not insist on knowing, what was not intended to be published merely because a writ or production had been made the subject of judicial procedure. The right and the interest of the public were concerned not with the statements which one party in a cause might make against his adversary, but with the proceedings in open court, by which, between both, justice was to be administered.

292.   The defenders appealed unsuccessfully to the First Division. Lord President Inglis in his judgment said the duty of the clerk in charge of the process was plainly not to part with the summons or give access to it, except to the parties to the suit or their agents. The parties and their agents must use proper caution. If they were to make the contents of the summons public at this stage, they would undeniably be subject to an action of damages if it contained statements which were defamatory of any other person. If the agent of either party were guilty of publishing it in any way he would not only be liable, like his principal, but would also be answerable to the court for his misconduct. At the stage where no defences had been lodged, no one except the parties or their agents could lawfully obtain access to the summons.

293.   An important change in reporters' right of access to information under qualified privilege takes place when the summons is founded on in a hearing in open court, even though it is not read out. In the case of *Cunningham*, debated on procedure roll in November 1986, Mr David Cunningham, a former advocate, sued *The Scotsman, Courier & Advertiser* and *Glasgow Herald* for £600,000 damages, alleging they had defamed him in reporting an *ex parte* hearing in the Court of Session on March 30, 1984, when interim interdict was granted against him dealing in certain shares. (That action was later abandoned). Mr Cunningham complained that the reports contained passages from the summons which had not been read out in court and were thus not covered by privilege. Lord Clyde, upholding the newspapers' plea that their reports could be protected by qualified privilege, said that previous Scottish cases (including *Richardson*) did not affirm that a report must be limited to what was said and read aloud in open court. Courts sat to hear cases and give judgment "with open doors," he said. The public must have at least the opportunity of understanding what was going on and if they did not have that opportunity he did not consider the hearing was a public one. Where a document had been incorporated into what counsel had said, the proceedings could not be said to be open to the public unless the terms of the document could be seen by the public. So great was the danger of secrecy seen to be, that it was considered preferable to secure publicity, albeit at the cost of private hardship. Furthermore, there was a clear advantage in enabling the public to know with certainty and accuracy what had passed in court rather than leaving them to rely on rumour or speculation, and the reporting of proceedings might be found to be unfair or misleading if access to the pleadings which had been founded upon in open court was not allowed. In order to make a realistic application of the principle to the circumstances of the present case, Lord Clyde said he could not restrict the availability of the privilege to a report of what was actually read out in court.

294. The test was not what was actually read out—although all that was read out was published—but what was in the presentation of the case intended to be published and so put in the same position as if it had been read out. If it was referred to and founded on before the court with a view to advancing the submission which was being made, it was to be taken as published. By making publication depend on whether or not a document founded on in open court was or was not read out in open court by counsel or judge (as counsel for Mr Cunningham contended), suspicion of secrecy might more easily be invited and the broad purpose which lay behind the principle of openness might be put at risk of frustration. It might be that in this matter the reporter had a responsible role to play in enabling those within and those without the walls of the court to be equally well informed of what had taken place.

295. Lord Clyde's judgment, which was not appealed, significantly enlarged the scope for reporters, as previously understood, to enjoy the protection of qualified privilege for what they write by having access to court documents (not only summonses) which have been founded on but not read out in court. It is important to note, however, that Lord Clyde made the reservation that it might well be that documents other than pleadings, such as productions, stood in a different position.

Adjustment roll

296. After the stage of the summons and the lodging of defences—all of which is private—an action appears on what is known as the "adjustment roll." This simply means that at intervals fixed by the court, the case is entered on the roll of a particular judge who has to decide whether a further continuation should be granted to allow one side to answer pleadings tendered by the other. He will at a certain stage decide that no further adjustment of the pleadings is to be permitted and order that the record be closed.

297. The distinction between an open record and a closed record is all-important to the safe reporting of civil actions. The record (containing the parties' written pleadings) remains open so long as the case is on the adjustment roll, and it must be the automatic practice of the court reporter handling such documents to check from the front cover that it is in fact a closed record before he proceeds to report excerpts from it. In the sheriff court, however, the cover of the record may not indicate whether it is open or closed and may merely bear the word "Record," when it is essential to check with court officials or lawyers in the case whether it has in fact been closed.

298. It will not always be safe to publish the occupation or calling of any of the parties as stated in an open record, since even this may be a matter of dispute between them. The pursuer may be suing in order to assert that he holds or held a certain position of employment, which is contested by the defender. Similarly, at this stage of the proceedings, the sum sued for should not be published, unless (as also applies to occupations of parties) it is for some reason mentioned in open court.

299. The closing of the record has the effect, once the case has come into open court, of enabling the reporter to publish its contents without fear of repercussions, provided he does so fairly and faithfully—and, of course, provided the case does not come within the classes of proceedings covered by the Judicial Proceedings (Regulation of Reports) Act 1926 (see Chapter 11).

Open record

300. It was judicially decided in the case of *Young* v. *Armour*, 1921 1 S.L.T. 211 (see also para. 651); that the publication of the contents of an open record constitutes an interference with the administration of justice. The action was one for damages for breach of promise of marriage and extracts from the record were published in certain English newspapers and by one Scottish paper, the *Weekly Record* on February 5, 1921, before it had been closed. Under the heading "Love on the Golf Course," the report gave a detailed account of the facts stated in the open record. Both sides agreed there had been an interference with the due course of justice, because the case might have been settled without any of the facts having been made public.

301. Lord Blackburn held that the appearance of the article amounted to contempt of court since the record, being open, was not public property. The editor was ordered to appear personally at the Bar of the court to tender an explanation. Through counsel he apologised and explained that, although he knew that the contents of an open record should not be published, he had seen the article in certain English papers and had assumed, wrongly but quite honestly, that the case had been heard in court. The apology was accepted, but the judge said that if the explanation had not been satisfactory, the fine inflicted would have been severe as both he and his brother judges considered that "the contempt which resulted from publication of this sort was a serious offence and one which should be met with a severe penalty."

302. While sounding a warning about the dangers of trespassing on the preserves of the unadjusted pleadings, it is necessary to point out that the reporter should not, at the very mention of the words "open record," take fright and flee. The Contempt of Court Act has to some extent relaxed the *Young* v. *Armour* rule; it is now contempt to publish from an open record only when proceedings are active under the strict liability rule (*e.g.* at a preliminary hearing—see Chapter 9), but even before the case becomes active publication from the open record could still be contempt by common law if *intended* to impede or prejudice the administration of justice. There are occasions when a point of some importance is debated before the closing of the record, and a full-scale hearing takes place in open court. It would be taking too strict a view to say that nothing of such proceedings could be safely published.

Closed record

303. A closed record is sometimes referred to as a public document, but this does not mean that its contents may necessarily be freely published at any stage in the proceedings. It was made abundantly clear in a decision in 1892 that, until a case has come into open court, it is not proper to publish excerpts from even a closed record. In practice, this caution will refer particularly to passages from a closed record which might in themselves be actionable. The position is that the privilege which protects a newspaper from an action of defamation in respect of what it publishes from a closed record operates only from the time the action has come into open court. This is dealt with more fully in Part III.

304. In the case of *Macleod* v. *Lewis Justices* (1892) 20 R. 218, it was held that publication in a newspaper of a closed record containing defamatory statements not referred to publicly in discussion in open court was not privileged. The record contained in that case certain statements about two justices of the peace which would, if untrue, be grossly libellous. The justices, who were defenders, answered the statements with a general denial. Immediately after the record was closed an agent for the pursuer handed to a reporter for the *North British Daily Mail* a record containing pursuer's contentions but not the defenders' general denial. A summary of the record was published in the paper and also in the *Scottish Highlander*. The papers later published a letter from the justices stating the allegations about them in the record were "a tissue of libellous falsehoods." The pursuer complained to the Court of Session that the publication of these letters was contempt of court. The matter was dealt with by the Second Division, who held there was no contempt, but made observations of some general assistance in this aspect of court reporting.

305. The Lord Justice-Clerk, Lord MacDonald, said it might be a practice to hand complete records to the newspapers, but it was not one to be looked on with favour, and certainly to hand an incomplete record to anyone for the purpose of publication was a very gross irregularity. Such an act, he said, was quite different from that which occurred in all the courts of the country, namely the publication by the newspapers of what occurred in a case when it had been brought to that point when it was openly litigated in court—evidence led, and the parties pleading. He was not prepared to say there was any contempt in the case before the court; considering that the fault was originally in the pursuer, and that the terms of the letter of denial were censurable, the proper course was to refuse the motion to summon the editor of the paper to appear before the court.

306. Lord Young, in agreeing, said it was clear that statements made in pleadings were privileged, however libellous they might be on their face, but there was no privilege whatever in the publication of pleadings. Reporting of proceedings was simply an enlargement of the audience which heard them in court, but which was limited by the size of the courtroom. It was therefore quite right to report such discussions as those on relevancy (a plea to the relevancy of an action may be taken by one party in an attempt to establish that even if his opponent's averments in his pleadings were proved he would still not be entitled by law to the remedy he seeks), and the report would be privileged if it was fair; and therefore, though a litigant was privileged in the statements he made on record, he was not privileged if he sent his pleadings (and it was to Lord Young's mind of no moment whether the record was closed or not) to a newspaper for publication. If the pleadings published were slanderous, then the paper publishing them, and the person sending them for publication, were liable in damages for slander.

307. It is not surprising, therefore, that reporters sometimes find solicitors reluctant to hand over to them closed records in cases which have not reached the stage of a hearing in open court. Yet, where such a document is made available, and where it contains no statements which could reasonably be regarded as slanderous, or the reporter is careful not to reproduce such statements if they do appear to be slanderous, there is still scope for the safe reporting of cases from this source.

308. The effect of the ruling in the case of *Macleod* might be said to have been to some extent modified by practice in the intervening years, and it is difficult to believe that many practitioners in our courts, if they are familiar with the case, regard it as still literally applicable in all particulars. For example, when an action of damages opens before a judge or jury in the Court of Session it is usual for solicitors willingly to let the Press have a copy of the closed record without any reservations as to which passages may be published. They do so in many cases voluntarily, although at a proof or jury trial the whole, or even a major part, of the closed record is seldom read out in open court. Since this in many instances is the first hearing in open court after the closing of the record, it may be said that the passages in the pleadings which form the substance of the case are not read out in public at all. A literal reading of *Macleod* in such cases would therefore make adequate reporting impracticable. True, the evidence led may be directed towards proving what is contained in the pleadings, but this does not enable the reporter to divine, by listening to witnesses, what precisely each party's contentions are.

309. Since the closed record is the only reliable and practicable means in such cases of preparing a fair and balanced report, it is not surprising that solicitors engaged in a case frequently surrender a copy to reporters at the opening of the evidence and often at a preliminary legal debate. Indeed, it would surprise many of them to learn that by so doing they were providing the media with something they had no legal right to publish.

310. The point made in the case of *Macleod* seems to assume that in all cases the closed record will sooner or later be read out in open court. In fact, since the judge has a copy, as do counsel and instructing solicitors, and since the jury are not normally allowed access to a record at all, there may be no occasion for counsel to read it out, except to draw attention sometimes to a particular passage. Were the reporter to be dependent solely upon such desultory readings, often out of context, from one side of a case, he would indeed have difficulty in ever attaining any semblance of fair or balanced reporting.

311. It seems a fair interpretation of the position, taking *Macleod* into account, to say that a reporter publishes the contents of a closed record at his peril if the case has not yet come into open court; but from the moment a hearing has begun (whether legal debate, proof or jury trial) he is entitled to regard a fair and accurate report of its contents as privileged, even though the contents of the record itself may not have been read out in open court. This must particularly be the position when the judge, because he has already read the closed record in preparation for the hearing, tells counsel expressly that he need not trouble reading it out in court; in such a situation the record may properly be "taken as read."

Commonsense

312. As in so many other aspects of court reporting, the journalist requires to exercise a high degree of care and commonsense in determining which passages, if any, he is safe to reproduce from the record before the hearing of the case in open court—remembering that if he publishes something that is slanderous he cannot invoke the protection of privilege. Where, as happily often happens, the pleadings are read out by counsel during the proceedings, these passages, when published, are of course privileged, no matter how slanderous the statements they contain might be if uttered outside the courtroom.

313. It is safe to assume that a lawyer who hands over a closed record

83

to a reporter without reservation is tacitly conceding that the statements, so far as his client is concerned, may be published without fear of reprisals. But the reporter has to keep in mind the interests of other parties to the case. He will be wise, where the pleadings contain matter that might be objectionable, to consult also the legal advisers of those other parties. He will then have a clearer idea of whether there is a potential danger of legal consequences if he publishes the pleadings before a public hearing of the case, and will be the better equipped to avoid such consequences.

Open court

314. Once the case is in open court the situation is entirely changed, and the reporter can normally expect to obtain a closed record from the solicitor for one party or the other. If he fails to do so, and the case is worth the trouble, his next step will be to approach the clerk of court. If the clerk is unable or unwilling to provide a copy, the reporter's next line of approach is to the Principal Clerk of Session. In the unlikely event of his refusal to help, an appointment should be requested with the Lord President. Only on exceptional occasions, where a matter of principle appears to arise, will it be necessary or appropriate to trouble the head of the judiciary.

315. Such a situation did, however, occur in 1953 when, not only did both parties to a large property dispute decline to surrender a record, and the clerk feel unwilling to supply one to the Press, but one of the parties offered a newspaperman a sum of money if he would undertake to publish nothing about the case. It clearly became imperative that a report should be prepared, and, as it was impossible to do so without the assistance of the printed pleadings, the matter was pursued to the ultimate conclusion. Lord President Cooper instructed the Principal Clerk that in such a situation the court staff should provide the Press with a closed record. Otherwise, he said, the parties would be, in effect, enforcing a closed-doors hearing at their own hand.

316. It is to be noted that this intervention by the Lord President occurred at the stage of the hearing of evidence, and it is not to be assumed that he would have taken a similar course had the case been at a preliminary stage, such as a hearing of debate on relevancy or competency.

317. A solicitor's refusal to supply reporters with a closed record does not always signify his non-co-operation. There occurs sometimes a shortage of copies of such a document, owing to the number of parties and legal representatives engaged in a case. In such an event the reporter may be able to borrow a copy from the clerk at the end of the hearing.

318. In a similar position to the closed record at the stage of proof or jury trial is the transcript of evidence taken on commission. Although, during a proof, such evidence may not be read out, since the judge will have the actual transcript, it should, for media purposes, be taken as read, and treated as being covered by the same kind of privilege as spoken evidence. The reporter in this situation is entitled to have access to a copy of the transcript, unless it contains the type of evidence which the court would ordinarily have heard behind closed doors.

Petitions

319. In contra-distinction to actions which proceed upon a closed record adjusted between the parties, there are a wide variety of proceedings which are taken by way of petition. The procedure is different, and a separate department is set aside in Parliament House for the handling of such documents in the Court of Session.

320. Whereas an action is initiated by the pursuer serving a summons on the defender, who in turn replies (if he proposes to contest the case), a petition is addressed to the court which orders intimation to other parties having a potential interest to lodge answers, and allows them time to do so. Petitions are directed usually towards obtaining such remedies as interdict, custody of children, authority to vary trust purposes, confirmation of reduction of capital of a company, presumption of death of some missing person and company liquidations or amalgamations.

321. A long-standing procedure by which a copy of each petition was displayed on the wall of Parliament House, as part of the system of intimation to all interested parties, ceased in 1961 when the court altered the practice by Act of Sederunt. Such display in public of petitions is now not permitted and instead only a bare notice that a petition has been lodged, along with the petitioner's name and that of his solicitor, appears on the wall. This offers such scanty information about a case that it is quite inadequate to form the basis of a report. The change of practice probably was brought about by the excessive publicity given by certain organs of the Press to interdict and custody cases, where the information gleaned from the petition pinned on the wall was sometimes used to seek out parties, have them photographed, and generally interfere with their peace of mind early in the proceedings, and while matters were *sub judice*.

322. The change is unfortunate for quite a different reason. It was

85

customary for the Press to publish, in certain petitions for presumption of death, particulars which could do nothing but aid the search for the missing person; indeed, publication of such petitions on the wall was originally designed to attain this end, if the person were alive. There had been more than one case where Press reports led to the discovery of the missing party, and the court was saved the embarrassment of setting aside its own decision declaring dead someone who, as it turned out, was alive. In another large category of petitions, interdict cases, there were many instances of publicity through the newspapers having the effect of assisting in the enforcement of a court order (for example, in preventing some fugitive spouse from hurriedly leaving the country with a child, who was the subject of a custody dispute, before an officer of the court had time to serve notice of the court order).

323. The revised procedure has at least the advantage that the court has relieved reporters of the responsibility of deciding what is and is not safe to publish from petitions at the stage of intimation; and publicity is not altogether silenced, since before the court may make a substantive order there is normally a hearing in open court. Since petitions do not appear on the Calling List, the bare intimation appearing on the wall, in place of the actual petitions as formerly, is sometimes a useful guide as to what may be available for reporting at a later stage.

324. When (and if) answers are lodged to a petition, these go through the kind of adjustment which occurs in an action, and eventually a document equivalent to a closed record (usually entitled "petition and answers") is drawn up. This may normally be treated, for purposes of publicity, in the same way as a closed record.

Interim interdicts

325. An order of interim interdict, the urgency of which will often lend weight to its news value, may be pronounced on a summons or on a petition. The only practical difference for purposes of reporting the case is that the documents are handled by a separate office and care will have to be taken to direct media inquiries to the appropriate department. There are, of course, also certain terminological niceties: the parties are pursuer and defender, not petitioner and respondent, and time may be allowed for lodging defences, not answers, as to a petition. In cases where the court makes an order on an *ex parte* application (in the absence of the party interdicted) it is advisable, in the interests of fairness, to indicate in a report of the proceedings that the other party was not present or represented in court and was allowed a stated period in which to answer.

326. The use of the expression "temporary order" or "temporary ban" is not always a satisfactory way of referring to an interim interdict. "Interim" is not necessarily synonymous with "temporary." An interim order is made to restrain a party from some specific act or behaviour until some further development may take place in the case. This may not occur for weeks or for months; it may never happen at all. Without any order having been expressly made by the court pronouncing a perpetual interdict, therefore, the interim interdict may continue in operation indefinitely and could not properly be called temporary. It is attributing to a court more power than it possesses to state in a report of interdict proceedings that it has issued an order to *prevent* some specific act; an interdict can only *prohibit* it. Otherwise breach of interdict could not occur, when in fact we know it quite often does, and is punishable as contempt of court.

327. As part of a general improvement of press facilities in Parliament House in 1973–74, an instruction was issued by authority of the Lord President that applications for interim interdict must be called by the macer over the address system (which is relayed to the Press Room). This practice, which does not normally operate during court vacations, has largely solved the problem of covering such hearings which, because of their urgency, are usually not intimated in the Rolls of the Court.

328. Because of its urgency interim interdict cannot await the cumbersome process of adjustment of pleadings; the consequence is that the petition may be sometimes in a distinctly raw state. A further difficulty arises from the fact that there is usually no opportunity for the alleged wrong-doer to be represented at the application for an interim order against him. The court's decision has then to be reached upon an *ex parte* statement which, for the reporter, requires special care. Only as much of such a statement as is necessary to demonstrate the basis of the court's decision may be safely published.

329. If the court refuses to grant any order on an application for interim interdict, the case for publishing no more than is absolutely necessary is even stronger. Indeed, unless there is some compelling reason why the result should be reported—for example the situation where the case may have been reported at an earlier stage and there is an obligation to publish the result—petitions for interim interdict which fail on an *ex parte* application should not be reported. It will usually be found that in such a case the court authorities will not provide any information for the use of the media, and parties' legal representatives will usually be equally reticent. The reason is pretty clear;

allegations have been made which have not even been accepted by the court on a *prima facie* basis, so that they can be regarded as being without substance as viewed from the aspect of news.

330. If, however, there is a satisfactory reason why the decision refusing an interim order should be published, the decision alone should be given, and it would generally be unwise to go in detail into the allegations made by counsel *ex parte* in seeking the order. Logically, where the court takes no action, it can be taken that it has regarded the allegations as being, for the purposes of the decision, without foundation; this is clear indication to reporters not to publish. On the other hand, where, in refusing such an order, the court reaches a decision which is in itself of such importance as to make news, then the reporter is justified in seeking from the court staff such particulars of the case, including names and addresses of parties, as are necessary to prepare a report. An example of this situation arose in a case in the Court of Session in 1968 (*Hoy and Others* v. *Hoy*, 1968 S.L.T. 413) in which Lord Robertson (upheld on appeal by the First Division) refused interim interdict to stop the marriage of an English girl,who had been made a ward of the English Court of Chancery, to a man domiciled in Scotland who had been prohibited by the Chancery Court from marrying her. The case raised intriguing questions of international law, the point of special interest being that the Court of Session held that, as the orders of the Chancery Court were pronounced when the girl and her prospective husband were both outside the jurisdiction of that court (both being in Scotland at the time), the Scottish courts were entitled to disregard those orders and find there was no impediment to the marriage.

331. It is not unusual to find counsel throwing a whole string of allegations at his opponent for good measure, in the hope that one of them, or the combined force of all, will persuade the judge in his favour. The reporter has to be astute to notice the case where the judge upholds only one or certain of the allegations and rejects others, and to reflect this fractional success in his report.

332. By the same token, a party may come into court with a series of claims for interim interdict. Where only one—or any number short of the total—is sustained, it is necessary that the report must not go beyond the limits of the case as accepted and acted upon by the court. It may indeed be necessary to consult the clerk of court or counsel or solicitors in the case to ascertain precisely which part of the claim has been sustained. The petition, it has to be remembered, is an unadjusted document; in other words, replies have yet to be put in by the person or persons who are the subject of the complaint—if they are in, the whole pleadings remain to be finalised and fall into the category of an open record.

Marriage interdicts

333. Yet the reporter should not miss the opportunity, in an interesting case, of publishing what is safe and proper of proceedings at this stage, for, by the very nature of petitions brought for some urgent or interim remedy, they may never go further. The party obtaining the order may be satisfied, and if the reporter were to wait until there was a closing of the record and a hearing of evidence, he would be able to report only a small proportion of such cases.

334. Until 1959 many cases of "runaway marriages" came to the Court of Session by way of interdict petitions seeking to stop marriage ceremonies in Scotland involving parties from other countries (including England) where the laws of consent were more strict. Many such elopements occurred to take advantage of the freedom of young people in Scotland to marry under the law without parental consent provided they were not subject to any other legal prohibition. In many cases interim interdict was granted by the court to enable the disputed matters to be inquired into and to prevent possibly irreparable harm by allowing a marriage to take place that might later have to be annulled. In many such cases an interim order was sufficient to enable the parties to reconsider their position and decide to make other arrangements.

335. These were peculiar to Scotland where, unlike most European countries, no parental consent is necessary for the marriage of a person over 16 years of age. Understandably a great deal of interest was created in the media of the countries concerned when young people eloped to Scotland and found themselves the centre of court proceedings.

336. But the flow of cases of the kind effectively came to an end with the case of *Bliersbach* v. *MacEwen*, 1959 S.C. 43, in which the First Division held that where in the absence of parental consent, a young person over 16 seeks to marry in Scotland, the law to be applied is that of the land where the proposed union is to be celebrated and not that of the party's domicile. Absence of parental consent would only be an impediment to the marriage if parental consent were required by the law of Scotland.

337. In practice, where there is in existence, for example, a valid English court order making a person under 18 a ward of court, the Court of Session will grant interim interdict to prevent any hasty act

89

causing a breach of the English decision. To do otherwise would be to allow the whole issue before the English court to be put beyond judicial decision (see para. 330.)

Court Rolls

338. The Rolls of the Court of Session, published along with the Calling List daily during the sittings and on certain statutory dates in vacation, contain lists of the cases set down for hearing before the individual judges in the Outer House of the court (*i.e.* judges of first instance) and before the Inner House (comprising the First Division and Second Division). Proceedings which have come to court by way of a petition are usually indicated by the contraction "Pet." before the name of the petitioner. The name of the party initiating the proceedings comes first. Parties' names are followed by the names of junior counsel (the names of senior counsel do not appear) and solicitors for all parties represented in the case. Where it is a case of a defender appealing in the Inner House, this is indicated by: "Appeal for defender *in causa* . . . " In an appeal from the Outer House to the Inner House, the term "reclaiming motion" is used and accounts for the initials "R.M." which appear in front of all such entries in the Rolls.

339. Only in a small minority of cases do the Rolls give any indication of the nature of the proceedings, but an inference may often be drawn, from experience, as to the class of case it *may* be. Where the pursuer's and defender's surnames are the same, and only one counsel's name appears, it may usually be assumed that the case is an undefended matrimonial suit, probably a divorce action.

340. Proceedings between husband and wife which are not for divorce, are usually designated "sep. and alt" (separation and aliment), "decl. of null." (declarator of nullity of marriage).

341. Outside the sphere of matrimonial cases, an occasional indication will be found of the type of action by the appearance of such contractions as: "C.R. & P." (count, reckoning and payment), "MP" (multiplepoinding), "S. & I." (suspension and interdict), and "Prov. the ten." (proving the tenor of a deed).

342. Another form of procedure, indicated in the Rolls by the abbreviation S.M. & A., is the summons, minute and answers form of proof. This will usually occur where, after the hearing of evidence in a divorce action, a further dispute arises on a subsidiary issue, such as payment of aliment for the children, or on whether interim interdict should be granted to one party for protection against ill-treatment by the other. A separate proof is heard on the summons (containing the case originally brought by the pursuer), a minute outlining the nature of the complaint raised in the subsidiary matter, and the answers tabled to the minute. Following this secondary hearing the judge may deliver a judgment, which will be subject to the same restrictions, under the terms of the Judicial Proceedings (Regulation of Reports) Act 1926 (see Chapter 11), as his judgment on the main issue of divorce. The minute and answers are not normally made available to reporters and are in a similar position in this respect to the summons (see paras. 287–295).

343. In the Outer House incidental motions, which often give rise to reportable material, are marked with an asterisk if counsel are due to appear to make verbal submissions. Where there is no asterisk, there is no public appearance, and the entry in the Roll indicates merely a formal step in procedure which is not as a rule reportable at all. In the Inner House motions are called "single bills" and the same procedure with regard to asterisks operates. Although the two Divisions are concerned largely with appeals from the Outer House and from the sheriff courts (always easily identifiable as such), they deal also with a wide variety of petitions as well as applications to the *nobile officium* (see paras. 598–600); the latter is an equitable power possessed by the court to grant a remedy in certain circumstances where none is otherwise provided.

344. At the appeal stage the court will have before it not only the closed record, or petition and answers, but also, where there was a hearing of evidence in the court below, an appendix containing a transcript of that evidence and a copy of the judgment delivered by the judge or sheriff, which is under appeal. Where, as is usual, the evidence has been given in open court, it may be useful and is permissible to refer to this and the judgment of the inferior court where necessary to prepare a report of the appeal. Regard must be had, however, to the limitations set in matrimonial cases by the Judicial Proceedings (Regulation of Reports) Act 1926, which is dealt with more fully in Chapter 11. An appeal in any of the classes of cases to which the Act applies may be reported to the extent only of submissions on any point of law and the judgment of the court (as well as the judgment of the court below where this may be necessary).

Avizandum

345. After the hearing of evidence in the Outer House, or debate either there or in the Inner House, the court may give an *ex tempore* decision or may "make avizandum." The latter peculiarity of Scottish law is simply a term signifying that the court desires time to consider the case before issuing judgment. In due course the opinion is issued. In the sheriff court such documents are usually issued from the sheriff clerk's office during term as well as vacation.

346. In the cases in which only the bare decision is announced in court, this may convey little to the layman, for it may amount merely to the answering of certain set questions to which he may not at the time have access. In such cases the reporter cannot begin to prepare his report until he is in possession of the actual opinion (or opinions in the case of the Inner House) and other relevant documents. We are not concerned here with the merit or otherwise of the practice as it affects the interests of the general public to know what is happening in our courts of law, but its introduction would appear to heighten the responsibility upon court reporters to provide adequate coverage of the decisions in cases of public interest, where this may be the only means by which members of the public are enabled to have access to judgments of the courts and the reasons on which they are based. On the other hand the preparation of reports from written opinions is in practice a much less exacting and more reliable method of coverage than the shorthand note taken in court often under conditions of great difficulty. The practice of reading out judgments from the bench had already been departed from some years earlier in the House of Lords (where they are called speeches). There, however, a copy of each opinion is made available for inspection by any interested member of the public.

347. Strictly speaking, the judgment of the court comprises two documents—the interlocutor and the opinion of the judge(s). In practice the opinion is the source of news. The interlocutor is a minute kept by the clerk of court recording in formal style the precise terms of the decision. This is normally not of the slightest use for publication and the reporter may refer to it only as a guide as to the true effect of a decision if this should not be apparent to him from a reading of the opinion. Decisions do not become operative until the interlocutor is signed by the judge. In certain circumstances a judge will grant a decree but for specific reasons will agree to delay operation of his decision for a stated period. He does this by "superseding extract" of the decree, in other words, delaying the process by which the successful party may obtain the extract copy of the decree which will enable him to enforce it. Where such delay is granted, reports of the case will require to make it clear that the decision does not become immediately operative.

348. It is not unusual to find in reports from local correspondents covering civil cases in the sheriff courts passages from what is described as the sheriff's interlocutor. This arises from a confusion of the interlocutor (which is in such formal terms as to be entirely useless as copy) with the note appended to it which contains the sheriff's reasons for reaching his decision and is, for the media's purposes, his judgment, and should be referred to as such. Nevertheless, the interlocutor is an important document in all proceedings, and every decision of the court (whether the Court of Session or the sheriff court) is embodied in one. It contains the record of what the court has decided (or, in some instances, refused to decide) available for reference at any subsequent stage of the proceedings. When a reporter is doubtful about the effect of a judge's opinion, he will most probably get help by asking the clerk to explain to him the terms of the interlocutor.

Criminal cases

349. In criminal proceedings the document with which the reporter is mainly concerned is, in cases dealt with in solemn procedure, the indictment, and in summary cases, the complaint or charge-sheet. In the district court the complaint contains the name and address of the accused person as well as the charge against him. In the High Court where bail has been allowed the address of the accused for citation purposes is normally available from the court documents (see Chapter 3), and where he is in custody his address, if known, can usually be obtained from court officials.

350. In the case of indictments, the first point in time at which the media are fully entitled to publish the whole contents of the document is when it is read out to the jury at the opening of the trial, or when the accused pleads guilty to the charge(s) contained in it (but see para. 63). This practice has not, however, been strictly adhered to, and it is not unusual for the indictment to be published at the pleading diet, at which the accused tenders a plea of "not guilty." This practice may be attended by certain risks, since it is still possible after a plea of "not guilty" for the charges or some of them to be dropped.

351. A person cleared in this way (without trial) of a charge which has appeared in the newspapers may feel sufficiently maligned to threaten proceedings against the papers which published the charge, but there is no record of such a complaint succeeding. The situation will usually be met by subsequent publication of the fact that the proceedings have been dropped. (William Watt was an example; he was cleared, without trial, of charges of murder of which Peter Manuel was later convicted.) Where the Crown Office have formally libelled a charge they will normally be willing to tell the media if it is later dropped.

352. The reporter is on more doubtful ground where he published a charge at the earliest stage of criminal proceedings—a holding charge libelled by the police, which is liable to considerable alteration before a formal charge is made in the name of the Lord Advocate. Reports of such charges are not privileged, since they are not the subject of public proceedings. The procedure up to this stage has been in private. When, however, the accused appears in public at the Bar of the court, the fact that he is charged with a certain offence may be published, even though the case may be continued for further inquiry. At this stage, however, the details of the charge should not be published, only the bare offence alleged—whether assault, theft, murder, etc. It is usual practice to publish a brief report about a crime that has been committed (taking care not to infringe the law of contempt dealt with more fully in Chapter 9) and to add to this the fact that a named person has appeared on a charge in connection with the affair, but not to elaborate the charge.

353. Where no plea is taken from the accused and his case is continued for one reason or another, these facts may and should be included in such a report.

354. Difficulties have not, so far as is known, arisen in obtaining copies of indictments and complaints in the High Court and sheriff courts at the stage of proceedings where the case is being actually disposed of. In the former Burgh Court in Edinburgh, however, the Press more than once met a flat refusal, without reasons, from the clerk when they asked to see a copy of a complaint after a case had been dealt with (see also paras. 651–652).

355. On one occasion, when the Press were refused access to a burgh court complaint the principle involved seemed important enough to require the attention of the then Lord Advocate, Mr John Wheatley, Q.C. His opinion was that, although reporters had no statutory right of access to complaints, it was a matter of public policy that they should have this facility in the interests of accurate reporting of cases. He suggested that in the event of a recurrence editors should raise the subject with the Scottish Secretary.

356. To sum up on the matter of documents, it can be said that, whereas the general right of a newspaper reporter to attend any legal proceedings is the same as that possessed by any member of the public, it is recognised that the reporter requires for the proper and fair discharge of his duty to the public access to certain court documents at the appropriate stage in proceedings. It is as a matter of public policy that the media is accorded access to certain papers, both in criminal and civil cases, or at least to certain of the information contained in them. Where both access to the documents necessary for the fair and accurate reporting of a case heard in open court and the opportunity to obtain the necessary information from them are refused, the reporter has a duty to raise the matter, in consultation with his superiors, with the appropriate court authority. In practice this is a difficulty which will rarely be found to occur, and where it does it will usually be possible to trace it to the fact that refusal has resulted from lack of experience on the part of an official or a genuine desire to protect himself against the consequences of disclosing information without the authority of a superior possessing sufficient experience to know the position.

357. A fuller appreciation emerged during 1973–74 at a high official level of the legitimate need of reporters to have access to documents and information necessary to enable them to do their job effectively. The Lord President of the Court of Session showed a sympathetic interest in removing several long-standing obstacles facing journalists working in the courts and took certain important steps to ensure Press facilities were improved. The Faculty of Advocates and the Law Society of Scotland also had begun to show, at top level, a desire to assist the Press in their task of reporting legal matters of public concern, and became noticeably more helpful and approachable. Each body established officially a liaison with the Press through, respectively, the Clerk of Faculty and an Assistant Secretary of the Law Society with Press matters as a specific duty. These advances must have two important effects—to facilitate news media coverage of legal affairs and to improve the public image of the legal profession in all its branches.

358. It has always been assumed (certainly in Scotland) that it is in order, if not even obligatory, to include the identity of the judge in any published report of a court case. Even in divorce cases in which, strictly read, the Judicial Proceedings (Regulation of Reports) Act 1926 seems not to allow the naming of judges, it has been the regular practice to name them and no one has been prosecuted for it. After all, if one of the media's functions is to satisfy the public that justice is in the right hands and being properly administered, that purpose is largely frustrated if the larger audience outside the courtroom is not to be told who in fact is on the Bench. But this fundamental assumption was called in question by the magistrates at Felixstowe, Suffolk, in a case in 1985 when they issued an order forbidding the media to identify them. (A similar attitude was reported to have been taken by 10 other magistrates' courts in England and Wales.) The official reason given was "security," a number of magistrates apparently having been harassed by threatening telephone calls. The matter was taken before the High Court of Justice by the *Observer* and one of its senior reporters, David Leigh.

359. Giving judgment in October 1986, Watkins L.J. (with whom Russell and Mann J.J. concurred) ruled that the magistrates acted unlawfully in seeking to conceal their identities. He said: "There is in my view no such person known to the law as an anonymous J.P." What the Felixstowe magistrates had done, he said, was inimical to the proper administration of justice and an unwarranted and unlawful obstruction to the right to know who sits in judgment. Judges and others had to put up with criticism, vilification and telephone pestering as part of the job. Anonymity for those presiding in court could defeat the principle of open justice. The *Observer* and Mr Leigh, whose application for review was supported by the National Union of Journalists, the Guild of British Newspaper Editors and the Society of British Editors, were awarded their costs against the magistrates.

DATA PROTECTION ACT 1986

360. Under the Act data users who store information on computer are required to register, and from November 1987 newspapers or others operating such systems are required to give any person named in their data base access to the information they hold about him or her. Anyone who can establish damage from storage of inaccurate information may have a claim for compensation. A ground of action may lie if the stored information is wrong (but it is a defence to prove that reasonable care was taken to ensure the accuracy of the stored data), misused, irrelevant or kept insecurely.

361. Section 21(5), however, allows computer users to withhold from disclosure the names or other identifying particulars of those who provided them with information about the person applying for access to it—*i.e.* the source. This protection from disclosure may not, however, cover the situation where the source is an organisation rather than an identifiable individual.

362. The right of access applies only to data held in computer files and does not afford access to written or typewritten notes taken by journalists—*e.g.* reporters' notebooks. Disclosure of obituaries of living persons can be avoided by storing these by a traditional filing system rather than on computer.

363. Data users may charge inquirers for information held on file and have up to 40 days to supply it. They are prohibited from altering stored information before disclosure. Main public libraries will keep microfiche copies of the register of users for public inspection.

364. The Act's requirements of registration and disclosure are of particular concern to newspaper and other media organisations which operate computerised direct input systems. The Act applies, in addition to news or editorial comment referring to individuals, to personal data stored for sales and advertising purposes, information used in connection with customers' orders and accounts, credit checking, identification of bad debts, market research, and filed material about the employer's own personnel. It applies also to data stored on computer by freelance journalists working on their own behalf. The requirements of disclosure can be simply avoided by retaining sensitive matter on paper, typed or handwritten.

365. The Data Protection Registrar has power to enforce the terms of the Act by proceedings before the Data Protection Tribunal. Further details may be obtained from his office at Springfield House, Water Lane, Wilmslow, Cheshire, SK9 5AX.

NEW TECHNOLOGY

366. A number of mechanical or electronic aids have come into use in the law courts which affect reporters to a greater or lesser degree. Tape recorders are now regularly employed by judges in the High Court of Justiciary and the Court of Session in place of shorthand writers for recording *ex tempore* judgments. While section 9 of the Contempt of Court Act 1981 makes it an offence to bring a tape recorder into court, without the leave of the court, to record the proceedings for publication, or to use recordings for this purpose, it goes on to provide for the court to grant leave for the use of such instruments for this purpose subject to such conditions as the court thinks proper. The section also gives the court discretion to withdraw leave, once granted, and power to forfeit any instrument used in breach of the conditions laid down (see Chapter 9). The courts themselves have not been able to eliminate human agency for the purpose of recording evidence, shorthand writers being still generally engaged for this purpose. While some of these write shorthand, others use shorthand machines, which are at least as fast as the older method.

367. Access by the media to shorthand notes taken by the official writers, while not formally recognised, will usually be available when reporters need to check their own notes and if they have taken the trouble to cultivate good relations with the staff concerned.

368. The problem of acoustics, the reporter's bogie, is the main obstacle to the installation of modern amplifying equipment in the older courtrooms. To be of maximum use where accuracy and efficiency are of prime importance, sound reproduction in court must be installed as part of the design of the room where it is to be used, and for this purpose the installation of microphones and loud speakers forms part of the acoustic planning of the most modern court buildings. Nevertheless, systems of the kind have been in use for some years in a few older sheriff courts with some success.

369. During 1972–73 closed circuit television was brought into use at certain sittings of the High Court at which reference had to be made in evidence to numerous documentary productions. The object was to enable the judge and jury, counsel and solicitors, witness, and the Press to see productions on television screens simultaneously and thus save some of the cost of copying documents and photographs required for reference during a trial. The system has proved to be most effective in protracted hearings of complex cases such as fraud trials.

370. Until the 1950s cases were called in Parliament House by macers announcing them, by the unaided voice, from a small rostrum at one end of Parliament Hall. More recently, however, a public address system has been installed, with loud speaker outlets in many parts of the building, including the Press Room, enabling reporters and others concerned to learn when and in which courtroom a particular case is about to be heard.

371. An invaluable addition to the equipment available to reporters in the supreme courts is a photo-copying machine, installed in the Press Room. By this means journalists may make copies of indictments, judgments, closed records etc., reproduce material for filing purposes, and are no longer dependent on the slower and less reliable method of carbon-copying.

372. The use of computers by the legal profession as an aid to rapid retrieval of stored material, such as statutory references and case citations on specific topics, has become a practical reality, but the usefulness of these facilities is regarded as very limited so far as the courts themselves are concerned. Judges, who must have access to actual statutes, cases, or texts, rely for their citations largely upon counsel who, with their instructing solicitors, may well carry out their researches with the help of a computer. The prospect of a "judgment bank," on the lines of that now employed, for example, by the Italian Court of Cassation, forming a significant part of the judicial system of Scotland, at present appears remote. Journalists may therefore safely dismiss the thought that they may soon be covering computerised courts where the judicial process is carried out by a machine.

373. It may be that advances in development of more sophisticated video cameras has brought nearer the day when, with the court's permission and without disrupting the proceedings, it will be possible to relay them to a central office where they would be monitored by journalists to enable fuller coverage to be given to the increasing numbers of courts which it is no longer possible to attend with the limited reporting staffs available. More immediate, however, is the use of video techniques by the police in gathering evidence of suspected offenders in riot situations or outbreaks of crowd violence at sporting events.

CHAPTER 9

CONTEMPT OF COURT

374. The Contempt of Court Act 1981 makes important and far reaching changes in the law of contempt as it affects publicity and replaces much, though not all, of the case law accumulated over the years. Fundamentally the principle remains the same: as was laid down by the High Court in 1954 (*Macalister* v. *Associated Newspapers Ltd.*, 1954 S.L.T. 14), the court has a paramount duty to ensure that a person indicted before it shall receive a fair and impartial trial—except that the court now has to do so under the requirements of statute, which makes some important innovations. The law is designed, however, to protect not only the person in the dock, but also the prosecution, although instances of contempt arising from publicity creating a risk of prejudice to the prosecution are very rare (see para. 423, case of Michael Fagan).

375. It is the first statute passed by Parliament on the subject as it concerns Scotland, and it deals with civil as well as criminal proceedings. One of the essential changes which it enacts is that, whereas formerly newspapers were in serious danger of committing contempt if they carried out their own investigation of crime while the criminal authorities were engaged in their investigations, now the risk (and it has to be a substantial one) can arise only once someone has been arrested in connection with the case, or a warrant has been granted for an arrest, or, if there is no question of arrest, from the time a charge has been served upon a suspect. This alteration of the law effectively began in Scotland with the judgment of the High Court in the case of *Hall* in 1978 (*Hall* v. *Associated Newspapers Ltd.*, 1978 S.L.T. 241); the rule devised in that case has been enshrined in the Act as U.K. law.

376. The risk of contempt of this sort being committed had formerly been derived from the judgment of the High Court in the case of *Stirling* (*Stirling* v. *Associated Newspapers Ltd. & Another*, 1960 J.C. 5), which laid down that once a crime was suspected—even if no arrest was eventually made—the media could not safely investigate a suspected crime or publish the results of their efforts. The problems for the journalist were accentuated by the vagueness of the rules governing the degree of risk which might be assumed before the contempt law began to bite, a situation that created a serious danger of suppression of information and comment about crime the public had a right to have access to. The new definition of the risk significantly relaxes those rules and it is important to be familiar with the legal requirements laid down in the Act, particularly those concerning when cases—both criminal and civil—become "active" (a new term to replace the more familiar *sub judice* rule) and when cases cease to be "active." This is explained in detail later.

377. The Act introduces for the first time a statutory right for reporters to attend and report the courts, criminal and civil, but also gives the courts new powers to direct non-publication of certain matters "where necessary." It gives the courts no power to exclude reporters from the courtroom for this purpose. It recognises the freedom of the media to comment on matters of public interest, even though this may create some risk of prejudice to court proceedings. It sets up a new defence of innocent publication, where the publisher can satisfy the court he was unaware that a case was "active" at the time of the offending publication.

378. A step towards recognition of journalistic privilege is the new provision about non-disclosure of sources, but with the reservation that the Act goes on to lay down that the protection will not apply where the court is satisfied that disclosure of the source " is necessary in the interests of justice or national security or for the prevention of disorder and crime."

379. On what, to the media, is the debit side the Act extends the contempt law to cover cases, both criminal and civil, at the appeal stage, as if judges were as susceptible as jurors to influence from what they may read in the Press or see on television. It also lays down that the contempt restrictions apply to a wide range of tribunals and "other bodies" without specifying these bodies, and gives the courts new powers to restrict reports in a way that is unnecessary in Scotland and arises in an attempt to check the activities of certain of the more adventurous English publications.

380. Because a detailed understanding of its provisions is so important to the journalist, it has been thought appropriate to reproduce the whole of the Act, so far as it applies to Scotland, as an Appendix. Within weeks of its introduction the Act produced a crop of cases, mostly in the English courts, some of which displayed scant knowledge of the new statute in the media. Some of those cases which bear some relevance for the Scottish media are referred to in the following pages. While the Act does not mention pictures, its terms are wide enough to

101

include them along with textual matter; this aspect of the subject is dealt with in Chapter 10.

381. The Act does not replace the whole of the common law on contempt. For example it does not deal with contempt committed in the face of the court, such as hurling abuse (or objects) at the judge, creating a disturbance in court or with conduct falling short of actual publication. It is still possible for a journalist to be guilty of contempt even though he publishes nothing, provided what he does impedes or prejudices the administration of justice. Section 6(c) of the Act indicates that to cover this form of conduct the old common law can still be invoked. There are also provisions in the criminal law, other than contempt, to deal with publicity that interferes with the administration of justice before a case becomes "active."

382. The "strict liability" rule defined in s.1 of the Act is not new; it has been applied by the courts in cases where a publication created a risk of prejudice to proceedings regardless of what the intention of the publisher may have been. For the purpose of applying this rule, s.2 lays down that publication includes any speech, writing, broadcast or other communication in whatever form, which is addressed to the public at large or any section of it. This means that a speaker who makes a statement in public that raises the issue of serious prejudice to proceedings in court risks breaching the Act. So, of course, may any newspaper or broadcast report of what he said. This section contains the only passage in the Act capable of covering pictures. It must be assumed that when the section refers to "other communication in whatever form," it is intended to cover pictorial communications as well as text, that it covers television as well as sound radio and printed matter, and that it has to be taken into account in relation to pictorial comment as well as what might be called factual pictorial representation.

Headlines

383. An aspect of the subject not specifically dealt with by the Act concerns headings. Care has to be taken to apply the same rules for avoidance of contempt as relate to the body of a report or article. A story which is within the permitted limits may step outside them if the headline introduces an element of prejudice to active proceedings (what is meant by "active", as used in the Act, is set out below). Especially to be avoided is the heading which may suggest a person may be guilty of an offence when proceedings described in the report have not resulted in a conviction, or imply he is implicated in a crime other than the one with which he is charged, or that a person involved in active proceedings has a criminal record (even though this may be well known). The result may often be that the temptation to use a lively, witty or original heading has to be resisted.

The public

384. The reference in s.2 to the public deserves special mention. Publications that may raise the question of contempt are usually directed at the public at large, but the section makes it clear they need not necessarily be so. They may be issued only to a section—"any section"—of the public. Statements or pictures distributed for special purposes to limited groups of people might not, however, come within the definition of the section if they were intended only for consumption among a restricted class of individuals, as in the case of medical magazines or circulars issued solely to members of a profession for their own exclusive use. The recipients of such information would not normally be treated in this situation as members of the public and could not thus form "any section" of it.

Substantial risk

385. The Act introduces a new and important test by which it is to be decided whether publicity coming within the strict liability rule risks causing prejudice or impediment to the course of justice so as to justify a finding of contempt. Section 2(2) lays down that the rule can only apply to a publication which creates a *substantial risk* that the course of justice in the proceedings in question will be *seriously impeded or prejudiced*. This transforms the previous situation, which was vague and open to varied interpretations, though in the case of *Atkins* (*Atkins* v. *London Weekend Television Ltd. and Others*, 1978 S.L.T. 76) the High Court did hold that the question for consideration was whether the publication gave rise to a *real* risk of prejudice to the fair and impartial trial of the complainer.

Active proceedings

386. Section 2(3) states the strict liability rule arises only if the proceedings in question are active at the time of the publication—the old *sub judice* rule in a new guise. The stages at which proceedings become, and cease to be, active for the purposes of the Act have to be considered in relation to each class of proceedings, whether criminal or civil, under solemn procedure (with a jury) or summary (without a jury), in the Court of Session Inner House or Outer House, sheriff civil court at first instance, before a district court, or on appeal from any of these courts, or before a tribunal. The rules about all this are contained in Sched.1 of the Act. Two points should be noted here. The strict liability rule (which involves publication regardless of intent) operates when the proceedings in question are active; the crucial factor in regard to timing is publication, and it can be vital to know at the time of writing an article or preparing a picture whether the case will have become active by the time it is published. The time lag between these two events could be vital, especially in the case of periodicals issued once or twice weekly.

387.   Schedule 1 divides all proceedings into three categories—criminal, "other", and appellate. Where it deals with more than one step in proceedings, the case becomes active when the first of these takes place.

Criminal cases

388.   In criminal proceedings the case becomes active with arrest without warrant, the grant of a warrant for arrest, the grant of a warrant to cite, or the service of an indictment or other document specifying the charge, whichever of these steps happens first (In this respect the Act affirms the existing law in Scotland—*Hall* v. *Associated Newspapers Ltd.*, 1978 S.L.T. 241.)

389.   Criminal proceedings cease to be active when the accused is acquitted or sentenced or with the return of any other verdict, finding, order or decision which puts an end to the proceedings. They may also cease to be active as the result of some other process causing the proceedings to be discontinued or by other "operation of law." Or proceedings are discontinued when they are expressly abandoned by the prosecutor or deserted *simpliciter* (*i.e.* absolutely or without qualification).

390.   An accused is sentenced for the purpose of the above provisions when he or she is made subject to any order or decision consequent on conviction or finding of guilt which disposes of the case, either absolutely or subject to future events. This provision covers deferred sentences, but not those where the deferment is for a short period only to enable the court, for example, to obtain background reports on the accused; in the latter situation the proceedings remain active during the short deferment.

391.   Under the strict liability rule criminal proceedings before a court-martial or standing civilian court (see para. 177) are not concluded until the completion of any review of finding or sentence.

392. Criminal proceedings against a person cease to be active also if the accused is found to be under a disability rendering him or her unfit to be tried or to plead or is found insane in bar of trial and a hospital order is made under the Mental Health Act 1959 or a transfer order ceases to have effect under the Mental Health (Scotland) Act 1960. But such proceedings become active again if they are later resumed.

393. The Government gave an assurance during the passage of the measure through Parliament that instructions had been issued to court officers to give Press and broadcasting inquirers information about specific cases necessary to enable them to find out whether or not they are active. The Attorney-General (Sir Michael Havers, Q.C.) indicated failure to get such information after reasonable inquiry would be a good defence to a charge of contempt.

394. There is a limit on the period during which criminal proceedings remain active after the grant of a warrant for arrest. The proceedings cease to be active 12 months after the date of the warrant unless the person in question has been arrested within that period. If he or she is arrested after the expiry of the 12 months, the proceedings become active again.

Tribunals of inquiry

395. In regard to tribunals to which the Tribunals of Inquiry (Evidence) Act 1921 applies, the proceedings become active when the tribunal is appointed and remain so until its report is presented to Parliament. (It was under the 1921 Act that the Vassall inquiry (*Att.-Gen.* v. *Mulholland, Att.-Gen.* v. *Foster* [1963] 2 Q.B. 477) was held in 1963, when two reporters called as witnesses were committed for contempt for refusing to answer questions put to them as to the sources of their information.)

Civil cases

396. Civil proceedings become active either from the time when arrangements for the hearing are made or from the time the hearing begins, whichever happens first. This provision covers any motion or application made in or for the purposes of the proceedings, and effects an important change in the stage at which the contempt law begins to operate under the strict liability rule in the Court of Session and sheriff courts. The previous position was that the rule began to operate from the appearance of the case in the Calling List of the Court of Session or in the official list of cases intimated in the sheriff court. The rule is now relaxed to the extent that it does not begin to operate until, at the earliest, arrangements for a hearing are made, or if no such advance arrangements have been made, when a hearing actually begins. This need not be the hearing of the case on its merits or for disposal of the central or substantial issue in the case, but may be a hearing to deal with an incidental or preliminary matter, such as interim interdict, interim custody or access, amendment of pleadings, appointment of curator, etc.

397. The making of arrangements for a hearing is defined in Sched.1 as meaning, in the case of an ordinary action in the Court of Session or sheriff court, when the record is closed; in the case of a motion or application, when it is enrolled or made; and in any other case, when the date for a hearing is fixed or a hearing is allowed. Again, it is the step which happens first that has the effect of determining when the case becomes active. Since some of the steps referred to—such as closing the record, enrolment of a motion or allowance of a hearing—take place usually in the offices of the appropriate court without public intimation, the journalist will have to check with either court staff or lawyers in the case whether any of the stages in question has been reached.

398. One important consequence of the above provisions is that in many cases where no preliminary motion or application is arranged in a civil case, and the first relevant step under the schedule becomes the closing of the record, the strict liability rule does not begin to operate until this takes place. This is a considerable advance from the position which formerly applied in such cases, which usually was that the rule began to apply when an action appeared in the court lists.

Status of summons

399. The provisions restricting prejudicial publicity in civil proceedings have an important bearing on the summons as a possible source of information for journalists. Before the passing of the Act it was understood to be the law that a summons was a private document—on the authority of *Richardson* v. *Wilson* (1879) 7 R. 237. Publication of material from a summons in that case, which had only appeared on the Calling List, led to a newspaper being sued for slander. The First Division, in upholding a complaint against the paper, also ruled it would be contempt for a lawyer to make the contents of a summons available to the Press before the case had come into open court. Publication from a summons could therefore lead to a risk of contempt as well as proceedings for defamation. The 1981 Act appears to preclude the risk of contempt by the media under the strict liability rule arising from publication from a summons before a date for a hearing has been fixed or other relevant step under Sched.1 has caused the case to become active. But the Act does not alter the pre-existing law that it is contempt to publish matter *intended* to prejudice the proceedings. So far as clerks of court and lawyers in possession of summonses are concerned, it may still be contempt at common law for them to disclose the contents at that early stage.

400. The law requiring the summons in civil cases to be treated (by court staff and solicitors as well as reporters) as a private document has been relaxed significantly by the 1981 Act and, more especially, by the judgment of Lord Clyde in 1986 in the case of *Cunningham* v. *The Scotsman Publications Ltd. and Others*. The judicial view (*Richardson* v. *Wilson* (1879) 7 R. 237) was previously that where a case had reached only the stage of the Calling List it would be contempt for a lawyer to make the contents available to the press before the case came into open court. Publication from a summons could lead to a risk of contempt as well as proceedings for defamation. The risk of contempt cannot now arise, however, before a case becomes active under the 1981 Act, unless there is a deliberate intention to interfere with the course of justice. In the case of *Richardson*, Lord President Inglis said the duty of the clerk in charge was "plainly not to part with the summons or give access to it, except to the parties or their agents, who must use proper caution." If the agent for either party were "guilty of publishing it" in any way, he said, he would be answerable to the court for misconduct.

401. The position can be quite different legally when a case has reached the stage of a hearing in open court upon a summons and before adjustment of the pleadings, the situation in the case of *Cunningham*, in which a former advocate sued three newspapers for £600,000 damages for alleged defamation in respect of statements they published which had been made by counsel at a hearing before a judge in open court in the Court of Session, at which an order was made interdicting Mr Cunningham from dealing in certain shares. The complaint against the newspapers was based on the proposition that, as the statements alleged to be defamatory, which were not read out in court but were published by the newspapers, were taken from the summons, they were not protected by privilege (see also paras. 254, 289–295.)

402. Civil cases remain active until they are disposed of or discontinued or withdrawn. Any motion or application in a case is a "proceeding." If a motion or application is all that takes place in a case, therefore, it ceases to be active when the motion or application has been disposed of, discontinued or withdrawn, but it has to be noted that such proceedings are usually only preliminaries to the hearing of the action proper. Where an application for interim interdict fails, no application is made for an appeal and the proceedings end there; so does the state of "activity" of the proceedings under the Act.

403. It is also worth noting that when an action is adjourned or interrupted to enable negotiations to take place, the case meantime remains active in terms of the Act and until the proceedings are settled, disposed of or withdrawn. But s.5 of the Act is designed to ensure that this fact does not preclude comment on a case while active, provided it is published "as part of a discussion in good faith of public affairs or other matters of general public interest".

Appellate provisions

404. Contrary to what was previously the situation in practice, if not in legal theory, the strict liability rule is reapplied if a case enters the appeal stage. Schedule 1, para. 15 says that appellate proceedings are active from the time when they are commenced. This stage is attained either by application for leave to appeal or apply for review, or by notice of such an application; by notice of appeal or of application for review; or by other originating process, whichever happens first. A case ceases to be active when the appeal is disposed of or abandoned, discontinued or withdrawn. In criminal proceedings where the appellate court remits the case to the court below or grants authority to bring a new prosecution, any further or new proceedings which result are active from the conclusion of the appellate proceedings. In other words, the state of activity of the case is continuous throughout the period from the start of the appellate proceedings to final disposal of any further or new proceedings arising from them.

405. Application of the strict liability rule to appeals does not cover the period between the time when a trial or other hearing at first instance ceases to be active and the beginning of the appeal stage, when the case again becomes active. Here, however, a problem arises of interpreting what the Act means by the words it uses to define the resumption of the activity of a case when it enters the appeal stage. When, indeed, for this purpose does it enter that stage? The scope of Sched.1 seems to be wide enough even to cover a case where papers for an intended appeal are lodged with the Justiciary Office at the earliest possible moment after return of the jury's verdict, or similar event. A defence lawyer, therefore, whose anxiety for the interests of his client may extend to preventing publication of any background material about him which might conceivably cause substantial risk of prejudice to an appeal, can seek to attain his objective by having his appeal papers ready for immediate lodgement. There would thus be no interval between trial and appeal during which the media were free from the risk of contempt if what they were to publish could cause the necessary degree of prejudice. Where no step has been taken to initiate an appeal, the strict liability rule does not bite, since the case for the time being has ceased to be active, but it can be seen that the new provisions concerning appeals could be used to gag publicity pending hearing of an appeal.

406. The extension of the contempt law into the appeal stage was, according to a Government spokesman during the passage of the measure through Parliament, intended to restrain the media from "whipping up public feeling pending an appeal," creating the impression in the minds of parties to the proceedings that the scales were loaded against any of them, and to remove the risk that the fear would be created by publicity that it *might* influence the appeal judges. It is a motive which may be considered unworthy and an insult to the judiciary, and we are bound to agree with that view, though we have to state the law as it exists and seek to have it applied as Parliament intended. It appears less restrictive than at first blush, however, when we come to consider s.6(*b*).

407. To keep matters in focus, it is also worthwhile reminding ourselves that the new rules about publicity in relation to appeals are not a total prohibition of all comment during the time a case is active, but only restrict that which creates a *substantial* risk of impeding or seriously prejudicing the proceedings. Circumstances alter cases, and arguably in a case where an editor was satisfied there was no substantial risk (possibly no risk at all) because appellate judges were immune from being influenced by what he published, he might feel justified in taking risks that the Act, taken literally, may appear to make illegal but which the judges themselves, if it came to an issue, might laugh out of court.

Right of appeal

408. In the event of a conviction on a charge of contempt under the Act, there is the same right of appeal as belongs to anyone convicted of a statutory charge. The opinion of the High Court (*Hall* v. *Associated Newspapers Ltd.*, 1978 S.L.T. 241) that contempt of court under the strict liability rule is not a crime but an offence in a separate category

(*sui generis*) appears to have been superseded by the Act, which makes
it a crim: nal offence.

409. Any doubt that existed about the right of a publisher to appeal
against findings of contempt in connection with criminal proceedings
was dispelled by a judgment of the High Court in 1982 (*Kemp and
Others, Petitioners*, 1982 S.L.T. 357), setting aside convictions against
the *Glasgow Herald* and the *Scotsman* in respect of passages included
in reports the papers published of a High Court trial in Glasgow in July
1981. The case involved eleven accused who were indicted on charges
of conspiring to further the aims of the Ulster Volunteer Force by
illegal means. The reports of the case included reference to a Mrs. Gibson and her husband (witnesses at the trial) being surrounded by police
as they left the building and were taken in an unmarked police car to a
secret address. Lord Ross, the trial judge, held there was a risk that
jurors might be influenced by the reference in their consideration of
the credibility of the two witnesses, and admonished both papers. They
appealed by petition to a bench comprising the Lord Justice-General
(Lord Emslie), Lord Stott and Lord Dunpark, who, in the exercise of
their *nobile officium*, said they had no hesitation in holding there had
been no contempt. It was understood to be the first case of an appeal
by any newspaper against a conviction for contempt in Scotland.

410. The judgment stated that Gibson was a self-confessed accom-
plice in the crime, admitted being a commander of the U.V.F., and
implicated several of the accused. The appeal judges agreed with the
newspapers' submission that it was mere speculation to say the jury
might be influenced by the passage about the two witnesses. The
reports, they said, fell to be read in the context of the particular trial
and of the extraordinary security precautions obviously being taken
throughout its course, which were a matter of public knowledge. The
passage was a simple narrative of fact and did not carry any implications as to the attitudes, fears or beliefs of the Gibsons or insinuation
bearing upon their credibility. Any reasonable juror would, in the
judges' opinion, have found the passage quite neutral in that matter.

411. Apart from establishing the procedure for appeal in such a case,
the occasion created an important precedent in relation to publication
of extraneous matter in a report of criminal court proceedings. The
passage in question did not form a part of a report of the actual proceedings and would, therefore, not qualify for the protection given by
s.4 of the Act; but to make such a complaint stand up it was necessary
to satisfy the court that there was a real risk of prejudice to the fair trial
of the accused. That was the criterion employed by the High Court in

the case of *Atkins* (*Atkins* v. *London Weekend Television Ltd. & Others*, 1978 S.L.T. 76), which was the state of the law at the time the alleged contempt arose in July 1981. The Act has since heightened the requirement to "a substantial risk of serious prejudice."

412. The inclusion of extraneous matter in reports of court proceedings calls, nevertheless, for special caution. It will usually involve no substantial risk where it consists of a "simple narrative" of facts which are likely already to be well known to members of the jury and will not therefore influence their minds in reaching their verdict. And it should always be made clear to the reader that it is a statement of known fact and does not form part of the proceedings as such.

Innocent publication

413. Section 3 creates the defence of innocent publication or distribution. It makes this defence, new to Scots law (a similar defence was introduced into English law by s.11 of the Administration of Justice Act 1960, and was repealed by the 1981 Act), available not only to those who publish material alleged to be in contempt of court but also to the distributors, whether of a newspaper or other periodical, or of a broadcast programme, by radio or television. The defence can be applied to any charge of contempt brought under the strict liability rule and, if established, will rebut a contempt complaint if the court is satisfied the publisher or distributor did not know (having taken all reasonable care) that relevant proceedings were active, and had no reason to suspect this was the case. The passage in parentheses is important. A newspaper, for instance, could not successfully advance this defence if it sat back passively before publishing the material complained of, without taking any reasonable steps to find out whether such a case had become active. It must exercise all reasonable diligence to ascertain what the position is in relation to what stage the case has reached before taking a decision whether or not to publish.

414. It will be necessary for the smooth working of the Act that the Crown Office and procurators-fiscal accept some responsibility to keep the media informed, when asked to do so, on whether specific cases are at a particular time active, and that journalists develop procedures for obtaining the information to which they are entitled to enable them to keep within the legal limits laid down by the Act.

415. If a defence of innocent publication or distribution is put forward in response to a charge of contempt, it is for the party making it to establish it in court, and not for the complainer to prove that the defence is bad (s.3(3)).

111

Fair and accurate

416. Section 4 enacts the important common law principle that no one can be held guilty of contempt under the strict liability rule for having prepared and published a fair and accurate report of legal proceedings held in public, published contemporaneously and in good faith. The requirement of contemporaneous publication is new in Scottish contempt law, although it was always accepted in regard to defamation that publication of reports unduly long after the event could expose the publisher to the risk of proceedings for damages, for instance on grounds of malice (see para. 650 in relation to defamation). Reports, to be protected from contempt prosecution under the strict liability rule, must be fair *and* accurate. The safeguards given by s.4 apply only to reports of cases heard in public. They are not intended to extend to publication of matter prohibited by other statutory restrictions—for example, those laid down by s.22 of the Criminal Justice (Scotland) Act 1980 (concerning identification of children, dealt with in Chapter 12) or those which operate in relation to civil actions, such as the Judicial Proceedings (Regulation of Reports) Act 1926 (see Chapter 11).

"Pending and imminent"

417. New restrictions are enacted by s.4(2) to protect other proceedings "pending or imminent" at the time a report of a case is published, but these are not automatic. (The "pending and imminent" rule is strange to Scots law, and comes in here from English law. It will be for the court, however, and not the journalists, to decide whether proceedings are "pending or imminent.") They will be applied only where the court sees fit. It has power to order that a report of a case, or of any part of it, be postponed for as long as it thinks fit to avoid the risk of prejudicing those other proceedings or any later stage of the same case. A postponement order may be issued only where this "appears necessary" in view of a *substantial* risk of prejudice to the other proceedings. When such an order is made, the report postponed will, when published, be treated as contemporaneous under the Act if published as soon as practicable after the order has expired (which will usually mean publication in the first edition issued after its expiry). There is a right of appeal against postponement orders. (*West Sussex County Times* and the National Union of Journalists successfully appealed to the High Court in London against a postponement order on reports of committal proceedings made by Horsham Magistrates in November 1981.) As will be seen below, it is also possible for newspaper publishers to make application to the court for withdrawal of a s.4(2) order.

418. Because of the absence of preliminary committal proceedings, which have produced a crop of postponement orders in the English courts, such orders are much less common in Scotland. One Scottish case given the s.4(2) treatment in 1986 involved two partners in a Glasgow firm of solicitors who were charged before the High Court with fraud and embezzlement. When one partner, Thomas McCool, was convicted and sentenced to five years' imprisonment on July 30, Lord Mayfield, the presiding judge, made an order delaying reports of the case until after the trial of his partner, William Carlin, due to open four days later. Because Carlin was ill the trial had to be postponed and on September 9, when he had still not recovered, on an unopposed motion by the Crown and supported by counsel appearing for the Scottish Daily Newspaper Society, Lord Allanbridge lifted the s.4(2) order, and the case of McCool was duly reported six weeks after the event.

419. A case which came before Maidstone Crown Court in December 1980 provides an illustration of the kind of situation in which (had the Act then been in force) a judge would be entitled to exercise the power now enacted by s.4(2). Henry Gallagher, wanted for two killings in Dundee, appeared in the Maidstone Court on two charges of manslaughter, which he admitted. During the hearing prosecution counsel stated the killings, which occurred in Ramsgate, were similar to an earlier attack in Dundee. Gallagher had been allowed home on leave to Scotland from Maidstone Prison, where he was serving three years for burglary. He failed to return, and killed two people in Dundee. As the Scottish proceedings were still pending, reporting of the English hearing caused Scottish editors some anxiety, but in fact—although some newspapers decided to exclude all reference to the Dundee killings—it was safe to report what was said in court. Section 4(1) now provides statutory grounds for this right, but subsection (2) gives courts throughout the U.K. new powers to delay reports which might create the degree of risk of prejudice which the Act sets out to prevent.

Public discussion

420. In some ways the most notable provisions of the Act appear in s.5 and concern the freedom of the media to comment on matters of public interest despite the fact that legal proceedings exist in relation to them. The intention of Parliament was to give effect to the ruling of the European Court of Human Rights in April 1979 in the case of the *Sunday Times* against the U.K. Government, which was instrumental in persuading the Government that a statute on contempt, to deal with this and other aspects in need of reform, was necessary and could not be further delayed. (The report of the Phillimore Committee recommending changes in the contempt law was issued in 1974.) The *Sunday Times* postponed publication of articles it had prepared commenting on the use and effects of the drug thalidomide under threat of contempt proceedings if publication took place while negotiations for settlement of damages actions arising from the use of the drug were going on. The negotiations continued for nine years, and contempt proceedings to determine whether the paper would be guilty of an offence if it published the articles in the meantime went through all stages of appeal, the House of Lords ruling it would be contempt to publish. The European Court held by a narrow majority the Lords were wrong.

421. The Act provides that publication of comment as part of a discussion in good faith of public affairs or other matters of general public interest is not contempt under the strict liability rule if the risk of impediment or prejudice to particular legal proceedings "is merely incidental to the discussion." The immunity from contempt proceedings which the section affords would not extend to published comment which *set out* to influence or prejudice particular proceedings. A consequence appears to be that contempt could arise where comment is published during negotiations between parties for an out-of-court settlement if the comment will seriously prejudice the pending case and does not form part of a discussion in good faith of a matter of general public interest. Section 5 can also be used to meet the case of the "gagging writ," more familiar in England than in Scotland, whereby publicity could be deliberately muzzled by the procedural device of raising a separate, bogus, action for the purpose of bringing the *sub judice* (active proceedings) rule into operation.

422. Application of the s.5 defence in any particular case arises only where prejudice caused to particular proceedings by published comment is merely incidental to the discussion in good faith of some matter of general public interest. The section intends no contempt will arise where the discussion of a topic of general public interest causes the kind of prejudice or impediment to legal proceedings that is liable to happen as a subsidiary, and not as a main, consequence of the discussion. It places priority in favour of the need for free public discussion instead of, as formerly, on the side of protecting particular proceedings from prejudice at the expense of public discussion. The matter was put to the test in a case of contempt brought against the

Daily Mail and its editor, Sir David English, in 1981 for publishing an article by Malcolm Muggeridge in support of a "Pro-life" candidate in a by-election during the trial of Dr Leonard Arthur, a paediatrician, on a charge of attempting to murder a mongoloid baby by use of drugs. The publishers were fined £500 but no penalty was imposed on the editor when the Queen's Bench Division of the English High Court found there had been a substantial risk of prejudice to the trial caused by the article. The House of Lords on July 15, 1982 unanimously set aside that finding. They agreed there was a substantial risk of serious prejudice to the trial but ruled that the defence provided by s.5 of the 1981 Act applied. The article, they held, was written in undisputed good faith as a discussion of public affairs and was part of a wider discussion on a matter of general public importance—the moral justification of mercy killing. The risk of the jurors' minds being prejudiced was *merely incidental* to any discussion of the candidate's election policy or to any meaningful discussion of the wider matters of general public interest involved in the controversy as to the justification of mercy killing. To decide otherwise, they held, would mean all Press discussion of that subject would have been stifled from the time Dr Arthur was charged in February 1981 until his acquittal in November. Such gagging of *bona fide* discussion in the press was what s.5 was intended to prevent. They also ruled that it was for the Attorney-General (who brought the contempt proceedings) to show that the risk of prejudice to the fair trial of Dr Arthur was not "merely incidental" to the public discussion.

423. In 1982 reports following Michael Fagan's intrusion into Buckingham Palace resulted in five English newspapers being brought before the Divisional Court in London charged with contempt. The *Sunday Times* and *Daily Star* were found guilty, but proceedings against the *Sun*, *Mail on Sunday* and *Sunday People* were dismissed. The *Sunday Times*, which "apologised without reservation," was fined £1000; the *Daily Star* was not penalised because its story had been the result of what the court treated as "an acknowledged if unaccountable mistake." The three judges emphasised the cases were considered against the exceptional background of the Fagan case and that they were not giving general guidance on how the new provisions should be interpreted. It is impossible, however, not to treat the cases as creating an important precedent in several respects. All five newspapers had been accused of "going beyond permissible grounds" in covering the story of Fagan, who had twice entered the palace and on the second occasion reached the Queen's bedroom. It had been alleged by the Attorney-General that the reports, commenting and speculating on

Fagan's actions, background and state of mind, had created a substantial risk of serious prejudice to the proceedings pending against him. Lord Lane, Lord Chief Justice, in his judgment, said the *Sunday Times* wrongly reported that Fagan had been accused of stabbing his stepson; the report, which exaggerated the case against Fagan, was bound to result in serious prejudice. Inaccuracy on its own did not amount to contempt, but when it occurred to this extent and was given front-page prominence, the publisher put himself at risk. The newspaper, the judge held, created a substantial risk of serious prejudice to the prosecution by later publishing an untrue report that proceedings against Fagan for taking and driving away a car without consent had been dropped; this was in fact the charge to which he subsequently pleaded guilty. The newspaper could not avail itself of the public interest defence in s.5. In the case of the *Daily Star* the report complained of referred to Fagan's having admitted stealing wine from the palace. No one could explain how this came to be printed; it was an admitted error. Lord Lane said it created a very substantial risk of serious prejudice, but the damage it caused was minimal, and the court imposed no penalty. In the case of the *Mail on Sunday* the court held that the newspaper was covered by the s.5 defence. Lord Lane said the references to the appalling state of safeguards designed to protect the Queen were matters of the gravest public concern and examples *par excellence* of "affairs or other matters of general public interest" (Contempt of Court Act 1981, s.5) covered by the section. Any prejudice to Fagan could only be described as incidental to a necessary and unavoidable part of the discussion on the Queen's safety. It could not have been written at all if the risk of prejudice was to be avoided. In the two remaining cases references by the newspapers to Fagan's background and alleged drug addiction were held to be too remote to involve any risk that he would be deprived of a fair trial.

The old law

424. So far we have been concerned with those sections of the Act that deal with contempt under the strict liability rule, and before passing to other provisions of the Act it should be stated that s.6 makes it clear that certain pre-existing principles of the contempt law survive in parallel with the new measures. The defences the Act provides under the strict liability rule therefore cannot be argued against a case of contempt brought outside that rule, *e.g.* throwing a missile at a judge, threatening a witness, causing a disturbance in court, suppressing evidence, or prevarication. Section 6 states in effect that (a) any defence available under the old law to a charge of contempt under the strict liability rule is not diminished by the Act, (b) nothing is to be punishable as contempt under that rule which would not have been before the passing of the Act, and (c) the new provisions do not alter the existing liability for contempt in respect of conduct *intended* to impede or prejudice the administration of justice. One effect of this is that it could still be contempt to publish from an open record before proceedings are active if this is intended to have that result.

425. The provision in s.6(*b*) is also worth noting since it can be read as taking most, if not all, of the sting out of the new rules covering appellate proceedings, and it is reasonable to cite this passage of the section as a defence to any charge of contempt alleged to have been committed at the appeal stage of proceedings. There may be scope for an argument that what was not actually punished under the old law in this regard could nevertheless have been punishable, but it would probably be hard to convince most judges on this point.

Juries

426. The Act introduces new measures (s.8) to protect the confidentiality of juries' deliberations. Except for certain limited reservations, it prohibits as a contempt of court any disclosure of statements made, or opinions expressed, arguments advanced or votes cast by members of a jury in the course of their deliberations. Equally it is prohibited to obtain or solicit any such particulars, and the provision applies to juries "in any legal proceedings." In other words, it operates in civil as well as criminal cases. Thus, to interview a juror, but later decide not to publish what he or she said (or carry out such an interview without any intention to publish) would be contempt. Section 8 was applied in a case at the Old Bailey in November 1981 when, during a drug smuggling trial, a journalist was ordered by the judge to be detained on a charge of contempt after the court was told he had approached a woman juror during the lunch break and questioned her about the case. The juror told the court she had left the jury room to make a telephone call within the court precincts when the journalist approached her, questioned her about a witness whose evidence had been taken *in camera* but also told her "not to worry" because he could not publish anything she told him.

427. The Act does, however, permit publication of statements disclosing particulars of jurors' deliberations where these are brought out in open court as part of the original trial or during subsequent proceedings for contempt arising from it. Section 8 reverses the legal position in England created by the decision that it was not contempt for the *New Statesman* to interview a juror in the Jeremy Thorpe case. The section is not intended to prohibit genuine research into the working of the jury system. Publication of general discussion of the subject, including the merits of juries as such, would not amount to contempt so long as it did not include material obtained in contravention of the section, that is, any particulars of a jury's deliberations in any particular case. It has to be realised, however, that the effect of the section is bound to be to make useful research based on actual experience of the working of the system more difficult than under the law as it stood before the passing of the Act.

Tape recorders

428.   Apart from their permitted use for making official transcripts of proceedings, the Act (s.9) makes it contempt to use tape recorders in court, or bring them into court for use, except with the leave of the court. This prohibition is less restrictive than it may appear, since the judicial attitude is tending towards a limited use of recorders as an aid to accurate reporting of court proceedings, provided the instruments can be prevented from interfering in any way with the proceedings or distracting the attention of witnesses, jurors or other participants by mechanical or electrical noise or other interference with the proceedings. Opposition to their use subject to these safeguards may be expected to diminish as advances in technology bring improvements in design and operational standards. One condition judges could be expected to impose is that recorders would not be used in court in such a way as to record private conversations in court between solicitor or counsel and client or between lawyers. It is an important advance that the Act does not impose a total ban, but permits the use of recorders subject to the leave of the court, with conditions.

429.   The section prohibits as a contempt the use or publication of any recording obtained without the leave of the court, as well as its disposal to someone else with the intention that it should be made public. It is to be within the discretion of the court to decide whether or not to grant leave to use a tape recorder in the courtroom, and the judge is to have authority, where he does grant leave, to impose such conditions as he thinks proper. The court also is given the power, having given leave, to withdraw it wholly or in relation to part of the proceedings. In the event of a breach, the judge can order forfeiture of the instrument or any recording made by it, or both.

430.   It can be expected the practice of different judges will vary in the application of the new provisions, and it may be only through resort to the Appeal Court that consistency will be attained and a set of standards or practical guidelines for the permitted use of tape recorders in court be laid down.

Journalists' sources

431. Section 10 prohibits any court from requiring a person to disclose the source of information contained in a publication for which he is responsible, subject to this important exception: that disclosure may be required where this is "necessary in the interests of justice or national security or for the prevention of disorder or crime." No person refusing to make such disclosure is to be guilty of contempt of court unless the court holds it is established to its satisfaction that the exception applies.

432. It can be seen that in practical effect the exception is larger than the rule and could be used in virtually any case to require disclosure since it may be argued that disclosure of any evidence in the witness-box is required "in the interests of justice" if it is found by the court to be admissible. Something may have been gained, however, by the fact that a right of protection of journalistic sources (subject to the exception) has for the first time been established by statute, and it could only be displaced by bringing the exception into operation in any particular case.

433. The reasons for which a court is entitled to withhold the protection of sources are substantially the same as those used by the courts in the few cases in which, under the old law, they decided to require disclosure (Vassall case, *Att.-Gen.* v. *Mulholland, Att.-Gen.* v. *Foster* [1963] 2 Q.B. 477). In Scottish cases the reason has been either national security or prevention of crime, or both, in combination with the interests of justice (*H.M.A.* v. *Airs*, 1975 S.L.T. 177).

434. In an English case in 1982 Jack Lundin, a journalist working for the *Observer*, who gave evidence in a case involving corruption in the conduct of a casino business, was accused of contempt for refusing to disclose to the High Court in London the source of information he had about an alleged scheme to lure gamblers away from rival casinos. Lord Justice Watkins, with whom Mr Justice Glidewell agreed, held that, while the information Mr Lundin had was relevant to the case, its disclosure could not serve any useful purpose, and the journalist was accordingly not guilty of contempt. The case was the first judicial ruling on an alleged contempt under s.10—which lays down that a witness shall be required to disclose his source only where this is "necessary in the interests of justice."

435. Following a decision of the European Court of Human Rights in 1986 in favour of Harriet Harman, Labour M.P., that she did not commit contempt of court by handing to a journalist confidential documents which had already been read out in court in a civil case in which she acted as a solicitor, the Government agreed to amend the law of contempt to make it clear that journalists had a right to see documents already made public in court. Miss Harman, then legal officer of the National Council for Civil Liberties, was representing an ex-prisoner who sued the Home Office in respect of his alleged ill-treatment while in jail. She was held by the House of Lords in 1982 to be guilty of contempt by handing documents already read out in court to a journalist preparing a feature article for the *Guardian*. They ruled that she was in breach of an implied undertaking not to use them for purposes other than the court action in which she was engaged. (No contempt proceedings were taken against the journalist or the paper.)

436. Miss Harman took the matter to the European Court of Human Rights on the ground that the Lords' decision violated the European Convention on Human Rights, and as part of a settlement the Government agreed to amend the law to make it clear it was not contempt to disclose to the media the contents of a confidential document already disclosed in public during civil court proceedings. The Government also agreed to pay Miss Harman's expenses, said to amount to £39,000.

Required anonymity

437. Section 11 gives any court, which already has power to "allow" a name or other matter to be withheld from the public in proceedings before it, authority to prohibit publication of that name or other matter in any report of the proceedings where this appears necessary. (The *Socialist Worker* disclosed the name of a blackmail witness where the court had ordered otherwise, the paper maintaining it had no power to make such an order—*R.* v. *Socialist Worker* [1975] 1 All E.R. 142. *Leveller* magazine named a plaintiff referred to in court as "Colonel B" in an Official Secrets case—*Att.-Gen.* v. *Leveller Magazine Ltd.* [1978] 3 All E.R. 731.) In other words, courts now have power not only to stop disclosure in court of names or other matters emerging during the proceedings, but can also prevent this being made ineffective by disclosure of the withheld details in the media. Significantly, though, this new power belongs only to those courts which already have power to "allow" such particulars not to be disclosed in court. The section is intended to clear up confusion which arose in certain English cases regarding the extent of the power judges actually had to control disclosure to the public through the media.

438. An example of the type of case where the new provision may be applicable, but which was formerly regulated by long-standing arrangements between the Judiciary and the Press in Scotland, is where the presiding judge at a rape trial excludes the public but permits reporters to remain in court provided they do not identify the alleged victim. Parliament has now removed any doubt about the courts' authority to act in such a situation by giving them power to impose a prohibition against publication of the particulars in question where they consider this is necessary to give effect to the existing power they have to allow non-disclosure to the public in court. The new provision applies also to preserving the anonymity of the alleged victim in blackmail proceedings or any other case where the judge already has power to allow non-disclosure of particulars exempt from disclosure in court.

439. Cases, other than rape or blackmail, where witnesses have previously been allowed to withhold their names or addresses in court have been relatively rare in Scotland, but where they have occurred there has been no illegality involved in reporters obtaining the particulars from another source and publishing them. Under s.11 a court has power to stop reporters doing so if it considers this necessary for the purpose for which it allowed the witness to withhold the information in court. This latter prohibition does not, however, follow automatically; the Act states the court "may give such directions" in this respect, as appears to the court to be necessary. The case for allowing non-disclosure of a person's identity during court proceedings may be quite distinct from any question of disclosure in subsequent media reports. The above provision is not to be confused with that for automatic anonymity of children contained in s.22 of the Criminal Justice (Scotland) Act 1980.

Fixed term sentences

440. Where a court imposes a prison sentence for contempt it must, under s.15, be for a fixed term although the court retains its power to order discharge at an earlier date. The maximum prison sentence which may be imposed by the High Court or a sheriff court in cases taken on indictment is two years, but a fine (without statutory limit) may be imposed as well or as an alternative. Where the contempt is dealt with by a sheriff in proceedings other than on indictment (*i.e.* in cases brought on summary complaint or in civil proceedings), the maximum penalty is three months' imprisonment or a fine of £2,000 or both. In the district court the maximum is 60 days or £1,000 or both. The provisions in the Criminal Procedure (Scotland) Act 1975, prohibiting the imposition of prison sentences on persons under the age of 17 or on persons suffering from mental disorder defined in that Act, are extended to cover anyone in those categories found guilty of contempt under the 1981 Act.

Tribunals and other bodies

441. Tribunals and "bodies exercising the judicial power of the State" are now treated as courts for the purpose of applying the law of contempt under the Act (s.19). This innovation met strong opposition during passage of the measure through Parliament. The Government, which promoted it, could not undertake to provide a list of the tribunals and other bodies which fitted the definition. If the Government with its resources found the task beyond it, it is not one this book can be confident of achieving, having regard to the great number and variety of bodies possibly involved. (The provision is understood to have been included in the Act because of a controversial English decision arising from a BBC television discussion of a valuation tribunal case while it was *sub judice*.) The problem may be simplified to some extent, however, by excluding from the definition all those tribunals set up to deal with disputes or complaints concerning the conduct of members of professions, trades or specialised bodies for their internal regulation where no judicial power of the State is involved; in most such instances the body in question is concerned with determining questions of discipline, ethics or practice within the profession or trade in question. The definition does, however, cover a judicial appeal from a tribunal which is not itself within the category.

442. It also covers tribunals of inquiry set up under statute or by ministerial order, fatal accident inquiries, the Lands Tribunal for Scotland, industrial tribunals, rent tribunals, inquiries into deaths at sea, shipping casualties or railway accidents held under statutory provisions laid down for the purpose, local planning inquiries, inquiries into objections to Private Acts of Parliament, and inquiries held under statute dealing with safety in mines and collieries, but this list is not exhaustive. In marginal cases it may be necessary to inquire into the nature of the powers possessed by a tribunal or body in order to decide whether the contempt jurisdiction applies. Where substantial doubt exists or the body's actual powers are difficult to ascertain, journalists are entitled to seek the advice of the Crown Office in Edinburgh on whether a particular tribunal or other body comes within the definition in s.19. During Parliamentary debate the Attorney-General gave assurances, so far as England was concerned, that assistance of this kind would be provided, where possible, by his office.

Coroners' inquests

443. These are confined to England and Wales, analogous functions in Scotland being performed by the fatal accident inquiry, but because the 1981 Act applies to the whole U.K., it is of some importance for journalists and publishers in Scotland, whose work may circulate elsewhere, to know the position of the inquest in the context of contempt law. In 1986 the English Court of Appeal upheld a ruling by a High Court judge, Gatehouse, J., that it would be contempt for London Weekend Television to screen a programme about the death of a man in police custody during an adjournment of an inquest into his death. The Police Federation and six policemen had successfully applied to the High Court of Justice to stop transmission of a TV programme dealing with events leading up to the death of John Mikkleson, aged 34, at Feltham police station. The inquest had been opened at Hammersmith and adjourned; police investigations were proceeding to ascertain whether there were grounds for criminal charges. Watkins, L.J. in the Appeal Court said there was a high probability that if the programme was shown there was a substantial risk to the course of justice; proceedings which were "active" might well be prejudiced.

Scottish proceedings

444. In defining "Scottish proceedings," the section indicates that a court (*e.g.* the House of Lords) need not sit geographically within Scotland to exercise the jurisdiction which brings it within the definition.

Common law and police sources

445. The Act being designed to deal with aspects of contempt concerned with published matter, certain other matters remain to be considered which are still subject to case law and the powers of the prosecuting authorities to deal with breaches of the criminal law intended to protect the administration of justice. The Act offers little assistance in deciding what special considerations apply to the possible publication of information obtained from the police, for example at a Press conference, during investigation of a crime. The leading case on this topic is *Hall* (*Hall* v. *Associated Newspapers Ltd.*, 1978 S.L.T.

241). One of the essential points made clear by that case is that a piece of information, should it prejudice proceedings by its publication, is no less of a contempt of court because of the fact that it emanated from a police source. Nor would this fact be a defence in the event of the publication meeting the standard of prejudice or impediment to the course of justice set out in the 1981 Act.

446. There can be actual danger in reliance by a journalist upon the belief that information given him by the police about a crime or its circumstances is necessarily safe to publish. The responsibility on whether to publish belongs to him, the writer, editor or publisher, or all of these. The aim must be to prevent publication of anything that will cause substantial risk of serious prejudice to a subsequent trial. As an example of the kind of material it would be unsafe to publish, we may imagine the police have released details to the media of injuries sustained by the victim of a crime or the condition or circumstances in which he was found, for example, bound hand and foot and gagged. When a suspect is ultimately apprehended and questioned by the police, if he volunteers information about those circumstances, it could be made almost valueless as evidence if the accused could have read it in the Press or heard it on radio or television. If, however, no such information had been published, its disclosure by the suspect would point strongly towards his implication in the crime.

447. So special care has to be taken to avoid the danger of publishing any matter even before arrest, grant of a warrant, or service of a charge, which could give grounds for a charge of attempting to pervert or interfere with the course or administration of justice. This is a criminal offence, separate from the law of contempt. The judges in the *Hall* case pointed out that publication of prejudicial material before the special jurisdiction of contempt arose (now by statute the point when a case becomes active), either by the Press or by anyone else, might be just as damaging to the interests of justice as publication at a later stage. That, if it arose, would be dealt with under the existing criminal law—as an attempt to pervert the course of justice, a common law charge. This caution applies equally to pictorial and textual publicity.

Pre-trial publicity

448. Even where allegedly prejudicial pre-trial publicity has taken place, the High Court is reluctant to intervene on a plea that a fair trial has become impossible. In the *Stuurman* case (see next para.) the court held that it would only intervene to stop a trial taking place in special circumstances which were likely to be rare and must be such as to satisfy the court that, having regard to the principles of substantial justice and of fair trial, to require an accused to face trial would be oppressive. The point arose also in a case where a justice in Inverness District Court in 1984 had upheld a plea in bar of trial on the basis of publicity given by local newspapers to disciplinary proceedings taken by Inverness Amateur Football Association against a footballer, Christopher Bernardi, who assaulted another player on the field. The justice decided that the pre-trial publicity—which occurred before Bernardi was served with an assault complaint—was sufficient to influence his judgment and the recollection of witnesses with the result that a fair trial could not take place. The High Court upheld an appeal by the procurator fiscal. Lord Justice-Clerk Wheatley said it was a trite part of the training of a judge at any level that a verdict had to depend solely on the evidence before the court, and that the decision thereon must not be affected by any extraneous considerations. It was not to be assumed that justices who had been appointed to discharge judicial duties would be incapable of exercising the self-discipline to observe these basic rules simply because they were justices. The case was sent back to the district court to proceed.

449. Another signal for special caution must be recognised when the information about a Scottish case originates outside Scotland, either through a news agency in England or in a foreign country, or has come from a police source south of the Border, where the rules and practice concerning avoidance of prejudice are different. An instance of this kind of situation arose in the case of *Stuurman and Others*, 1980 S.L.T. (Notes) 95, which arose from an article about a drugs case which the High Court held to be a substantial contempt. The material in the article which led to this conclusion was stated to have been mainly derived from a Press Association release which, the court was told, was based in turn on information supplied by the English police. The court stated that the source could not be relied upon in mitigation of the offence.

Legal advice

450. Experience has shown it is not enough that journalists, especially editors, should rely solely on their legal advisers in deciding what is or is not likely to involve their paper or company in contempt proceedings. It is clear from the *Stuurman* case, though it is not the only one in which such a situation has arisen, that the judges expect a high degree of expertise and responsibility on the part of those making the editorial decision. They were highly critical in that case not only of the editorial decision to publish but also the fact that a lawyer previously consulted had passed the article as safe. They expressed themselves as "astonished and indeed appalled" to learn that publication was apparently approved by the newspaper's legal adviser. This displayed "almost certainly a lamentable ignorance" of recent decisions of the court or "a total lack of responsible professional judgment." Nevertheless the publishers were fined £20,000 and the then editor of the *Glasgow Herald* £750. Radio Forth was also fined £10,000 and its chief executive £1,000 for contempt arising from its report of the same case.

451. The judges of the High Court have made it clear in several cases that the law places a heavy duty on those responsible for organisation within a newspaper or other organ of publicity to see that a proper system is operated and maintained to prevent an occurrence like that of the *Stuurman* case, so far as this is possible. Indeed the court stated in that case that even the raw recruit to journalism ought to be familiar with this branch of the law.

452. No amount of special knowledge of this difficult area will be of much practical use, however, unless the journalist obliged to apply it is in possession of the facts essential to enable him to make a decision. For example, and in particular, has anyone been arrested, or a warrant been granted for an arrest of anyone, or a charge been served? Or, if it is a summary case, has a warrant been granted to cite the accused to appear in court? These are matters about which those working in the media may be uninformed unless given the necessary assistance by the police or the prosecuting authorities. An approach to the Crown Office or the local procurator-fiscal is obligatory.

453. The necessity for appropriate information to be given to the media has been recognised by the Lord Advocate who, in 1983, made it known to the police that in his view information on whether proceedings are active in any particular case should be given to the media, on request, in order that they may comply with the Act. He thought it right for the police to release the name of any person who has been arrested (unless there are operational reasons for not doing so), but not at this stage any details of a charge; and also to release, subject to the same conditions, the identity of any person after a warrant for his arrest has been obtained. In either case, the naming of the person concerned is to ensure that the media are aware not only that proceedings are active in any particular case but that they are active in respect of a particular person. It is not only the publication of information about the case which may be prejudicial to an accused. The publication of information about that person, even if it relates to other matters unconnected with the particular case, may also be prejudicial. The Lord Advocate also considered that the media are entitled to be told, on request, when a person (without identifying him) is detained under s.2 of the Criminal Justice (Scotland) Act 1980. Although detention does not make proceedings active, this last facility is intended to put the media on their guard and to be a warning that proceedings may become active in respect of that particular case. The purpose of the release of the information is not that it be published. Indeed in certain circumstances, where a suspect is still being sought, publication may create difficulties for the police by making it harder for them to catch him.

454. The most that can usually be safely published after the arrest stage and pending a public appearance in court is what the procurator-fiscal is prepared to disclose—the name and address and usually the age of the accused and the general nature of the offence of which he is accused. In the case of a young offender, the information he is able to release may be even more restricted. An example of the dangers attached to any enlargement of the basic factual disclosures he makes at this stage was the case of a Scottish weekly paper which in 1977 was summoned before the High Court for contempt. In reporting a case of two men who appeared on petition in chambers at Dumbarton Sheriff Court on charges of assault and robbery, the *Milngavie and Bearsden Herald* stated that when caught the accused, whom they identified, were both wearing masks. Crown counsel submitted to the High Court this was "a fair indication of their guilt." For the paper it was stated the story was a last-minute filler produced under considerable staffing difficulties. The court held the story was calculated to interfere with the administration of justice and, although this was not deliberate, it was condemned by the judges as "a disgraceful publication." The publishers and the editor were each fined £250 (see para. 557).

455. Although the Act, by s.3, has created a defence of innocent publication, it at the same time places a duty on journalists to take "all reasonable care," which must involve reference to an authoritative and entirely reliable source for the information necessary for a decision to be made about when or whether to publish. The High Court in the case of *Hall* observed that, as the risk of prejudicial publication would arise only in relation to crimes attracting wide public interest, those in the media considering the issue of publication had a duty to make the necessary inquiries. In this respect, especially in view of the terms of the 1981 Act, they are entitled to expect the necessary co-operation of the Crown Office. Officials of that office cannot, however, be expected to give legal advice, merely to supply the basic information to enable an editorial decision to be made.

456. Among the principles surviving from the case law is that laid down by the High Court in the case of *Caldwell* in 1960 (*Caldwell* v. *Daily Record Ltd.* February 12, 1960)—that punishment for contempt arising from publication may be imposed upon a member of the editorial staff of a newspaper (and of a broadcast organisation) below the rank of editor. In that case the court were satisfied that the editor was absent through illness at the time of the preparation of the offending publication. Where contempt is established, therefore, punishment goes with actual editorial responsibility on the spot.

Freelance's responsibility

456a. So much for staff; freelance journalists bear responsibility for their own work, as was judicially established in a case in 1987. A High Court murder trial at Paisley was abandoned when the court learned that Radio Clyde broadcast a report, before the judge had charged the jury, which stated (inaccurately) that the accused offered to plead guilty to culpable homicide. Seven members of the jury later told the court they had heard, or been told of, this report. The freelance who supplied it, Gavin Bell, was fined £5,000 for contempt of court. Colin Adams, the Radio Clyde duty news editor, was fined £20,000, but on appeal this fine was quashed. Lord Allanbridge, the trial judge, said it should have been known to an experienced journalist that if there had been an offer of a plea to a reduced charge, it would have been made outwith the presence of the jury. After retrial before a fresh jury at the High Court in Edinburgh, the accused, Joseph Trainer, aged 37, was acquitted. Reporting of the contempt proceedings was delayed by order of the court until the end of the second trial. Bell decided not to proceed with an appeal. In the case of Adams, however, the Court of Criminal Appeal, presided over by Lord Justice-General Emslie, held that there was no culpability attached to him, Lord Allanbridge having expected of a person in his position much too high a standard of conduct in the assessment of the accuracy of a news report submitted by an experienced source of a specialist nature. The freelance journalist was in a totally different position. His degree of culpability was of a grave order.

Contempt in court

457. If a party or witness or member of the public commits contempt by his behaviour in court or makes offensive remarks amounting to contempt, it will not normally be contempt for a report of the incident to be published, including quotations of what was said by the offender, provided his remarks can be treated as relevant to the proceedings before the court. It may be a matter of degree to decide in which cases remarks not relevant to the case are safe to publish, but proceedings for contempt against the publisher are unlikely where the report is accurate. No action was taken, for instance, against newspapers which in the 1950s published accurate reports stating a litigant in the First Division of the Court of Session called the judges "Nazis."

458. Where a person sentenced for contempt is a witness found guilty of prevaricating or otherwise obstructing the proceedings he can appeal by invoking the jurisdiction the High Court and Inner House of the Court of Session possess, the *nobile officium*, which can be used to provide a remedy where none is available by other means (*Wylie* v. *H.M. Advocate*, 1966 S.L.T. 149).

Investigative journalism

459. The other side of the contempt coin is the right which the media have, and which is recognised by common law, to publish material drawing attention to suspected crime. An important element of this function of the Press and broadcasting, however, is its limitations. Once the crime or legal abuse which has been exposed is being investigated by the criminal authorities and an arrest has been made, a warrant granted for arrest or a charge served, publication of media revelations or comment must cease.

460. The leading case on the point (*Smith* v. *Ritchie & Co.* (1893) 20 R.(J.)52), though about a century old, still applies as a valuable authority for the journalist's right to publish the fruits of his inquiries into suspected crime so long as he knows when to stop. The case concerned the uttering of forged documents and, in giving judgment, Lord Justice-Clerk Macdonald said it was not only allowable but right for a newspaper to call public attention to such matters when they arose. The publishers at the same time took the risk of making comments and accusations against individuals and being liable in the civil courts if what was published was defamatory. Publicity which might prejudice a subsequent trial must cease once the matter was in the hands of the public authorities (and under the terms of the 1981 Act, a case has become active). Agreeing, Lord Trayner said if a newspaper had information which enabled it not only to assert that certain documents were spurious, but also to indicate a certain person as the one guilty of uttering them as genuine, it was doing a public service in laying that information before the public. But such publicity must cease when the person accused was apprehended. It need only be added that the case sets up a principle which applies not only to cases of uttering forged documents.

Dignity of the court

461. Another area where the media have certain rights and duties to the public, but with associated responsibilities, is that concerned with criticism of the judiciary. This may take many forms. That least likely to raise any question of contempt is criticism of court decisions provided it is expressed responsibly and reasonably and does not attack the integrity or authority of the judge. Fair comment on a court's judgment is not contempt. Criticism undermining the dignity of the court or bringing ridicule on the judge may amount to contempt by common law. Murmuring of judges, as it was known in Scots law, would now be dealt with as contempt, and this branch of the law need not be limited to publication, being available to protect the courts from intemperate attacks upon them from whatever quarter.

Clear infringement

462. Proceedings for contempt are rarely taken unless there is a clear infringement of the law. The High Court in 1973 (*Royle* v. *Grey*, 1973 S.L.T. 31) emphasised that the power to punish for contempt should be exercised only with care and discretion. In their judgment the court quoted with approval what Lord President Normand said in an earlier case in the Court of Session (*Milburn*, 1946 S.L.T. 192):

" . . . the greatest restraint and discretion should be used by the court in dealing with contempt of court, lest a process, the purpose of which is to prevent interference with the administration of justice, should degenerate into an oppressive or vindictive abuse of the court's powers."

Escaped prisoners

463. Care has to be exercised in publishing reports about prisoners who have escaped from prison or from custody, lest what is said will prejudice their subsequent trial or proceedings taken against them in respect of having escaped. An accused charged with attempting to defeat the ends of justice by escaping has the same basic right to protection from prejudice by publicity as any other person awaiting trial, but the extent of this right may be modified through his own violent behaviour. There is the important distinction that in cases where the escapee has a record of violence he may be a danger to members of the public, and the media may be entitled (indeed may feel under a duty) to publish details sufficient to warn them. In deciding how much to publish, journalists must be guided by official sources—the Scottish Information Office, the Crown Office or the procurator-fiscal—who may authorise publication of a fugitive's dangerous propensities in appropriate cases. In certain instances, by authority of the Lord Advocate or Solicitor-General, the media may be allowed, or encouraged, to publish a photograph or photo-fit picture of a violent person at large.

464. A policy statement issued to the media in 1966 by the then Secretary of State for Scotland, that official information about escaped prisoners would be restricted, was revised in 1981, but the practice continues to be that such statements will not contain reference to the crime for which the escapee had been convicted, or the charge for which he awaits trial, except where a departure from this practice is justified by considerations of public safety. The basic information—name, home area, date and place of sentence and term of sentence—will normally be issued for publication. The 1966 practice was reconsidered in 1981 after a man serving life for murder was allowed out of Saughton Prison to visit his family under escort, escaped and, while at large, raped a woman. At the time of his escape an official of the Scottish Prisons Department was quoted as saying he was not considered dangerous. Next day a public warning was issued through the media, along with his photograph, authorised by the Lord Advocate for publication. After the man was caught and sentenced for the rape, the Scottish Home and Health Department stated that in future cases of the kind, their advice to the media would be that, although a person's behaviour in prison did not suggest he would be a danger to the public, his record involved violent crime.

CHAPTER 10

PHOTOGRAPHY

465. The Contempt of Court Act 1981 made important changes in the law concerning photography and the publication of pictures in relation to judicial proceedings. In particular it clarified aspects of the contempt law in this area and removed much of the uncertainty existing before the passing of the Act, when rules had to be derived from court decisions, not all of which were consistent with each other. The Act does not, however, deal with the whole law of contempt as it affects photography, and it is still necessary to refer to the old common law for guidance on specific aspects of the subject, particularly those relating to the restriction on taking or making pictures within court precincts. It must not be assumed that, although the Act is a United Kingdom statute, the same standards will be applied by the Scottish courts in interpreting it as those applicable in England in relation to publication, for example, of pictures of criminal suspects. English newspapers have formerly, without repercussions, exercised much greater freedom than those published in Scotland in this respect, and even since the passing of the Act they have continued publishing this kind of picture to an extent that would be inviting contempt proceedings in a Scottish case. An outstanding instance was the case of Dennis Nilsen who, after the unearthing of parts of a number of human skeletons in London in 1983, appeared in pictures published in English newspapers handcuffed to two detectives. Lord McCluskey, former Solicitor-General for Scotland, asked the Lord Advocate in the House of Lords whether Scottish newspapers were therefore free to follow the example of the English Press and to publish photographs of persons accused of murder, allegedly committed in Scotland, without risk that the Lord Advocate would petition the High Court to treat such publication as a contempt of court. Lord Mackay of Clashfern, the Lord Advocate, in a written answer, said they were not. There is no doubt about this continuing risk in Scotland, but it would be wrong to treat it as a total certainty in every case, having regard to the undoubted fact that in a minority of cases there can be no possible issue of identification of the suspect in question and that the element of risk of prejudice to his trial is therefore non-existent, far less substantial. Judging by the crop of cases in which the Attorney-General has been reported to be investigating the possibility of contempt where pictures of suspects have been published south of the Border, the risk of contempt proceedings in such cases exists in England to an extent which it did not before the passing of the Act, and it is ignored by the media at their peril. It has to be borne in mind that the defence of "discussion of matters of general public interest," (see Contempt of Court Act 1981, s.5 and case of Michael Fagan at para. 423) which may excuse a report or article that would otherwise be treated as contempt, is unlikely to protect a picture which creates a risk of substantial prejudice.

466. We must deal first with the statutory limits now placed on publication of pictures in connection with court proceedings, being the aspect of the subject most likely to cause difficulty or call for guidance in practice, and later in the chapter offer some help with the problem of photography and the making of pictures within judicial precincts. The Act makes no distinction between pictorial and textual contempt, which is discussed in detail in Chapter 9. Indeed, the Act makes no specific mention of pictures at all. It sets down rules which apply to "publications," and goes on (in s.2) to explain that by this term the Act includes "any speech, writing, broadcast or other communication in whatever form, which is addressed to the public at large or any section of the public."

467. "Other communication in whatever form" must be intended by Parliament to include photographs or other pictorial matter. This applies in particular to television pictures as well as Press reproductions of photographs, sketches, drawings or cartoons, although, as is noted later, some consideration of common law may still be necessary to derive practical implications from what is now laid down by statute.

468. The Act introduces the important principle that, to amount to contempt in relation to court proceedings, a publication must create a *substantial* risk that the course of justice in the proceedings in question *will* be *seriously* impeded or prejudiced. This statement is made under what the Act calls the strict liability rule, which makes it an offence to create such a substantial risk regardless of what intention may lie behind the decision to publish. In other words, if publication of a picture breaks the rule, it is not relevant that the publisher did not intend to prejudice or impede the course of justice.

469. This s.2 rule introduces advantages particularly for journalists and photographers working in Scotland, where formerly the law of contempt was considerably stricter than in the rest of the United Kingdom. Under the Act the law applicable under the section is the same on both sides of the Border, although it may prove in practice that the judges will still employ the underlying principles of the common law to construe the Act where difficulty or dispute arises as to its application in specific cases in Scotland.

470. On the basis of judicial decisions, contempt could formerly be committed by the publication of a picture of an accused person during his trial although there was no real possibility of any issue of identification arising in the case.

471. Even before the Act was passed the position had been radically altered by the judgment of the High Court in the case of *Atkins* v. *London Weekend Television Ltd.* in 1978 in which the court stated: "So far as the photographs were concerned, said Mr Bruce (counsel for LWTV), there is no hard and fast rule that the publication of a photograph of an accused person will always constitute contempt. We have no difficulty in accepting this proposition and we accept, too, the further proposition that the publication of a photograph of an accused person will constitute contempt only where a question of identification has arisen or may arise and where the publication is calculated to prejudice the prospect of fair trial. This appears also to be the law of England."

472. It is worth noting that the Act, in setting the time limits within which prejudicial publicity must not occur, has adopted the principles laid down in the Scottish five judge decision in the case of *Hall* (*Hall* v. *Associated Newspapers Ltd.*, 1978 S.L.T. 241). In this respect the Act brings the English law into line with that laid down by the Scottish High Court. In ruling in the *Hall* case that the point of time at which the contempt rule begins to bite is when a suspect is arrested or a warrant is granted for arrest, the High Court held that the decision in the case of *Stirling* ("Lord Clyde's judgment" of 1959) was based on a wrong interpretation of the law, having laid down that the restriction began when a crime was suspected and was being investigated by the criminal authorities. The *Hall* ruling that that is not the law is confirmed by the 1981 Act.

473. Whether the degree of "substantial risk" stipulated in the Act is involved in any particular case must depend on the facts of the case, but it is important to keep in mind that the rule is applicable at the time of publication and not after the event, when a case has been heard and it has become possible to assert that in fact no such risk was involved.

Degree of risk

474. So the two most important considerations to be taken into account in deciding what it is safe to publish are the point of time of publication in relation to the stage court proceedings in the case in question have reached, and the degree of risk created if it is decided to publish. The Act deals with civil as well as criminal proceedings, and lays down precise rules as to when the contempt rule begins or ceases to operate in each type of case. It also lays down rules restricting publicity in relation to appeals and to proceedings before tribunals and various other unspecified bodies exercising the judicial power of the State. The implications of these innovations are discussed in Chapter 9.

When a case is active

475. The term *sub judice* is not used in the Act. Instead it creates a system of time limits by reference to when a case is *active*. When a case becomes active, the strict liability rule prohibiting publicity under threat of contempt proceedings becomes operative. When it ceases to be active, the restriction under the Act is lifted. The bar may come down more than once in the course of a case.

476. The detailed implications of the rule (see Chapter 9) apply to pictures equally as to reports or articles or broadcasts. It is imperative to know what stage proceedings have reached in any particular case, or will have reached when the intended publication takes place. This question is most likely, on the basis of past experience, to arise in relation to criminal cases, and in such a situation, the Crown Office, local procurator-fiscal or the police should be best qualified to supply the necessary information. It is fair to assume that the criminal authorities will be prepared to deal with media inquiries about whether particular proceedings have become active. To find out when a case is no longer active, or when it has been reactivated by intimation of an appeal, reference should be made to the clerk of the appropriate court or to defence lawyers.

477. Unless specific authority for publication of a picture of a suspect sought by the police has been given by the Lord Advocate or his depute, it is most probably not safe to publish it, even though no proceedings have yet become active under the terms of the Act. In this respect the law restricting publication of pictures differs from that on reports; while a picture in itself identifies the person it depicts, a written report may be published without doing so.

Care with captions

478. The same care has to be taken in writing the caption to a picture it is considered safe to publish as applies to reports, with the object of avoiding the substantial risk of prejudice the Act aims to prevent. At the risk of underlining the obvious, it has to be an invariable practice to check that the caption matches the picture. In a libel case before the High Court in London in December 1986 Dr Abdel Yassine, director of research at the Arab Institute for Socio-Economic Studies in Jordan, won undisclosed damages after a picture identifying him as the notorious terrorist Abu Nidal was published in *The Times* and the *Guardian*. Both newspapers and the Press Association, who distributed the picture, agreed to pay substantial damages and costs. The court was told the photograph had been distributed and published in good faith.

Civil cases

479. While hitherto contempt cases arising from publicity in civil cases have been extremely rare, it should not be assumed no risk exists. The Act lays down definite rules for the protection of parties in civil cases; but here again the risk of prejudice or impediment to the course of justice must be substantial before there can be a successful prosecution for contempt.

480. One effect of the Act is to relax to some extent the former rule that the risk of contempt under strict liability began to operate when a civil case was intimated in the official court rolls. Under the Act the restriction begins to operate when the case becomes active, and the earliest stage when this can happen (Sched. 1 of the Act) is either when the record is closed, or a motion or application is made or enrolled, or when a hearing is fixed or allowed. During the interval between the raising of the action (official intimation) and the earliest of any of the above steps, therefore, the strict liability rule, restricting publicity including pictures, does not apply.

Criminal cases

481. Schedule 1, which contains the rules on when cases are or are not active, states that in criminal proceedings, they are concluded, and therefore cease to be active, when the accused is acquitted or sentenced or by the return of any other verdict, finding, order or decision which puts an end to the proceedings, or by discontinuance or by operation of law (these terms are explained in Chapter 9). The Schedule lays down that proceedings are concluded also when any order is made consequent on conviction or finding of guilt which disposes of the case, either absolutely or subject to future events, or by deferment of sentence. In other words, for example, a case ceases to be active when the court makes an order deferring sentence and not when the case comes again before the court on expiry of the period for which sentence has been deferred. (See para. 390).

482. Proceedings before a court-martial or standing civilian court are not concluded until the completion of any review of finding or sentence.

Arrest

483. In the event of a warrant for arrest being granted but no arrest being made for some time, the Act lays down that the case ceases to be active after 12 months from the date of the warrant, unless an arrest is made within that period. Arrest, however, reactivates the case for the purposes of contempt law.

484. Civil cases remain active until disposed of, continued or withdrawn. Appellate proceedings (criminal or civil) are active from the time an application for leave to appeal or apply for review, or notice of appeal, is made, and remain active until disposed of or abandoned, discontinued or withdrawn.

485. There are situations not covered by the Act which call for care to avoid possible prejudice in civil cases even before the proceedings are active. For example, in a case where a defender maintains the wrong party is being sued, his defence could be prejudiced substantially by publication of his picture. Other instances of civil actions where questions of identification could be crucial to the issue in dispute in the action would call for special caution in considering whether to publish a picture of a party or parties. It is prudent to avoid publishing any picture which could provoke a party to an action to lodge a complaint that his case has been substantially prejudiced. The provision in the Act which requires that proceedings for contempt under the strict liability rule may be taken only by the Attorney-General does not apply to Scotland.

Inside the court

486. If the Act has clarified the law in relation to publication of prejudicial matter, uncertainty remains as to the precise objects and effects of aspects of contempt which lie outside the scope of the Act: where there has been no publication and possibly none is intended. While it is easy to understand the aims of those provisions now in operation which are designed to prevent prejudice by publicity, it is less obvious why,

for example, it should be contempt merely to bring a camera into a courtroom without actually using it or possibly even intending to do so.
487. There is no statute specifically to deal with the taking of photographs, or having the equipment for this purpose, in Scottish courts. The Criminal Justice Act 1925, which under s.41, prohibits the taking of photographs, and the publication of photographs taken in court, expressly applies only to England and Wales. There is no corresponding legislation for Scotland. It is generally accepted that, at the time when the Act was passed, there was no necessity for the introduction of such a law in Scotland either because the remedy where such a problem might arise could be found in the common law, or because the authorities had reason to believe that the matter could be left to the good taste and sense of the Scottish papers. However that may be, it is true that it is only in recent years that any serious possibility has arisen of a newspaper taking photographs in court for publication.
488. In a case in Glasgow Sheriff Court in 1975 a Mr. Peter Sweeney admitted being in contempt of court in respect that, during the proceedings in a criminal case in the court, he was in possession of a camera and took photographs in the court. He was stated by his solicitor to have wanted a souvenir of his first visit to a courtroom, but, after being told by an attendant to leave, which he did, he had been pursued by a detective, apprehended and detained in custody overnight. The following day the photographs he took were produced in court and Sheriff Archibald Bell, Q.C., admonished Mr. Sweeney for contempt of court and confiscated the camera. He stated: "Proceedings in court cannot and should not be subject to any interruption," although Mr. Sweeney's solicitor had said what his client had done was so quiet and unobtrusive that even the sheriff was "unaware and not troubled by the matter."
489. We would maintain that to constitute contempt a photograph must amount to an interference with the proceedings before the court; this could take the form of embarrassing the judge, or counsel or a witness, and could undoubtedly amount to contempt if persisted in. Obviously the taking of a photograph with flash equipment in a courtroom during the hearing of a case would invite swift retribution. At the other end of the scale—without implying that such conduct would be approved by the court—there can be no doubt that tourists visiting our courts have taken photographs with subminiature cameras, and the court has been none the wiser nor the worse for it. (The Criminal Procedure (Scotland) Act 1975 (which came into operation after the Sweeney case occurred) provides, by s.145(4) that "any person who
138

interrupts or disturbs the court (in solemn procedure) shall be liable to imprisonment or a fine or both as the judge thinks fit" and no maximum is specified.)

490. But in light of the case of *Sweeney* referred to above it would appear that the photographer may be held in contempt of court even though the judge was unaware that the camera had been used in court, or even that there was one in the courtroom at all, and there could therefore have been no actual interference with the progress of the proceedings as a result of Mr. Sweeney's conduct. The case raises points of some interest which may one day have to be tested. For example, would a man who took a trumpet into a courtroom during proceedings be in contempt of court even though he did not blow it? What would be the legal position of a person seen having a toy camera in court and apparently taking a picture with it when in fact it was incapable of taking one? It is very doubtful that the mere presence of a camera in court is a contempt by the person possessing it; but if its discovery resulted in an interruption of proceedings, even though no photograph was taken, quite a different situation would arise and contempt could well be held to have been committed.

491. Clearly there must be a distinction between photographs taken for publication and those taken for the private interest or pleasure of persons like holidaymakers visiting our courts. Neither form of photograph is officially approved in the Scottish courts, and indeed applications for permission to take photographs for purely personal and private use have on a number of occasions been refused.

492. When we come to the second stage in the process, the publication for commercial purposes, of a photograph taken in court, we may be sure—despite the fact that there is no statutory law against it—that this is strictly forbidden. It would probably not be an unfair inference from our deduction as to the reasons for the 1925 Act not being made applicable to Scotland (see para. 487) that, were Parliament now to consider the matter, it would indeed impose similar prohibitions throughout the United Kingdom. Although the 1925 Act does not apply to Scotland, therefore, its terms may be taken as a useful guide to the sort of rules which would be introduced in Scotland were the issue brought to a head. It seems far preferable that the desired results be attained by self-restraint on the part of the media.

English Act

493. Section 41(1) of the 1925 Act lays down that no person shall take or attempt to take in any court any photograph or, with a view to publication, make or attempt to make in any court any portrait or sketch of any person, being a judge of the court or a juror or witness in or a party to any proceedings before the court, whether civil or criminal; or publish any photograph, portrait or sketch taken or made in contravention of the foregoing provisions of this section or any reproduction thereof. Section 41(2) provides that the expression "court" means any court of justice.

494. Section 41(2)(c) lays down that a photograph, portrait or sketch shall be deemed to be a photograph, portrait or sketch taken or made in court if it is taken or made in the courtroom or in the building or in the precincts of the building in which a court is held, or if it is a photograph, portrait or sketch taken or made of the person while he is entering or leaving the courtroom or any such building or precincts as aforesaid.

495. Two examples of how the English and Welsh courts deal with such matters were given in 1986. One was the case of a woman—not a journalist, a member of the public—who took a flash photograph of Judge Malcolm Ward during a sitting of Wolverhampton Crown Court in July. Mrs Joan Maynard, recently married to a solicitor, had been taken to the court by her husband to see justice being administered and gain experience before taking up employment in her husband's office. Mrs Maynard, who said later she had no idea she was breaking the law, was detained in the cells until the judge dealt with her, fining her £500 (later reduced to £100 on appeal) and confiscating her camera. The other case occurred in June, when the publishers of the *Merthyr Express* were fined £200 for contempt when a staff artist was discovered sketching during a trial after permission to do so had been refused by Judge Lewis Bowen. The editor, Graham Jones, who was ordered to appear, told the judge he had sent the artist to sketch from memory and not during the case. Judge Bowen said he had refused permission to sketch in court because he felt it might make the jury uncomfortable and because it was unfair to the defendant (a hospital consultant) who had already had widespread publicity. He conceded the editor acted in good faith.

Precincts of the court

496. In a case in which official guidance was sought in 1964, the then Lord President issued a ruling which stated: "No photographing is permitted within the precincts of the Law Courts. The precincts of the Law Courts are defined as the areas occupied by the car park and the piazza." The reference was to the portion of Parliament Square, Edinburgh, lying between St. Giles' Cathedral and Parliament House, and offered no guidance in relation to the precincts of any other law court in Scotland. It also gave no assistance in defining the extent of the precincts at the rear of Parliament House where in some cases use has been made of the exit to the Cowgate to enable parties to escape the attentions of the Press. It was probably the first formal attempt to be made to define the precincts of any Scottish court for the purpose of guiding the Press in relation to restriction of photography. When invited to supply a definition of precincts of the court in an earlier case, the Lord Advocate (later to become the Lord Justice-Clerk, Lord Wheatley) stated that a definition was not possible because the extent of the precincts must vary with the circumstances and requirements of each case.

497. It is possible to imagine situations in which, while a court is on vacation and no judicial functions are being performed in the building, photography might well be permitted even inside the building, which would unquestionably be entirely within the precincts, and out of bounds to photographers, when the court was in session. It would, nevertheless, be wise to seek official authority before attempting to take pictures in such circumstances. On the other hand, there may be occasions when the precincts extend outside the limits of the court building itself. The degree and duration of this extension will vary according to the requirements of the case. For example, parties and witnesses approaching or leaving the building and crossing an open space forming part of the necessary access to it, may well be held to be within the precincts if the opposite would mean their harassment by photographers so as to interfere with their freedom or willingness to come and go for the purpose of taking part in court proceedings.

498. The 1925 Act, it has to be noted, restricts not only the taking of photographs but also the making in court of a portrait or sketch for publication. The theoretical situation in Scotland would seem to be that the law would frown on drawings no less than photographs; but there is an important distinction. Sketches or portraits of persons taking part in court proceedings may, by a person suitably skilled, be made from memory. Such activity could amount to contempt only if subsequent publication were to create the kind of substantial risk of prejudice envisaged in s.2 of the Act. It is also to be remembered the prejudice the Act aims to prevent is prejudice to the proceedings, so that any behaviour within the courtroom or the precincts which interrupted the proceedings or distracted the attention of any of those tak-

141

ing part could result in a contempt complaint. The use of photographic equipment is the most obvious example, but even the presence in court of an artist obviously making a sketch of the participants could bring the same result. Here the law is concerned not with publication, which is dealt with by the 1981 Act, but with behaviour of any kind which may interfere with the course of the proceedings, which is still a common law matter.

499. Any conduct which might lower the dignity of the court or embarrass any participant in the proceedings is liable to be dealt with as a common law case of contempt. In this field it is the accumulated opinions of Scottish judges which rule, and it is well recognised that they are likely to disapprove strongly of any conduct which would amount to treating the court proceedings as if they were a kind of public entertainment.

Common law

500. Contempt is not the whole story concerning restriction of publicity in relation to judicial proceedings. Conduct of any sort, including publicity, which interferes with the course or administration of justice, may be dealt with by the criminal common law. The five judges in deciding the *Hall* case (see Chapter 9) made it clear this instrument would be used where necessary to punish such behaviour where the law of contempt did not provide a remedy.

In the open

501. When the judge, jury, clerk and counsel leave the courtroom to inspect an exhibit outside, which it is not possible or convenient to take into the building, like a motor vehicle, it has to be remembered that the place where the inspection takes place becomes, for the time being, the equivalent of the courtroom, and the utmost care has to be taken not to take pictures which would incur the displeasure of the judge.

502. Parties or witnesses or counsel passing along the public street, having emerged from the court buildings and courtyard, or making their way there, are in a different position and there is no danger in the taking of photographs provided nothing is done that would amount to obstruction or molesting of the persons in question. It is also worth noting that any conduct by Press photographers which might so embarrass witnesses as to discourage them from coming voluntarily to court to give evidence might be regarded as an interference with the course of justice and punishable as a common law offence.

"Assault by photography"

503. In 1975 proceedings were begun, but later abandoned, against two Press photographers who took pictures of a solicitor in the street outside the Sheriff Court at Dunfermline, where he was appearing on behalf of a client at an inquiry into a suspicious death, and during an adjournment. The solicitor complained to the procurator-fiscal, on whose authority the photographers were later charged with assault and had their films confiscated. The case was without precedent.

504. Researches could produce only a civil case in 1916 in which a boy aged 17, charged with a minor offence, had his fingerprints and photograph taken by the police without his parents' consent, and brought proceedings against the chief constable for damages for defamation in respect of injury to his reputation from having his fingerprints and photograph filed by the police along with those of notorious criminals. Lord Salvesen, giving judgment, said he did not feel it necessary for the purposes of that case to consider the general proposition how far members of the public could complain of being photographed, when the photographer was able to take an instantaneous photograph from a place where he was legitimately holding his instrument, although he was of opinion there was no such absolute right. The circumstances of the case before the court did not raise that general question (*Adamson* v. *Martin*, 1916 S.C. 328).

505. In the Dunfermline case, the Crown Office in due course intervened and instructed the procurator-fiscal not to proceed with the case against the photographers and their photographic materials were returned to them. The case establishes with certainty no more than that there has been no instance in Scotland of a successful prosecution for assault by photography. It is not, however, inconceivable that a photographer could be charged with breach of the peace—a process whose use has been progressively extended over the years—were he to persist in photographing a person or persons in public against their wishes with results which led to a complaint by them or some kind of disturbance. (Whether a conviction ensued might be another matter.) It has to be noted also that the criminal law will take notice of any conduct in public which offends legal principles whether by physical attack or otherwise, and that the legal definition of assault does not require that the victim should suffer any injury (see para. 787).

Children

506. Special provisions are made by statute for the protection of children from publicity, and it is essential that Press photographers and others involved in decision-making on the publication of pictures in the Press or on television should be familiar with these, particularly where the issue of identification of any child may arise. What was formerly left to the discretion of the criminal courts by way of issuing a direction in an appropriate case has become automatic prohibition with the introduction of s.22 of the Criminal Justice (Scotland) Act 1980.

507. This prohibits the disclosure in any newspaper or broadcast report of proceedings in any criminal court of particulars calculated to lead to the identification of any person under 16 concerned in the proceedings. This refers not only to the person against whom, or in respect of whom, the case has been brought, but also any witness in the case who is under 16. The section specifically prohibits the publication of any picture in a context relevant to the proceedings which is or includes a picture of a person under 16 concerned in the case in the above sense.

508. The prohibition is not automatic, however, in the case of a child under 16 who is a witness only and where no one against whom the proceedings have been taken is under 16. In such a situation the court has power to direct non-publication of any matter (including pictures) calculated to identify the child in question.

509. Section 22 also provides that at any stage of the proceedings, if satisfied that it is in the public interest, the court may direct that the automatic prohibition be dispensed with either wholly or partially, as the court may specify. In addition, the Secretary of State for Scotland has power under the section to dispense with the prohibition after completion of a case, if he is satisfied this is in the public interest. The effect of this provision is that where the automatic prohibition has taken effect or the court has made a direction imposing a prohibition about a child concerned in the proceedings, the Secretary of State may make an order permitting disclosure of the child's identity—which could include publication of a picture—if he is satisfied this is in the public interest.

510. Although the Act does not specifically say so, this last provision could be used by the media as a form of appeal, by application to the Secretary of State, as a means of having judicial rulings on nondisclosure of pictures and other means of identification of children overturned. It also provides machinery by which the media could

144

attempt to have the automatic prohibition lifted in any specific case where it appeared this would be in the public interest.

511. Anyone who publishes matter (including any picture) in contravention of s.22 is liable on summary complaint to a fine not exceeding £1,000. The s.22 provisions replace those which formerly applied to children under 17 in summary proceedings in the sheriff courts.

512. An important factor to be kept in mind in applying the terms of the s.22 restrictions is that they will usually involve also prohibition of publication of pictures of any adult, particularly parent or other relation or relations, of a child concerned in a case which could lead to the identification of that child (see also Chapter 9). Adults are not referred to in the section, but clearly its terms are wide enough to cover any picture of another person whose identification in the media could lead to identification of a child, if that child is protected by the section. The prohibition could also extend to pictures of a school or any other subject-matter that could lead to the child's identification.

513. There is an automatic prohibition of publication of anything that could lead to the identification of any child concerned in a children's hearing, or appeal in such a case before the sheriff or Court of Session, under the terms of the Social Work (Scotland) Act 1968. The hearings are taken in private but *bona fide* representatives of the news media are allowed to attend, subject to the restrictions regarding identification.

Fatal accident inquiries

514. The sheriff presiding at a fatal accident inquiry has power to order non-publication of a picture of any person under 17 in any way involved in the inquiry (see Chapter 12).

515. The Civic Government (Scotland) Act 1982 (s.52) makes it an offence to take any indecent photograph of a child under 16, to distribute or show such a photograph (negative or positive), or to possess one with a view to its distribution. The prohibition covers also video-recordings and films (see also para. 809). Contravention can result in a fine of up to £2,000 or a jail sentence of not more than two years, or both. It is a defence to prove there was a legitimate reason for distribution or possession of the item in question or that there was no knowledge or suspicion it was indecent.

Official secrets

516. There is a voluntary system administered by a joint committee representing the media and civil service to restrict publication of sensitive material, and matters which are subject to restriction are listed under a series of "D Notices." These are dealt with in more detail in Chapter 30; the aspect most likely to concern photographers covers pictures of defence establishments, installations, dockyards and factories (see para. 863).

CHAPTER 11

MATRIMONIAL PROCEEDINGS

517. There appears to be a widespread impression in the legal profession that divorce actions and other matrimonial cases in Scotland are conducted in the glare of publicity. That was the phrase used in the Report of the Royal Commission on Legal Services which was published in 1980. It was also one of the reasons put forward by the Faculty of Advocates for keeping divorces exclusively in the Court of Session. The Faculty talked about the glare of publicity that would probably be focused on an examination of private lives in the local sheriff courts. This was contrasted with the "relative anonymity" of the Court of Session, an observation much nearer the mark.

518. The fact is that reports of divorce proceedings have been rare in Scottish newspapers and there are several reasons for this. First the media are extremely limited as to what they can publish about divorce cases and certain other matrimonial matters under the Judicial Proceedings (Regulation of Reports) Act 1926. Secondly the overwhelming majority of divorces in Scotland—about 95%—are undefended and since 1978 are not normally heard in open court at all. It is also undoubtedly the case that the breakdown of marriage is so commonplace in Scotland these days—about one marriage in four fails—that the average case is not newsworthy.

519. The situation has not changed with the passing of the Divorce Jurisdiction, Court Fees and Legal Aid (Scotland) Act 1983, which gave power to sheriff courts as well as the Court of Session to deal with divorces. There has been no explosion of publicity for divorce cases from sheriff courts around Scotland. Indeed, reports of sheriff court divorces have been almost non-existent. Local newspapers have not followed the practice of some of their English counterparts of publishing weekly lists of names of people who have been divorced in undefended cases. There have also been very few reports of judgments of the courts in defended cases. However, now that divorce is competent in the sheriff court it is important that journalists should be familiar with the terms of the 1926 Act.

520. The Act is unusual because rather than setting down that certain details about matrimonial cases may not be published it says that reports are prohibited altogether except for certain limited categories of information. Section 1(i)(*a*) is not restricted to divorce cases and applies to judicial proceedings of any kind. It prohibits the publication of any indecent material or any indecent medical, surgical or physiological details, publication of which would be calculated to injure public morals.

521. It is clear from evidence which was led at public inquiries before Parliament passed the 1926 Act that there was much concern at the time about the effects on public morals of unrestricted reporting of full details of some scandalous divorce cases. However, there has obviously been a shift in attitudes on the question of public decency and morals since the Act was passed and much of what would have been prohibited in the 1930s would pass without comment today.

522. The part of the 1926 Act which has most relevance to the working journalist is s.1(i)(*b*) which affects reports in relation to any judicial proceedings for dissolution of marriage, nullity of marriage or judicial separation. Nothing may be published about these types of case except: the names, addresses and occupations of the parties to the action and of witnesses; a concise statement of the charges, defences and counter-charges in support of which evidence has been given; submissions on any point of law arising during the proceedings and the court's decision on that and finally, the judgment of the court and any observations made by the judge in giving judgment.

523. The Act applies to both defended and undefended divorces and as undefended cases are by far the more common it would be appropriate to deal with them first. The maximum penalty for each contravention of the Act is four months' imprisonment or a £500 fine or both, liability lying with the proprietor, editor, and printer or publisher.

524. In undefended cases an important change in procedure affecting the working practice of journalists was introduced in 1978. Anyone seeking a divorce in an undefended case no longer has to attend court personally with his or her witnesses. Written evidence in the form of sworn statements or affidavits has replaced evidence in court and these cases are now normally dealt with by a judge in chambers. A list of the divorces granted in undefended cases in the Court of Session is published in the court rolls once a week. A similar list is published in at least some sheriff courts. Such lists of course do not contain sufficient information in themselves to provide the reporter with a story, and it will always be necessary to confirm details in a case of interest. A check can be carried out with the court department handling divorce cases, but only the brief details permitted by the 1926 Act should be used from the court documents. The few reports published in newspapers of affidavit divorces have run to only a few paragraphs setting out who has been divorced, on what ground and which judge granted decree.

525. The restrictions in the Act are not limited to reports of actual proceedings in court, and apply to reports "in relation to court proceedings." Any follow-up story, therefore, should avoid a mere rehashing of the evidence given in court, as this could arguably be caught by the terms of the Act. The dangers of defamation should also be kept in mind.

526. In 1983 a new, simplified form of procedure, popularly known as do-it-yourself divorce, was introduced in Scotland following a report of a committee under Court of Session judge Lord Cowie. It is available for undefended cases where there are no children under the age of 16 and no financial claims are made. The Divorce Jurisdiction Act meant that "Cowie divorces" were possible in the sheriff court, which emphasises the need for reporters covering sheriff courts to establish regular access to information about local divorces.

527. As far as defended cases are concerned the normal practice in the Court of Session has been to carry a report at the stage when the judge issues his judgment on the case. This is now normally given in writing and a copy is made available to journalists. As indicated earlier it is permissible to publish anything in the judge's opinion which may properly be regarded as an observation passed in giving judgment. Divorce judgments are normally in very full terms and give a reporter more than enough information to present a complete picture of a case.

528. There may of course be cases which are regarded as being of such interest and importance that it is felt they must be reported before the judgment stage. In these cases it is important to know exactly what the words of s.1(i)(*b*) mean.

529. There should be little difficulty about names, addresses and occupations. In both defended and undefended cases they should be available at the relevant court department. In defended cases these details are sometimes contained in the judge's written opinion. Where children of the parties involved are not parties to the action, have not given evidence and are not named in the judgment, according to a strict interpretation of the Act the children's names should not be used in any report.

530. "Charges, defences and counter-charges" refers to the condescendences contained in the summons or initial writ (in an undefended action) or the closed record (in a defended case). These contain the legal pleadings on which the action is based. The Act does not expressly provide that the ground of the action of divorce can be published but this must be included under "charges." However, the Act goes on to talk about charges in support of which evidence has been given which means that the ground of the action should not be published until this has become clear from the evidence. The position is slightly more complicated since the passing of the Divorce (Scotland) Act 1976 under which all divorces are granted on the one ground—that the marriage has irretrievably broken down. The practical effect for reporters seems to be that it can be said at an early stage that a divorce is on the ground that the marriage has broken down but the cause of the breakdown, such as adultery or unreasonable behaviour, should be left until evidence has been heard in the case.

531. The word "concise" in the subsection may present some difficulty in interpretation since its precise application will vary with the circumstances of each individual case. In practice, however, this problem will arise in only a tiny minority of cases since the charges, defences and counter-charges can normally be reported in full from the judgment when it becomes available. A recital of alleged incidents or allegations based on evidence given would not come within the permitted statement of charges and defences. Where there is doubt or the case is complicated the safest course is to err on the side of brevity and keep the summary to a single sentence for the charges and another for replies and counter-charges. The summary must be derived from the evidence so that the reporter must have heard enough to enable him to prepare a proper summary.

532. Submissions on a point of law arising in the course of the proceedings may in a minority of cases provide a good source of copy. There have been several outstanding instances, for example the question of whether artificial insemination by a donor (AID) was a good defence to an action of divorce for adultery. In the *Argyll* divorce case the issue arose as to whether a wife could be compelled to surrender as evidence passages in her diary containing references to her alleged association with men other than her husband.

533. In reporting this kind of submission, however, the reporter must be careful that what he is publishing is not in essence an argument on the facts but truly deals with a question of law. A legal argument must, of course, be based on a certain minimum amount of fact but any report, to come within the Act, must contain no more factual material than necessary for a proper report of the legal submissions.

534. The next permissible category is "decision of the court" on the submissions of any point of law. This brings in the judgment given by the court at certain preliminary stages in a case where the issue is a legal one but the judge is not necessarily being asked to give a final decision on the case. In the well known AID case referred to above Lord Wheatley heard preliminary debate on issues of great legal interest and public importance. The arguments contained a great deal of reportable and permissible material although very few newspapers took advantage of the opportunity, and of course the judgment was publishable.

535. In another case a wife made a preliminary application to the court for an advance of a very large sum of interim expenses to enable her to bring witnesses from various countries to Scotland to help her defend a divorce action. The judge, Lord Guthrie, gave his view that under the 1926 Act his judgment on the point could be legally reported provided that the only other matters published were the parties' names and addresses as they appeared on the calling list.

536. In reporting such preliminary matters, as well as the judgment, the provisions of s.1(i)(*a*) mentioned earlier in the chapter should not be forgotten. This prohibits the publication of any material calculated to injure public morals.

537. The Act does not say that the Press is allowed to publish in matrimonial cases the name of the judge or the court in which he is sitting or description of the parties or witnesses if this was thought necessary. Yet it seems a matter of commonsense that the Act cannot have been intended to prohibit such details, provided any descriptive material does not amount to evidence (see paras. 358–359).

538. The term "decree nisi" applies only in English law where, in divorce actions, decree becomes effective only after a certain period of time during which the authorities must be satisfied that no reason has arisen why decree should not be granted. Decree in Scotland becomes absolute when it is granted subject to a 21–day period to allow for any appeal to be lodged.

539. The granting of a decree is, however, delayed in certain cases where the court has to be satisfied about the circumstances in which the children of the marriage are being cared for before issuing decree.

540. It is important to notice that the restrictions imposed by the 1926 Act upon the reporting of matrimonial cases apply to the appeal stages as well as in the court which first hears the case.

541. No proceedings appear to have been taken under the Act. In 1956, however, a newspaper published material from a petition for dissolution of marriage on the ground of presumed death at the stage when the document was displayed on the wall of Parliament House.

The editor was required by the Lord Advocate to give a written undertaking that he would not allow a repetition, although the offence was a purely technical one.

542. The case was not a matrimonial one in the usual sense and publicity of this kind would more likely help than hinder the ends of justice being achieved. Parliament has since rectified the situation however: s.14 of the Presumption of Death (Scotland) Act 1977 states that, for the avoidance of doubt, s.1(i)(b) of the 1926 Act does not apply to an action of declarator of death under the Act.

543. The 1926 mechanism may be a trifle rusty through lack of use but it would be dangerous to ignore the Act at a time when there is a growing feeling in some quarters that reporting of divorces is an intrusion into private lives. There was a threat to invoke the Act in a case in 1983 involving the Scottish entertainer Billy Connolly. His lawyers claimed that a custody hearing in the Court of Session was part of the Connollys' divorce action and that reports in several newspapers had gone far beyond the scope of the Act. The threat was never carried out, so that the question remains unanswered. The case does, however, illustrate the care reporters must exercise in distinguishing between a custody hearing pure and simple (where there are normally no reporting restrictions under the 1926 Act) and divorce proceedings. As will be seen from the *Connolly* case, the distinction is not always an easy one to draw, and a decision on what can safely be published will depend on the circumstances of each particular case.

CHAPTER 12

CHILDREN

544. There are a number of provisions for the protection of children's interests which must be observed by journalists and photographers in the coverage of court proceedings, including children's hearings. (For statutory provisions for protection of children against publications such as "horror comics" see para. 838.) The provisions are of two types—those which lay down express prohibition of publication of the means of identifying children in court proceedings, and those which empower the judges to make a direction that publication of such particulars, in whole or in part, is prohibited.

545. Section 22 of the Criminal Justice (Scotland) Act 1980 brought about important changes in the statutory restrictions upon identification of any child concerned in criminal court proceedings. Before the passing of the Act the prohibition extended to children under 17 and applied only to summary sheriff court cases. It now applies to children under 16 in any criminal court in Scotland. It forbids disclosure in court reports of the child's name, address or school, or any particulars calculated to lead to the identification of "any person under 16 years concerned in the proceedings." The person the section is aimed to protect may be one against or in respect of whom the proceedings are taken or who is appearing as a witness. The provision applies to pictures as well as to Press, sound and television reports of cases. But where the person under 16 is concerned as a witness only and no one against whom the proceedings are taken is under 16, there is no bar on identifying him unless the court makes a direction to that effect. (There is no minimum age for children as witnesses.) Section 22 does not apply to proceedings in courts in England, Wales and Northern Ireland. In Scotland, a court may at any stage of the proceedings dispense with the statutory prohibition if satisfied this is in the public interest. The Scottish Secretary is also given power, after a case has been dealt with, to make an order lifting the prohibition or to overrule an order made by the court.

546. In a case before the High Court in Edinburgh in 1983 (*H.M. Advocate* v. *George Aitken*, March 8, 1983), on an application by the Crown for a ruling, Lord Brand held that s.22 does not apply to dead children; a "person" within the meaning of the section was a live person, he said. A dead person could not be "concerned" in the proceed-

153

ings. The judge added that, if he had been of the opinion the section did apply, he would have dispensed with the provision in the particular case in the public interest. (Had the defence submission that the section did apply to the child in the case been upheld, reports of the case could not have identified the father, who was charged with culpable homicide of the child, since this would have been "calculated" to identify the child.) Where there is a living brother or sister under 16 of a dead child in a case and that other child is concerned in the proceedings, the automatic prohibition might apply, but it would be for the court to decide whether in the particular circumstances the provision should be dispensed with in the public interest.

547. In an English case raising a similar issue, Lincoln Crown Court in June 1986 set aside an order made by local magistrates at committal proceedings that the press must not identify a dead child alleged to have been the victim of grievous bodily harm at the hands of a Lincoln couple. Judge George Whitehead, on hearing an application by counsel for the *Lincolnshire Echo*, ruled that the magistrates' order was a nullity. It appeared that they had acted on advice of their clerk, who had noted that the 1933 Act did not stipulate that a child, to be protected under s.39, must be living. Judge Whitehead rejected a plea for the Crown that he had no power to overturn the magistrates on the point.

548. The section also makes an exception to the automatic prohibition where the child in question is a witness only and where no one against whom the proceedings in which he is a witness have been taken is under 16. In such a case the prohibition does not apply unless the court makes a direction to stop publication of the child's identity. In each instance the consideration which the court has to have in mind in deciding whether or not to make a direction is the public interest. The court's power in this respect includes decision on the extent to which the prohibition should be dispensed with, and the Secretary of State's power includes a similar choice.

Broadcasting

549. All these s.22 provisions concerning identification of children apply to pictures in the Press, to sound broadcasting and to television reports of cases in any criminal court in Scotland.

Penalties

550. The maximum penalty on any person publishing in contravention of the section is a fine of £1,000.

154

551. One of the results of s.22 is that, while there is a mandatory bar against identification of persons under 16 in any criminal court (subject to the exceptions explained above), the courts no longer have power to direct non-publication of identity in cases where the person concerned is over 16 but under 17—the power formerly given to cover persons up to 17 by the Criminal Procedure (Scotland) Act 1975, s.169 (solemn procedure) and s.365 (summary cases). Section 169 is replaced by s.22 of the 1980 Act, and s.365 is repealed by Sched. 8 to the same Act.

552. The relevant age of a person concerned in proceedings is his or her age at the time the case is in court and according to the information accepted by the court as to his or her age. In the event of the person concerned having (to the court's knowledge) attained his or her 16th birthday on the day the case is before the court, the automatic prohibition flies off.

553. The question may arise as to the stage in criminal proceedings concerning a person under 16 at which the s.22 restriction takes effect. The section has to be read subject to its opening words—"No newspaper report of any proceedings in a court shall reveal . . . "—which means that the prohibition operates when the proceedings are in a court and does not apply, for example, at preliminary stages of a case before a hearing takes place.

554. The Act makes no express provision for appeal against a court's direction either permitting or prohibiting publication in terms of s.22, but the power given to the Secretary of State to make an order dispensing with the requirements of the section may provide a channel by which representations, *e.g.* by the media, could be made in individual cases for the strict terms of the automatic bar to be lifted in the public interest.

555. The full implications of s.22 will become apparent only with experience. For example, in a child custody case, in the event of either parent being charged with an offence in connection with some incident in the dispute, such as assault or breach of the peace, the reporting of these criminal proceedings would become subject to the automatic prohibition in order to prevent identification of the child thus concerned in the proceedings. Disclosure of the child's identity in the civil action would have to be withheld since, to disclose it, would defeat the purpose of s.22 in requiring anonymity in the criminal case.

556. The consequences of the section are further illustrated by the case of an adult convicted of shoplifting offences while acting alone who is exposed to unrestricted publicity, while one caught operating with his child aged under 16 may not be identified in reports of the case

155

lest this would create a breach of the section by disclosure of information "calculated" to lead to the identification of the child. Other examples may be figured, and will no doubt occur, of the customary even-handedness of justice being upset by extending protection against publicity to some privileged adults—when the object of the section was to protect children—while not permitting it to other adults. It is not difficult to imagine how s.22 could encourage parents indulging in shop-lifting expeditions to take their children along with them and thus enjoy unjustified protection from publicity for themselves.

557. When Parliament prohibits publication of matter *calculated* to have certain results, this should not be understood to mean that those results will be excused by the law if the journalist did not actually calculate they would ensue as a result of what he had written. The word should be interpreted as applying to an event (identification) following as a natural and likely result of the act prohibited (publication) (see para. 454).

558. In May 1982 the *Lothian Courier*, Bathgate, was fined £75 at Linlithgow Sheriff Court for naming a man in a report it carried in January 1982 of his conviction for assault on his 18-month-old daughter. The newspaper admitted a charge under s.22, that publication of the man's name was "calculated" to lead to the identification of the child.

559. There is no statutory provision in England equivalent to s.22, but the English courts have power under s.39 of the Children and Young Persons Act 1933 to prohibit identification of a child in terms similar to those which are mandatory in Scotland under s.22 of the 1980 Act. Magistrates at Felixstowe, Suffolk, for example, in April 1985 issued such an order in the case of a girl aged 11 months who was the victim of gross indecency at the hands of four adults, including a teacher. A similar order in relation to a child was made in the Old Bailey by Judge Michael Underhill in January 1986, in respect of a boy aged 15, convicted of raping two girls aged 14 and 10. The order was made at the request of defence counsel. On the other hand Mr Justice Owen, at Newcastle Crown Court in July 1986, at the end of a trial that lasted 11 days, lifted a ban he had imposed when it opened, against identification of the defendant, a boy aged 12, convicted of murdering a crippled widow. He did so on an application by a local newspaper, and while accepting this course might create difficulties for the boy's nine brothers and sisters, he said it did appear that the public had "a right to know."

Incest cases

560. In reporting cases of incest or other sexual offences it is desirable to protect the anonymity of persons of tender years who are innocently involved. Where the person in question is under 16 it is an offence to publish his or her identity under s.22, but over that age there is no such statutory protection. In 1966 the Press Council (Memorandum C304/D943) recommended a course which has been widely adopted. The object is to avoid the situation where two or more reports, each protecting the anonymity of a child, may disclose his identity when read together, for example, where one report names the accused but does not disclose his relationship to the victim, while another publishes a report indicating his relationship to the victim without identifying the accused. The Press Council proposed that editors should exercise their discretion in favour of a uniform formula by which the accused is named (if an adult) but the relationship to the child involved is not specified. In 1980 Scottish newspaper editors agreed that in such a situation they would apply a formula on the following lines:— Where a case of incest is reported the adult is identified but the word "incest" is not used, the offence being described as "a serious offence against a young child" or the like; the child is not identified and the report excludes anything implying the relationship between the accused and the child.

Children's hearings

561. The Social Work (Scotland) Act 1968 abolished juvenile courts and brought about important changes in the methods of dealing with children. It laid down that a child could be prosecuted for an offence only on the instructions of the Lord Advocate or at his instance, and that no court, other than the High Court of Justiciary and the sheriff court, has jurisdiction over a child for an offence (Social Work (Scotland) Act 1968, s.31(1)). It requires every local authority to set up a children's panel—a reservoir of suitably qualified citizens to hear cases concerning "children who may require compulsory measures of care (*id*.s.34(1)). This category of children includes those who have committed offences. The Act also requires each local authority to appoint an officer, known as a Reporter (the Reporter or his deputy, to be entitled to appear in a referral to the sheriff, must be legally qualified), to arrange children's hearings and to carry out other functions in relation to the panel and to hearings which, in effect, have taken over the functions formerly performed by the juvenile courts. Where the

Reporter considers that a child may be in need of compulsory measures of care, it is his duty to arrange a children's hearing.

562. Cases of the kind are heard by three members of the appropriate panel. This tribunal of three, consisting of a chairman and two other members, must include at least one woman. It is properly referred to in newspaper reports as a children's hearing and not as a children's panel, which, as already explained, refers to the complete list of persons from whom the members of any particular children's hearing are selected.

563. There is a right of appeal by a child or his parent, or both, to the sheriff against a decision of a children's hearing, and the appeal is heard in chambers, which is understood to mean that the Press is not entitled to be represented. Where the sheriff is not satisfied that the decision was justified he may remit the case back to the children's hearing for reconsideration, and the same rules then apply to newspaper reports of the proceedings as at the original diet.

564. The same restrictions, with certain modifications, so far as publicity is concerned, as formerly applied to juvenile court proceedings, now apply to children's hearings, brought into being by the 1968 Act. The Act lays down that these hearings are to take place in private (Social Work (Scotland) Act 1968, s.35(1)) but permits *bona fide* representatives of a newspaper or news agency to attend (*id*.s.35(3)). It prohibits any newspaper, radio or television report of any children's hearing, or of any hearing before a sheriff or appeal before the Court of Session in such a case, to reveal the name, address or school, or include any particulars calculated to lead to the identification of any child concerned. The maximum penalty for a breach by any person of this prohibition is a fine of £500 for each offence (Social Work (Scotland) Act 1968, s.58). The provisions apply also to pictures. The restrictions may be dispensed with wholly or partly by order of the Secretary of State in any case if he is satisfied this would be in the interests of justice; they apply also to reports of children's hearings published in England, Wales and Northern Ireland.

565. In cases coming before children's hearings, "child" means a person under 18 years, where a supervision requirement of a hearing is in force, and in other cases a person under 16 years (s.30(1)).

566. List D Schools provide residential education and care for children referred to them by children's hearings or sheriff courts. They are administered by local authority social work departments. (The term derives from the category to which approved schools formerly belonged.) In June 1985 a new species of functionary entered the field—the safeguarder—who may be appointed in certain cases where

CHILDREN

there appears to be a conflict of interests between parent and child in a children's hearing. He/she is usually a person, not necessarily a legal practitioner, qualified by knowledge of and interest in problems of children and suited to safeguard the interests of the child involved.

567. The Criminal Procedure (Scotland) Act 1975 lays down that no child under 14, other than an infant-in-arms, shall be permitted to be present in court during the trial of any other person charged with an offence, or during any proceedings preliminary thereto, except when required as a witness or otherwise for the purposes of justice; but this does not apply to messengers, clerks and other persons required to attend for purposes connected with their employment (s.165 (solemn procedure), s.361 (summary procedure)).

568. The Act provides that in any proceedings in relation to an offence against or conduct contrary to decency or morality, where a person who, in the opinion of the court, is a child is called as a witness, the court may direct that the courtroom be cleared, but *bona fide* reporters will be allowed to remain. This section does not affect the courts' ordinary powers to hear a case *in camera* (s.166 (solemn procedure, s.362 (summary procedure)).

569. Journalists should observe a specific code of terminology in reporting proceedings in relation to children dealt with summarily. The words "conviction" and "sentence" are not used (see s.429 of the 1975 Act). Instead the child is referred to as having been found guilty of an offence, and the court is said to have made a finding of guilt or an order upon such a finding. It is important to observe the geographical implications of the provisions forbidding publication of particulars calculated to lead to the identification of a child concerned in proceedings. In sparsely populated districts, for example, disclosure of the sex and age of a child in a named village or small community could well lead to his or her identity being disclosed to people in the locality. In such cases, to avoid a contravention of the Act, it will usually be necessary to exclude the local geographical name and give instead one embracing a much larger area—in some cases the name of the county or region may be used in order properly to conceal the child's identity.

Custody cases

570. While there is no restriction upon the reporting of custody proceedings as such in Scotland, where the dispute arises in the course of divorce proceedings, the reporter must be careful to observe the requirements of the Judicial Proceedings (Regulation of Reports) Act 1926 (see Chapter 11).

159

Adoption procedure

571. Adoption proceedings are normally heard *in camera*. Under the Rules of the Court of Session (Court of Session Rules of Court, rule 227) it is required that "All proceedings before the Court in relation to an Adoption Order shall, unless the Court otherwise directs, be heard and determined *in camera*; and, unless the Court directs otherwise, all documents lodged in process, including the report by the curator *ad litem*, shall be open only to the Court, the curator *ad litem* and the parties, and shall be treated as confidential by all the parties concerned and by the Clerk of Court; and the curator *ad litem* appointed by the Court shall regard all information obtained in the course of his investigations or otherwise as confidential, and shall not divulge any part of it to any person save as, in his judgment, may be necessary for the proper execution of his duty." The reporting of adoption proceedings at all, therefore, is very difficult, if not impossible, except where the court permits the hearing to take place in public. This rarely happens in practice, but very occasionally, where the merits or the facts of the case are not being discussed, the hearing may be public and the proceedings may be reported, provided, of course, the identities of the parties are not disclosed and no information is sought to be published from any of the documents regarded as confidential by the Rule of Court. An example of this was a case in 1973 where an important point affecting procedure to be followed in adoption cases in general was debated in the First Division. The proceedings were of sufficient importance to be reported in some newspapers, without names and addresses. Judgments of the court may sometimes be made available for publication by authority of the court, but subject to non-identification of the parties.

Other civil proceedings

572. So far as other civil proceedings are concerned, Parliament has made no provisions restricting publication of identity of any child involved. This is in sharp contrast to the position in England and Wales where, for example, restrictions are placed on publicity concerning proceedings for wardship of court for the protection of children. The matter has, however, been the subject of difference of judicial opinion in Scotland. (The power to direct non-publication of identity provided by s.46 of the Children and Young Persons (Scotland) Act 1937, as amended by s.57 of the Children and Young Persons Act 1963, is contained in Part IV of the 1937 Act which is headed "Protection of Children and Young Persons in Relation to Criminal Proceedings."

160

Custody cases, like other civil proceedings, therefore fall outside the scope of the power.) As a consequence, there have been cases in which directions have been issued by judges of the Court of Session requiring the media not to identify children involved in specific custody cases. Settled judicial opinion now appears to be that the complex rules laid down by the legislature (now to be found by reference to five Acts) on the matter of child identity do not cover civil proceedings in general and that there was no statutory basis for directions issued in the past. The law leaves the issue to the good sense, taste and sensitivity of journalists for the rights of children innocently involved in civil disputes. The media may feel justified in applying a voluntary code where Parliament has failed to act in civil cases, while having gone further in criminal cases than some may think justified

573. It may sometimes be necessary in Scotland for attention to be given to the anonymity rule applying to wardship cases in English courts. In a case before the English High Court Family Division in August 1984 Balcombe J. ruled that he had power to make an anonymity order "against the world at large"—*i.e.* the entire media. He was dealing with the case of a Scotswoman aged 27, who had been convicted of the culpable homicide of two boys, aged four and three, when she was 11 years old and living in Scotland. She was released on licence in 1980, moved to England, made a new life for herself under a different name, and had a baby daughter who had been made a ward of court. The judge issued an injunction against the *News of the World* revealing the woman's identity, that of her child or of the child's father, and extending his order to apply to all the media in the interests of the ward.

Fatal accident inquiries

574. The Fatal Accidents and Sudden Deaths Inquiry (Scotland) Act 1976 requires that inquiries held under its terms be in public (s.4(3)) unless a person under the age of 17 is *in any way involved*, a provision open to wide interpretation, in which case the sheriff may at his own hand, or on an application by a party, order that no report in any publication or broadcast shall reveal the name, address or school of that person or otherwise identify him. Section 4(4) empowers the sheriff to order that no picture of the person under 17 may be published "in any manner," which must be taken to cover television as well as Press publication. These provisions make even more anomalous the lack of clear statutory provisions relating to civil proceedings outlined above.

Advertisements

575. Non-statutory rules regulating advertisements aimed at children are laid down and enforced by the Advertising Standards Authority under a code with which publishers should be familiar (see Chapter 28: Advertisements).

CHAPTER 13

PROCEDURAL PECULIARITIES AND SPECIAL PROBLEMS

Civil juries

576. Although civil jury trial has been virtually dispensed with in England, it is still a statutory right of litigants in certain important classes of cases in Scotland. The historical background illustrates the kind of legislative anomaly that has afflicted the development of Scots law since the Act of Union, although the number of cases dealt with each year by this procedure has greatly diminished in recent years.

577. The right to jury trial in Scotland in both criminal and civil cases appears to date from the 14th century, but it fell into disuse in civil cases during the 17th century and was not reintroduced until the passing of the Jury Trials (Scotland) Act 1815. It was already in operation in England and was brought to Scotland experimentally and, at first, for a limited period only. The Scottish civil jury in modern times came to be based on the English model, which explains why there are 12 jurors and not the traditional Scottish figure of 15. Several other statutes were introduced to regulate procedure and, in 1830, it was enacted that the statutory requirement of jury trial in appropriate categories of civil cases in Scotland "shall be continued and remain in force until altered or revoked by Parliament." By section 11 of the Law Reform (Miscellaneous Provisions) (Scotland) Act 1980, however, civil jury trial in the sheriff court was abolished.

578. Meanwhile in England, where there was no statutory requirement for the continuance of civil juries, they gradually for lack of demand diminished in number, and it was eventually decided by the English courts themselves that jury trial in civil cases would not in future be permitted except by specific authority of the court. In Scotland, on the other hand, the position remains that, if a party with a statutory right to jury trial insists on this form of procedure, and unless there is some "special cause" why it should not be employed, then a jury trial there must be. "Special cause" usually consists of difficult questions of law or mixed fact and law which would be difficult for a jury to deal with, or undue delay in raising the action, resulting in special problems in assessing the reliability of evidence given by witnesses whose recollection is dimmed by the passage of time.

579. A virtue of the old Scottish jury was that it had (and still has in

163

criminal cases) 15 members and it was thus possible to achieve a majority verdict. (The traditional Scottish attitude, in favour of majority verdicts, has been based on the concept of determining the "sense of the meeting" rather than—according to the English approach—coercing every member of a jury to reach the same result.) In civil cases, because of the even number, derived from the English model, there is always the risk of a jury being equally divided—the "hung" jury. This occurred in a Court of Session case in 1973, when, after expiry of the statutory time of three hours, the jury, in an action of damages for personal injuries had failed to produce a verdict, and were discharged.

580.   In practice most frequent use of civil juries is made in the disposal of claims for damages for injuries arising from accidents of various kinds, in factories, collieries, on the roads and so on. Less numerous, though also entitled to be considered for trial by jury, are claims for damages for slander. (Actions of breach of promise of marriage, formerly tried by jury, were abolished in 1984.)

581.   Because of the passing of the Interest on Damages (Scotland) Act 1971, juries' verdicts in civil actions are less inscrutable than they used to be. The Act entitles the successful party to interest on damages he may be awarded, but the rate of interest and the date from which it is calculated varies with the category of damages and the circumstances of the particular case. The interest (fixed by the judge, not the jury) may be applied at one rate for past loss of earnings and at a different rate for future loss; other considerations may affect the rate payable on the solatium element of the award. So, under a change of procedure made necessary to put the Act into operation, juries are now required to return a verdict which (if any award is made at all) is divided into separate sums for each element of damages. The result not only produces a verdict which is subject to closer examination for purposes of considering an appeal; it also provides more detailed information for the preparation of media reports at the end of the trial.

582.   A few notes on the procedure at jury trials in the Court of Session may be of assistance, since this differs in certain important particulars from that before a judge sitting alone. The hearing is opened by an address to the jury by junior counsel for the pursuer who outlines the circumstances of the case and summarises the basis of his client's claim. After the jury have heard the evidence for the pursuer, they are addressed by junior counsel for the defender, who, in his turn, introduces the evidence for his client. At the end of all the evidence senior counsel for each side sum up the case to the jury, urging their respective contentions, and the hearing is completed with the judge's charge.

The judge, who is responsible for seeing that the whole proceedings are kept on a proper and competent basis, guides the jury on any question of law arising in the case, and may also express to them his own opinion on the evidence while making it clear to them that they are judges of the facts in the case.

583. It sometimes happens during a jury trial that the jury are taken from the courtroom while counsel make legal submissions to the judge on some point of procedure. These may result in the case being withdrawn from the jury; but, in the event of the case proceeding after such an interruption, care must be taken not to publish reports of the statements made by counsel (although in open court) which could be read by the jurors before having finished with the case. Such publication of arguments could be said to be an interference with the course of justice or to prejudice the case of one party or the other, and to amount to contempt of court. This is an example of the important caution that it is not necessarily safe to publish a statement merely because it was made in open court. In terms of the Contempt of Court Act 1981, s.4(2) (see Appendix), the responsibility for preventing such interference with the course of justice now lies with the judge, but in the event, through apparent judicial oversight, of the s.4(2) provision not being applied in an appropriate case, the reporter would be well advised to exercise his own judgment.

584. When a party is dissatisfied with the verdict of a jury, appeal is taken by way of a motion for a new trial. This is heard in the Inner House and may be on any of a variety of grounds, such as misdirection by the presiding judge at the trial, insufficiency of evidence, lack of corroboration or perverseness on the part of the jury. The appeal may be directed against the amount of damages awarded, either as to excess or inadequacy. The appeal judges, if satisfied that the verdict cannot stand, may order a re-trial before a new jury, or, in certain circumstances, where the judges are unanimously of opinion that the jury were not entitled to find for the pursuer and that there is no fresh evidence available to bring before a new jury, they have jurisdiction to enter their own verdict for the defender.

Proof before judge

585. The hearing of evidence before a judge in civil proceedings is called a proof—in other words, the judge hears evidence to ascertain the proof of the case one way or the other. There are no opening speeches by counsel; at the end of the evidence the judge hears counsel's submissions upon the evidence. The judge may give an immediate

165

decision or he may make avizandum, that is reserve his judgment. Since some judges have greater enthusiasm for *ex tempore* judgment than others, and every case has to be treated on its own merits—and to that extent is unique—there is no certain guide as to when to be prepared for an immediate judgment. The most that can be said is that where a proof is of comparatively short duration, say two days or less, and the issues appear to be relatively simple, it is wise to be prepared for an immediate judgment (for divorce procedures see Chapter 11).

586. In reporting cases decided by a judge, it is important to distinguish between those in which the action is dismissed and those where the defender is absolved. The latter is a higher degree of success for a defender than dismissal, since a decree of absolvitor precludes the pursuer from suing the same defender again in respect of the same matter. In the case of dismissal, however, the pursuer may find another remedy against the same defender in a different action. It is of some concern, therefore, to the successful defender to see whether he is reported as having won absolvitor or merely dismissal. No such distinction can, of course, arise with reference to juries' verdicts.

587. Apart from damages for financial loss or loss of property, the court, whether in cases tried by jury or by proof, may in appropriate circumstances make an award for pain and suffering incurred by an injured pursuer (solatium), or award a sum to compensate, as far as possible, a bereaved relative of a person who has died as the result of the defender's negligence (loss of society). In the latter instance the award is intended to cover a variety of kinds of loss, such as companionship and guidance besides the element of grief and sorrow.

Judicial review
588. A simplified procedure for disposal, before a single judge instead of a bench of three or four, of petitions for judicial review of administrative decisions came into operation in the Court of Session in June 1985. Cases, dealt with on petition and answers, may involve complex and technical questions but may also contain factual material of human interest. The first case under the new procedure, dealt with by Lord Ross in July 1985, for example, concerned a girl aged 16, who left home as a result of being assaulted by her father, and applied successfully to the court for reversal of a decision of Monklands District Council rejecting her claim for accommodation as a person with a priority need under the Housing (Homeless Persons) Act 1977. She had no assets and no income, had nowhere to go and had attempted suicide. The judge held that no reasonable authority could fail to con-

166

clude she was vulnerable, and ordered that she be given accommodation under the Act. She was also awarded damages against the council.

The procedure has proved a fertile source of copy, having been used also to test such diverse questions as the vesting of assets of the Trustee Savings Bank in Scotland, the nature and extent of Crown immunity in building a fence at a submarine base and the policy of the D.H.S.S. on the payment of special cold-weather allowances. Hearings are in public and judgment is usually given *ex tempore*. There is a right of appeal to the Inner House.

Judicial review was described by Lord McCluskey in the Reith Lectures in 1986 as one of the old forms of remedy now rediscovered by the judges to enable citizens to challenge infringements of their rights, especially infringements by public officials—a process by which, he said, the judges had armed the citizen with rights he did not know he had. If so, then clearly such cases deserve close attention from the journalist for their potential news value.

Standard of proof

589. There is an important distinction between the standards of proof required by the law in criminal and in civil cases. In criminal proceedings generally proof must be beyond reasonable doubt; but in civil cases the court has to be satisfied merely on a balance of probabilities—in other words, the judge or jury in the latter instance has to decide which of two conflicting stories is more probable.

590. An important change in the legal requirement of corroboration in civil actions for personal injuries was effected by the Law Reform (Miscellaneous Provisions) (Scotland) Act 1968. Section 9(2) of the Act provides that, if the court is satisfied that any fact has been established by evidence given in the case, it may hold that fact proved even in the absence of corroboration.

Trust variation

591. The Trusts (Scotland) Act 1961 introduced a novelty into the Court of Session by bestowing upon it (in the Inner House) the power to vary or "break" trusts which formerly were inflexible. It also resulted in a departure from the accepted rule applied to the reporting of court proceedings generally: that the Press was entitled to have access to, and to publish fair and accurate excerpts from, the pleadings put before the court in support of, and in opposition to, a particular course.

167

592. To take an example, the most usual kind of petition brought before the court under the Act is aimed at circumventing a provision in a trust which restricts a beneficiary to the income and puts the capital of the trust beyond his reach. The court may under the Act, where satisfied as to the interests of other beneficiaries, authorise payment of the capital of a trust to a person who previously was entitled only to the income. Such variation will usually be designed to enable the interested parties to save tax. This is legitimate tax avoidance, and must not be referred to as tax evasion. The court (First Division) have taken the view that the figures contained in this type of case must not be made public. For this reason reporters are not usually permitted to have access to documents containing figures.

593. The only means of reporting such cases—which from time to time produce copy of considerable interest, especially where the estates of well-known public figures are concerned—is usually to sit through the proceedings, and obtain the names and addresses of the parties from the clerk of court or solicitors. In some cases agents for the petitioner will allow the Press to see the petition; this occurred in a case in 1963 in which the petitioner was one of the Senators of the College of Justice (Lord Sorn) and the document was volunteered to the Press by his solicitor. But in an earlier case (*Colvilles*, 1962 S.C.185)— the first case under the 1961 Act to be reported in the general Press— the parties complained to the court about publication of figures not actually disclosed in court. The then Lord President (Lord Clyde) took the view that, since the court in such cases was performing what was in effect an administrative act on behalf of the parties, the figures should not be published. This is still the attitude of the court, except where the particulars in question actually emerge in court.

Remits

594. Special care has to be taken in the handling of reports of criminal proceedings in their early stages. When an accused person appears at the Bar of a lower court and pleads either guilty or not guilty to the charge, it is in order to publish his name and address and the contents of the complaints, although he may be remitted to another court for disposal of his case or remanded to await trial. Similarly, these details may be published in the case of an accused person who admits or is convicted of an offence in the sheriff court and, because of the seriousness of the case, is remitted to the High Court for sentence.

595. Where an accused appears on petition before a sheriff in chambers, the reporter's scope for coverage is strictly limited and, in

the matter of deciding how much he may safely publish, he must be guided by the procurator-fiscal, who will usually provide the name and, where available, the address of the accused (except where he or she is under 16) and the gist of the charge. Special caution is necessary at this preliminary stage of a case, since proceedings could still be dropped or the terms of the charge(s) altered before the case is called in open court.
596. One must have in mind not only the law of slander but the less predictable one of contempt of court. The essentials of defamation, as it concerns the journalist, are discussed in Part III; those of contempt in Chapter 9.

Fitness to plead

597. When a person who has been charged with a criminal offence suffers from such degree of unsoundness of mind as to render it doubtful whether he is capable of instructing his defence or of pleading to the charge, he appears before a judge of the High Court of Justiciary, who hears the evidence of two or more medical experts on the accused person's mental condition. Upon the evidence the court decides whether or not the accused is fit to plead. If he is, a diet for trial is fixed; if not, the judge will make the appropriate order for the detention of the accused in a state hospital or other suitable institution. The procedure is laid down in ss.25 and 330(1) of the Criminal Procedure (Scotland) Act 1975 as amended by the Mental Health (Scotland) Act 1984.

Nobile officium

598. This jurisdiction, belonging to the High Court and the Court of Session, has been invoked in a variety of cases in recent years to seek a remedy where none was provided by statute or precedent. A bench of at least three judges is required and normally in practice they reach their decision unanimously, but under Rule of Court 189(*a*)(3) certain matters may be dealt with by a single judge. For many years it was almost entirely in civil cases that the *nobile officium* was exercised but its use in criminal cases has become increasingly frequent. In one important case in 1966 two witnesses, who had been sentenced to three years' imprisonment for contempt of court for refusing to take the oath or give evidence at a High Court trial, presented a petition to three judges of that court with the object of having their sentences reviewed. The court (while refusing to alter the sentences) held that the petition was competent (which was not disputed by the Crown), since the petitioners—being witnesses and not the accused at the antecedent trial—had no statutory right of appeal.

599. It is useful for journalists to be familiar with this type of procedure, since it is quite distinct from any form of appeal laid down by statute. It is misleading to refer to such applications to the judges' special powers as an appeal, since the reason for using this method of review may be the absence of any right of appeal as such.

600. In a case in 1972 the High Court held that an application to the *nobile officium* was competent to give relief to an alien under the Extradition Act 1870, which provides for release, by the English process of *habeas corpus*, of a person claimed to be detained illegally, but makes no corresponding provision for Scotland. The *nobile officium* is therefore a valuable power inherent in the supreme courts in Scotland to provide a solution and achieve a just result within certain strict bounds where Parliament—as is by no means unknown or even unusual—has omitted to legislate for Scotland. It is of more than terminological importance that reports of such a case should not treat it as just another appeal.

Rape cases

601. Judges of the High Court of Justiciary (unlike their counterparts in the English courts) in accordance with practice "close the doors" while the evidence of an alleged victim of rape or attempted rape is being heard, the object being to protect the witness from influences which might be likely to inhibit her in the giving of evidence that would assist the court in reaching a decision. It has also become the practice of the judges to allow reporters covering the proceedings to remain in court provided they do not identify the witness in their reports. The above practice was judicially recognised in a case in 1983 in which Lord Avonside said, "In our courts a victim alleged to have been raped almost invariably gives evidence behind closed doors. In such a situation the public is not permitted to hear her evidence. It has been the practice, particularly in Glasgow, to allow the Press reporters to remain. They are asked to exercise a wise discretion, and, in my experience, this they do admirably. The trial judge could, of course, if he thought it desirable, exclude the Press and clear the court completely." (*H.* v. *Sweeney*, 1983 S.L.T. 48 at p. 61.) Besides the powers the judges have under statutes of the Scottish Parliament (see paras. 239–240) and in more recent statutory provisions (the Criminal Procedure (Scotland) Act 1975, s.145(3) gives the presiding judge power from the opening of the evidence in a rape trial "or the like," if he thinks fit, to clear the court of all persons except those actually involved in the proceedings), they may now give directions to *prohibit* publication of "a name or other matter" where they were already able merely to *allow* disclosure of it in open court.

602. Legislation, for which there was public clamour following a series of rape cases in England in 1975, would—so far as it affected non-publication of identity of alleged rape victims—appear to be unnecessary in Scotland. In England identification in court reports of the alleged victim of rape or attempted rape is prohibited by the Sexual Offences (Amendment) Act 1976, which also makes it an offence to identify the accused in such cases unless and until he is convicted. The absurd consequences of this latter provision emerged in a number of cases, in particular in a case in 1986 when a man charged and named by the police in connection with a series of murders became anonymous when he was charged also with rape. Apart from the difficulties this created for the media, the police were hampered in circulating descriptive details of the man wanted for the crimes. It became clear also that a man acquitted of rape and convicted of murdering his victim could be jailed for life but not identified by the media, which, however, would be free in law to name the victim. The (English) Criminal Law Revision Committee in April 1984 recommended that the anonymity provision should cease to apply to the defendant in rape cases, and the Government later stated it was actively considering whether the anonymity of defendants in rape cases should be taken away, while preserving that given to rape victims. Meanwhile the Attorney-General, in March 1986, decided to take no action against the *Sun* on a complaint that it had allegedly broken the law by publishing a front-page photograph of a rape victim before an arrest had been made; and Mrs Margaret Thatcher, the Prime Minister, in Parliament appealed to newspapers not to reveal the names of rape victims before charges were brought, saying there were "certain customs and conventions" which she hoped would be observed by the Press in such cases. (It is the observance of such conventions in Scotland, it might be added, which has made legislation like the 1976 Act unnecessary here.)

CHAPTER 14

TITLES AND TERMINOLOGY

603. The principal judge in Scotland holds the dual office of Lord Justice-General (in which capacity he is president of the High Court of Justiciary) and Lord President of the Court of Session. The Lord Justice-Clerk, who is next in order of precedence, holds office in both courts and carries the same title in each. In the Court of Session the Lord President presides over the First Division as well as over sittings of the full bench (which are not common); the Lord Justice-Clerk presides over the Second Division. He also deputises for the Lord President in his absence as head of the courts.

604. There are 22 other judges (including the Chairman of the Scottish Law Commission, who may perform his judicial function also from time to time). Each bears the title of Lord Commissioner of Justiciary when sitting in the High Court and Senator of the College of Justice when performing the functions of a Court of Session judge. In either capacity he is entitled to the courtesy title "Lord," but he is not a peer, unless he is one of the few judges who have been made Life Peers. There is no objection to the forms "Lord President Smith" or "Lord Justice-Clerk Black," styles which are in use in the legal textbooks. The term Lord Ordinary is used frequently in court with reference to a judge of first instance; the reporter will usually have to inquire or search in the documents of the case for the particular judge's name. The Court of Session sits only in Edinburgh, the High Court of Justiciary deals with criminal business in Edinburgh and on circuit in various parts of Scotland.

Sheriff court

605. When a sheriff principal or sheriff is a Q.C., this designation should not be omitted from the first mention of his name in a report. Sheriffs principal and sheriffs in court or when discharging their shrieval functions are addressed as "My Lord." They should be given their judicial titles only in reports of matters concerning their discharge of these duties. When a sheriff is reported as speaking or participating in any activity as a private individual, his shrieval title should be omitted. (This practice may be reversed in local papers, where "the

Sheriff'' tends to carry this style with him wherever he goes and whatever he does in the public eye.)

Faculty of Advocates

606. From the point of view of etiquette, to which the law attaches
much importance, it may be as offensive to describe an advocate as a
Q.C. as to call a Q.C. an advocate. This can be understood if it is
realised that when an advocate takes silk his junior practice comes to
an end. There have been instances of juniors losing briefs because they
were prematurely described in the Press as Q.C.s—and, of course,
members of the Faculty of Advocates may not advertise themselves,
even in order to rectify such inaccuracies. The former rule by which a
Q.C. could not normally appear without a junior was rescinded in
1977. In the High Court an advocate-depute who is a Q.C. may appear
alone. The title advocate depute belongs to several members of the Bar
who assist in the preparation and conduct of criminal prosecutions.
They are deputies to the Lord Advocate, and not advocates' deputies
(as the title might suggest).

Law officers

607. The Lord Advocate holds one of the most ancient offices in the
Scottish legal system. Besides having the supreme authority over all
prosecutions conducted on behalf of the Sovereign in Scotland, he represents various government departments where these are involved in
civil litigations in the Court of Session. He does not often appear personally to represent the Crown, although he will do so in important
cases. He is more often represented by his senior deputy, the Solicitor-
General for Scotland. These two law officers are allocated special
places in court—the Lord Advocate at the clerk's table on the right of
the chair, and the Solicitor-General in the corresponding place on the
left. It is usual for at least one of them to be a Member of Parliament,
where he answers Scottish questions on legal subjects and advises the
government on the conduct of Scottish Bills, but there have been
occasions when this has not been possible. Both appointments are
made on a political basis, and when a government goes out of office, so
do the law officers. When a vacancy occurs on the High Court and
Court of Session Bench the Lord Advocate recommends a successor
who may be himself. The Lord Advocate is in charge of the Crown
Office in Edinburgh (where criminal prosecutions are prepared) as well
as the Lord Advocate's Department in London (where Scottish legislation is largely drafted).

608. Members of the Society of Advocates in Aberdeen, who are solicitors, are not to be confused with members of the Faculty of Advocates. Aberdeen advocates do not share the right to plead before the supreme courts, which belongs to the members of the Faculty, and to parties who conduct their own case.

609. The term "counsel" applies only to members of the Faculty and is not accurately used in reference to solicitors appearing before the sheriff or other courts.

610. It is necessary in the reporting of Scottish court cases to avoid the use of English court terms. We use pursuer, not plaintiff; defender, not defendant. In England divorce proceedings are taken by way of a petition; in Scotland, by way of a summons. The distinction results in quite separate terms being used for the parties concerned in the proceedings. Thus, while in England the person who institutes divorce proceedings is the petitioner and the opposing party the respondent, these in Scotland are respectively pursuer and defender. The term respondent is used in Scotland in reference to a party contesting a petition as well as to one resisting an appeal. A third party who comes into divorce proceedings to deny allegations implicating him or her may do so by lodging a minute and is known as a party-minuter.

611. A number of Scottish and English court terms are interchangeable according to the particular requirements of the newspaper, having regard to its readership. For example, although in Scotland a court order prohibiting some act which is the subject of complaint is properly called an interdict, the reporter writing for an English paper might find it desirable to call such an order an injunction, the equivalent English term which would be more readily understood by his readers and is at the same time not entirely unknown in Scotland. The same might be said of such terms as aliment (English maintenance or alimony), arbiter (arbitrator) and expenses (costs).

Part III

DEFAMATION

CHAPTER 15

ESSENTIALS OF DEFAMATION

612. "I do not for my part, consider that any privilege whatever attaches to a newspaper report as such. If a newspaper gives circulation to a slander, it is simply in the position of any other party circulating a slander and the general rule is that a person circulating a slander is answerable equally with the author of the slander." (Lord Kyllachy in *Wright & Greig* v. *Outram* (1890) 17 R. 596 at 599.) The law has changed slightly since Lord Kyllachy said this at the end of the last century and newspaper reports of certain matters are now privileged by statute. But apart from these special cases the principle remains the same. The law of defamation applies to newspapermen as to ordinary mortals. There is no general privilege of journalism. "It would be a total mistake to suppose that the editor of a newspaper, who sits behind a curtain like another veiled prophet, is entitled to vote himself public accuser, to the effect of calling every member of society to account for his misdeeds and to confer upon every anonymous contributor whom he admits into his columns, the same privilege." (Lord Deas in *Drew* v. *Mackenzie* (1862) 24 D. 649 at 662.)

613. The second part of Lord Kyllachy's remark should also be noted. "A person circulating a slander is answerable equally with the author of the slander." This means that the author, publisher and printer of a book can be, and frequently are, all sued for the one slander. It means that both the writer of a defamatory article, report or letter and the proprietor of the newspaper in which it is published may be liable for damages and it means that the newspaper which merely repeats a defamatory statement already published in the columns of another is as liable to be sued as if it originated the slander. (By the Defamation Act 1952, s.12, however, a newspaper owner can prove in *mitigation of damages* that other newspaper proprietors have already paid damages in respect of the statement in question.) It would seem, however, that people such as newsagents and librarians who merely

175

disseminate a defamatory publication are not liable if they have no reason to think that what they are circulating is slanderous (*Morrison* v. *Ritchie* (1902) 4 F. 645).

614. It is sometimes thought that it is safe to publish a statement if it is stated clearly that it is merely being repeated for what it is worth. Nothing could be further from the truth. The newspaper which repeats a defamatory statement is asking for trouble if the statement is untrue even if it emphasises that it does not endorse the allegation.

Civil wrong

615. In Scotland defamation is a civil wrong giving rise to an action for damages and not a criminal prosecution. However, the Representation of the People Act 1983 makes it a criminal offence for any person before or during a Parliamentary election to make or publish for the purpose of affecting the return of any candidate any false statement of fact in relation to the personal character or conduct of such candidate. In theory, too, a publication tending to cause a breach of the peace might render the publisher liable to prosecution for this common law offence. In England and many other countries defamation can be a criminal offence.

Publication

616. You can shout a slander to the waves and write reams of libellous invective. If nobody hears or reads there will be no defamation. Publication of some sort is essential. In this respect there is a difference between Scots law and English law. Scots law allows an action for injury to the feelings caused by an insulting and defamatory statement even if it is not made known to any third party. English law requires communication to a third party before there will be civil liability. From the journalist's point of view the difference is not important. In his case there can seldom be any doubt about publication. There is no technical distinction in Scots law between words published in writing and words spoken. The terms libel and slander are often used interchangeably.

Falsity

617. Only false statements are actionable. Truth, or *veritas*, is a complete defence. But defamatory statements are presumed to be false

176

and, if the defender relies on *veritas*, the burden of proving the truth of his statements rests on him. If he makes one allegation, he must prove that it is true and not merely that it is partly true or that something less is true. If a man has been called a liar, it is not enough to prove that he lied on one occasion (*Milne* v. *Walker* (1893) 21 R. 155) and if a man has been called a thief it is no defence to prove that long ago, as a boy, he had two convictions for petty theft (*Fletcher* v. *Wilson* (1885) 12 R. 683).

618. On the other hand, if the pursuer founds upon two separate allegations, the defender can always prove the truth of one of them even although he may not also be able to prove the truth of the other (*O'Callaghan* v. *Thomson & Co.*, 1928 S.C. 532). Before 1952 this had the effect of diminishing the damages. Under s.5 of the Defamation Act 1952, it may absolve the defender from liability altogether. The section provides that: "In an action for defamation in respect of words containing two or more distinct charges against the pursuer, a defence of *veritas* shall not fail by reason only that the truth of every charge is not proved if the words not proved to be true do not materially injure the pursuer's reputation having regard to the truth of the remaining charges." It should be noted that, under the present law, a pursuer can choose to base his action on only one allegation out of several. If he does this, the defender has no opportunity to prove the truth of the remaining allegations so as to take advantage of s.5.

619. It was formerly the law, at least in England, that if a man was said to have committed a crime it was not a defence to a defamation action to prove merely that he had been convicted of that crime. It had to be proved that he had *in fact* committed the crime. However, in a defamation action proof that a person stands convicted of an offence by a United Kingdom court or British court-martial is now conclusive evidence that he committed the offence (Law Reform (Miscellaneous Provisions) (Scotland) Act 1968, s.12; Civil Evidence Act 1968, s.13). As we shall see later, the Rehabilitation of Offenders Act 1974 adds a new complication to *veritas* in relation to criminal offences. If the offence in question is the subject of a "spent conviction" the defender in an action of defamation by the rehabilitated person cannot rely on *veritas* if the publication is proved to have been made with malice.

620. The defence of *veritas* can be a very difficult one. Even where charges seem justified, they may not be easy to prove. It can also be an unwise defence if there is serious risk of failure as it means that the defamation is persisted in and this is a factor which can aggravate damages.

Defamatory

621. There is no clear rule on what is and what is not defamatory. Generally speaking, however, a defamatory statement involves some imputation against character or reputation, including business or financial reputation. The best way of answering the question "What is defamatory?" is to set out by way of example various types of statement which the courts have regarded as actionable. It must be emphasised, however, that this is only a guide. The fact that a statement has been regarded as defamatory in the past, does not necessarily mean that it will be regarded as defamatory now. Fashions in defamation change. Accusations of Sabbath breaking are less likely to be held defamatory today than they were in the last century.

622. To call a man a criminal in general terms is clearly defamatory. To call him a thief or accuse him of some other serious crime is also defamatory. The *Sunday Mail* once made an unfortunate mistake. In reporting a murder of which William Harkness and his wife had been found guilty, it said beside a photograph of the two murderers, "John Harkness and his wife, both of whom were condemned to die but the man alone paid the extreme penalty. The woman is serving a life sentence." John Harkness and his wife were allowed an action for defamation (*Harkness* v. *The Daily Record Ltd.*, 1924 S.L.T. 759). An accusation of a minor or technical offence, however, is probably defamatory only if the offence is regarded as socially or morally discreditable. It is hardly actionable to say that a man exceeded the speed limit.

623. An interesting case was that of *Leon* v. *Edinburgh Evening News*, 1909 S.C. 1014. The *Evening News* reported a police court case under the headline "The Edinburgh Licensing Prosecution: Prisoners Acquitted." One of the accused referred to, who had in fact never been in custody but had simply appeared in court in answer to a citation, sued for defamation, pointing out, quite correctly, that he had never been a prisoner. It was held that in the circumstances of the case the statement was not defamatory. Lord Kinnear observed that "the description was not technically exact. But a newspaper in a paragraph of this kind does not necessarily use technical language: and in ordinary language an accused person at the Bar of a court may not improperly be described as a prisoner. To an ordinary reader, the paragraph with its heading, would not in my opinion convey any more injurious meaning than that the pursuer had been accused and had been acquitted." There were also observations that it would not necessarily be defamatory to refer to a man as a prisoner in any event as a person may be a prisoner quite innocently. But clearly the word "prisoner" is not one to be recklessly bandied about.

624. Imputations of sexual immorality are clearly actionable. There can be no doubt about accusations of adultery or prostitution but, depending on the standards of the time and the views of reasonable people generally, very much less may suffice. Accusations of want of womanly delicacy have been held actionable. *Blackwood's Magazine* carried a story describing life in a Fife mining village. The author said that in the course of a social evening in one house, a girl of seventeen grew tired and in the presence of more than a dozen people of both sexes prepared herself for bed and got into it. She showed no embarrassment and the company took no notice. "Now this," said the author, "might be called 'indelicate'. Delicacy, however, is a standard of the more complex world, and this girl knew nought of it." The girl in question thought differently and brought an action against the publishers. It was held that the passage was actionable (*A.B.* v. *Blackwood & Sons* (1902) 5 F. 25).

625. Another celebrated action on this ground was that brought by Mrs. Cuthbert, better known as Wendy Wood, against Eric Linklater (*Cuthbert* v. *Linklater*, 1935 S.L.T. 94). In his novel, *Magnus Merriman*, Mr. Linklater referred to a woman called Beaty Bracken who had removed a Union Jack from a castle and placed it in a public urinal. Wendy Wood, having herself achieved some fame by removing a Union Jack from Stirling Castle and tossing it to a guard, read the statement as applicable to her and raised an action. The court held that the passage could be read as making an imputation of gross indelicacy and that an action should be allowed.

626. Actions have often been based on imputations of drunkenness or dishonesty—the latter covering anything from appropriating public funds to evading payment of rent. In one case two political lecturers engaged a hall. A newspaper commented later "Now one of them has left the town. Any information as to his whereabouts will be thankfully received by a sorrowing landlord, the proprietor of the hall, who now concludes that a Tory Cleon is no more profitable as a tenant than a Socialist Boanerges" (*Godfrey* v. *W. & D.C. Thomson* (1890) 17 R. 1108). An action was allowed.

627. To sum up, any charge of conduct which is usually regarded as discreditable or dishonourable may be defamatory.

628. It has been held defamatory to call a man debauched, corrupt, two-faced, a blackguard, "a low dirty scum", a coward, a calumniator, a scoundrel, a disgusting brute, a mansworn rogue, an infidel, a hypocrite, an informer, a glutton or a plagiarist,but it would be very much a question of circumstances whether any of these expressions standing alone would be regarded as defamatory today. The leaning of the law is now against actions based on words of mere general abuse.

629. Imputations on solvency are clearly actionable. They need not go as far as to allege bankruptcy. It is enough if they imply financial embarrassment.

630. Numerous defamation cases have been concerned with imputations on a man's fitness for his occupation or profession. To give only a few examples, it is dangerous to accuse a minister of brawling with his parishioners (*Mackellar* v. *Duke of Sutherland* (1859) 21 D. 222), a Christian missionary of being a Mohammedan (*Davis* v. *Miller* (1855) 17 D. 1050, 1166), a teacher of ignorance of his subject (*McKerchar* v. *Cameron* (1892) 19 R. 383), a medical practitioner of cruelty to a patient (*Bruce* v. *Ross & Co.* (1901) 4 F. 171), an accountant of being unfit to be a trustee in bankruptcy (*Oliver* v. *Barnet* (1895) 3 S.L.T. 163) or a solicitor of conducting cases for his own advantage and without regard to the interests of his clients (*McRostie* v. *Ironside* (1849) 12 D. 74).

631. False allegations of insanity are actionable. There is more doubt about physical disease but it would probably be defamatory to say that a person suffered from some obnoxious disease which rendered him repulsive in the eyes of his fellows.

Innuendo

632. An innuendo is a statement in which the pursuer sets forth the precise meaning which he places on words he alleges are defamatory. This is necessary where the words are innocent or ambiguous on their face. For example, a statement that a person "took" a thing has been held to require an innuendo that he "stole" it to make it actionable (*Moore* v. *Reid* (1893) 20 R. 712). An innuendo is also required in the case of ironical or technical words, or statements in a foreign language. In some cases an innuendo may be used where there is obvious defamation but where it is desired to crystallise the charges made or implied in a long statement or correspondence.

633. It is not enough that the words *could* bear the meaning alleged. It must be shown that they probably *would* bear that meaning when heard or read by a reasonable man. The innuendo must represent what is a reasonable, natural or necessary inference from the words used, regard being had to the occasion and the circumstances of their publication (*Russell* v. *Stubbs*, 1913 S.C. (H.L.) 14). With regard to news-paper articles, it has been said that the court must consider the mean-ing which the words used would convey to an ordinary reader reading them as newspaper articles are usually read (*Hunter* v. *Ferguson & Co.* (1906) 8 F. 574; *Stein* v. *Beaverbrook Newspapers Ltd.*, 1968 S.L.T. 401, 409). If they would not appear defamatory to such an ordinary reader, no action will lie. This, however, is subject to the qualification that the reader may have knowledge of special facts making an appar-ently innocent statement defamatory. It seems harmless to say that Mrs. M. gave birth to twins on a certain date but this becomes defama-tory when read by those knowing that she had been married for only a month (*Morrison* v. *Ritchie* (1902) 4 F. 645, and see para. 669).

Statement

634. There must be a statement. It need not however be in words. It may be inferred from acts, as where a waxwork effigy of the pursuer was placed in a waxworks among the effigies of notorious criminals (*Monson* v. *Tussauds* [1894] 1 Q.B. 671) or where a boy's photograph was placed by the police in their "rogues gallery" (*Adamson* v. *Martin*, 1916 S.C. 319). Of more importance for the journalist is the possibility of inferring a defamatory statement from drawings and photographs. An issue of the magazine *Lilliput* contained on a left-hand page a photograph of an outdoor photographer called Sydney Garbett with his camera. On the opposite page was a photograph of a naked woman. Under Mr. Garbett's photograph were the words, "Of course for another shilling, Madam" and under the other photograph, the words, "You can have something like this." Mr. Garbett alleged that after these photographs appeared, his friends stopped calling him "Sydney" and began to call him "Smutty." The court held that the arrangement of the photographs and captions was quite clearly libellous (*Garbett* v. *Hazell Watson & Viney Ltd.* [1943] 2 All E.R. 359).

About a person

635. The statement must be of and concerning the pursuer. He must show that reasonable persons would take the words to refer to him but need not prove that they were intended to refer to him (see below paras. 668–676).
636. Difficulties arise where a class of persons is defamed. The general rule is that members of the class can sue if and only if the class is sufficiently well defined for the defamation to be applicable to them

181

individually. A particular minister could not sue on an attack against ministers generally but could sue on a charge of drunkenness against the ministers of his particular presbytery (*Macphail* v. *Macleod* (1896) 3 S.L.T. 91).

637. A company can sue for defamation relating to its business interests but cannot, of course, recover damages for injury to feelings.

638. As a general rule only the person defamed can sue and hence no action will lie for defamation of somebody already dead. When a widow brought an action based on a newspaper statement that her late husband had attempted suicide, her action was dismissed on this ground (*Broom* v. *Ritchie* (1904) 6 F. 942). But if aspersions on the deceased cause actual patrimonial loss to a pursuer, he may establish a title to sue the person who cast them.

CHAPTER 16

DEFENCES

639. In defence to an action for defamation the defender may claim that one of the essentials of defamation is lacking—for example, that no statement was made, or that, if made, it is true, or is not defamatory or would not be taken by a reasonable man to refer to the pursuer. These points were considered in the last chapter. We must now deal with various other defences.

Rixa

640. Words spoken in *rixa* are words uttered in the heat of a quarrel. Even if apparently defamatory they will not be actionable, unless it would appear to third parties that a specific charge was being seriously made. This defence is properly applicable only to spoken words and is hence of little importance for the journalist.

Fair comment

641. The defence of fair comment is available to everyone but is particularly relevant for newspapermen. The Press is not only entitled, but also expected, to comment on matters of public interest. In performing this function it is allowed considerable latitude by the law, partly for reasons of public policy and partly on the theory that people can form their own opinions on facts generally known or accurately set forth.

642. Fair comment is often pleaded in cases concerning criticism of public men. While, as we saw, it is defamatory to say of an ordinary member of the community that he is unfit for his job, a similar statement made about a public official may well come under the umbrella of fair comment. Democracy and free speech would indeed be empty words if this were not so.

643. Certain conditions must be present before the defence of fair comment will succeed. First, the matter complained of must be comment: the defence does not protect defamatory statements of fact (*cf. Waddell* v. *B.B.C.*, 1973 S.L.T. 246). Secondly, the comment must be such as an honest man could have made. Comment, however, does not cease to be fair merely because it represents a stupid, partisan or eccentric point of view. Fools and cranks can have their say. Nor does comment become actionable merely because it is couched in strong or vituperative language (*Archer* v. *Ritchie & Co.* (1891) 18 R. 719). Thirdly, the comment must be based on facts and if these are set out, they must be set out accurately. Under the Defamation Act 1952, s.6, however, a defence of fair comment will not fail only because the truth of every allegation of fact is not proved, if the expression of opinion is fair comment in view of such facts as are proved. Fourthly, the comment must be on a matter of public interest. This gives plenty of scope. It clearly covers comment on affairs of central and local government, the administration of justice and the conduct of those holding or seeking public office. It also covers comment on sport and criticism of books, and of films, plays and other public entertainments. It does not, however, cover observations on matters regarded by the law as lying outside the legitimate sphere of journalism such as the private lives of private citizens. "While it is in the public interest that the Press should exercise freely its right of criticism in regard to public affairs, it is equally important that the right of a private individual to have his character respected should be maintained, and that people should not as private persons be exposed to unjustifiable and arbitrary comment" (*per* Viscount Haldane in *Langlands* v. *Leng*, 1916 S.C. (H.L.) 102 at 106).

644. It seems that proof of malice may vitiate a defence of fair comment (*Brims* v. *Reid* (1885) 12 R. 1016; *McKerchar* v. *Cameron* (1892) 19 R. 383). If this is so, then possibly a newspaper could not plead fair comment in respect of remarks contained in an anonymous letter the writer of which was not disclosed. The newspaper would be putting forward a defence and at the same time depriving the pursuer of an opportunity of overcoming it. "How can anyone prove malice on the part of a person of whom he knows nothing at all?" (*Brims* v. *Reid*, *supra* at p. 1021). On the other hand it is arguable that in this sort of case it is only the newspaper's malice which is relevant. It is the publication which is complained of, not the writing of the letter. If the newspaper has published without malice on its part, or on the part of its agent or employees, then it should be entitled to the defence of fair comment. The Scottish cases on this point (*Brims* v. *Reid*, and *McKerchar* v. *Cameron*, *supra*,) are old and unsatisfactory and reveal so much confusion between fair comment and privilege that it is difficult to interpret them with confidence.

Fair retort

645. A certain latitude is allowed to the man who denies charges made publicly against him. Even if his denial is not entirely true and is in strong terms it will not be actionable. But he must not pass from repudiation to the making of separate defamatory allegations against his accuser. The retort must be a shield and not a spear. The defence of fair retort is thus of very narrow scope. Its main practical effect is to prevent a man being sued for saying his accuser lied.

Privilege

646. There are two types of privilege—absolute and qualified. If a statement has absolute privilege, no action can be based on it, however false, defamatory or malicious it may be. If a statement has qualified privilege an action can be based on it but the pursuer must prove that it was made with malice. The theory behind both types of privilege is that in some circumstances the public interest demands freedom to speak without fear of an action for defamation.

Absolute privilege

647. Absolute privilege applies to statements made in Parliament, reports authorised by Parliament and statements made in court with reference to the case in progress by judge, advocate, solicitor or witness. The litigant, however, has only qualified privilege: he cannot indulge with impunity in malicious defamation simply by raising an action. By statute, absolute privilege attaches to certain communications by, or to, or arising out of an investigation by the Parliamentary Commissioner (see Chapter 6) commonly known as the Ombudsman, and Local Commissioners for Administration. Of most importance for journalists is the absolute privilege accorded to a fair and accurate report of proceedings in a public court of justice. This must be considered in some detail.

648. The report must be both accurate and fair. It need not be verbatim or even complete. Where a newspaper merely purports to report the result of a case and does so accurately it cannot be liable in damages because it fails to narrate the steps leading up to judgment. "There is no duty on a reporter in a report of a law suit to make his report exhaustive. It is . . . sufficient if the reporter gives the result of the litigation truly and correctly" (*per* Lord Anderson in *Duncan* v. *Associated Newspapers*, 1929 S.C. 14). When more than the result is reported, however, great care must be taken to see that the report is not one-sided. If one party's allegations are mentioned, the other party's replies should be given equal prominence (*Wright and Greig* v. *Outram* (1890) 17 R. 596). If reported allegations are found unproved

185

this must always be clearly stated as soon as possible. There is no objection to publishing daily accounts of a case lasting several days but the reports should be kept up to date. If both allegations and refutations are available there will be no privilege if the allegations are published one day and the refutations held over till the next. The burden of proving that a report is fair and accurate lies on the newspaper (*Pope* v. *Outram*, 1909 S.C. 230).

649. Care should be taken with headlines in reports of judicial proceedings. If these take the form of comment on the case, they cannot be regarded as part of the report and will not be privileged. They should therefore always be fair and justified by the facts reported so as to be protected by the defence of fair comment.

650. It has never been expressly decided in Scotland that a report must be contemporaneous in order to have absolute privilege (*Buchan* v. *N.B. Ry. Co.* (1894) 21 R. 379, indicates that a report need not be contemporaneous but the grounds of the decision are not clear; see also Contempt of Court Act 1981, s.4), but it might well be that the law would look less favourably on the exhumation of old cases than it does on the publication of current reports. Public policy demands freedom in the one case but not in the other. In England only contemporaneous reports have absolute privilege and if a Scottish paper circulates in England, there is always the possibility of an action being brought under English law. For these reasons it is prudent to publish only contemporaneous reports. In practice this means that a report should be published as soon after the proceedings as is reasonably possible. A report in the next edition of a daily paper would be contemporaneous and so too would a report in the next issue of a weekly or fortnightly paper although appearing some days after the proceedings (Gatley on *Libel and Slander*, 8th ed. (1981) para. 630).

651. Absolute privilege protects a fair and accurate report of statements made in open court. It is often impossible, however, to understand a case completely without reference to the various documents connected with it. How far are statements derived from this source protected? The answer varies with the circumstances. In civil cases a report of statements made in an open record is completely unprivileged and the same would seem to apply to reports derived from a closed record which has not yet been referred to in open court. In practice, of course, there are many circumstances where it may be judged safe to publish information from a closed record at this stage but the law seems clear. A litigant is not privileged if he sends his pleadings (whether the record is closed or not) to a newspaper for publication.

186

"If the pleadings so published are slanderous, then the paper publishing them, and the person sending them for publication, are liable in damages for slander" (Lord Young in *Macleod* v. *J.P.s of Lewis* (1892) 20 R. 218 at 221). The same principles would apply to the indictment or complaint in criminal cases. Once the case comes up in open court the position is different. Publication of a document actually read out in open court is of course privileged and privilege may also protect statements derived from documents which are merely referred to expressly or impliedly in open court. The test here would seem to be whether the information in the documents is an essential part of the case and is merely referred to for the sake of convenience. The point arose in *Harper* v. *Provincial Newspapers*, 1937 S.L.T. 462. A man called James Harper appeared in the Edinburgh Burgh Court. The clerk of court read out his name but not his address. He was found guilty of a fairly minor offence. A reporter verified the name and took down the address from the complaint, which was shown to him for that purpose by the clerk of court. In fact the address given in the complaint was not that of the accused but that of his father who was also called James Harper. When the report appeared the father sued the newspaper and the question then arose whether the statement derived from the complaint was privileged. It was held that it was. The address was an essential part of the case which was omitted from the proceedings in open court simply for reasons of speed and convenience. But it was observed that different considerations might apply to information taken from documents which were merely productions in a case.

652. In the case of *Cunningham* v. *Scotsman Publications Ltd*, 1987 S.L.T. 698, Lord Clyde held that privilege applies to a document which "is referred to and founded upon before the court with a view to advancing a submission which is being made," even if not read out in open court (see paras. 293–295).

653. No privilege attaches to reports of proceedings held in private. It is a question of circumstances in each case whether proceedings are in private or in public. In *Thomson* v. *Munro and Jamieson* (1900) 8 S.L.T. 327, it was held that when a statutory examination of a bankrupt took place in public in the sheriff-clerk's room this "was for the occasion a public court." An interesting question arises regarding children's hearings. They are not, strictly speaking, courts. They are not open to the public, but *bona fide* newspapermen are admitted. Do fair and accurate reports of their proceedings have privilege? The point has not been decided but it can hardly be doubted that such reports would enjoy at least qualified privilege. The newspapermen are there to

187

represent the public. There would seem to be the strongest reasons for according privilege to the only source of information on the proceedings available to the public.

654. Situations may arise where there is doubt whether remarks form part of the proceedings. Thus in one English case (*Hope* v. *Leng Ltd.* (1907) T.L.R. 243) a witness shouted from the well of the court that the plaintiff's evidence was "a pack of lies." It was held in this case that a report containing this statement was none the less privileged. It is clear on the other hand that a report of a conversation between two spectators at the back of the court would not be privileged. The journalist must exercise his discretion in deciding whether or not interruptions can properly be regarded as part of the proceedings (see para. 457).

655. What is meant by a public court of justice? The term certainly covers the ordinary civil and criminal courts in the United Kingdom and it can safely be assumed that it covers special courts such as the Lands Valuation Appeal Court, the Restrictive Practices Court, Election Courts, the Registration Appeal Court, the Scottish Land Court, the Lyon Court, and Licensing Boards. It also seems safe to assume that reports of proceedings before Courts-Martial sitting in the United Kingdom will be privileged. There is more doubt about the courts of the Church of Scotland. It may be that reports of their proceedings would have absolute privilege but in any event, they have a special kind of qualified privilege under the Defamation Act 1952. This will be dealt with later.

656. The position with regard to foreign courts is interesting. In two Scottish cases (*Pope* v. *Outram*, 1909 S.C. 230; *Riddell* v. *Clydesdale Horse Society* (1885) 12 R. 976) the Court of Session treated reports of proceedings in foreign courts on the same footing as reports of proceedings in United Kingdom courts and assumed that privilege would apply. The point, however, was neither expressly argued nor expressly decided. The question arose in England in connection with reports of the trial of Donald Hume in Switzerland in 1960 (*Webb* v. *Times Publishing Co. Ltd.* [1960] 2 Q.B. 535). It was held that there was not the same close public concern with the administration of justice abroad and no reason for allowing privilege to reports of foreign judicial proceedings unless there was "a legitimate and proper interest" in the proceedings "as contrasted with an interest which is due to idle curiosity or the desire for gossip." Even where there is a legitimate interest it should be noted that, in England, reports of foreign court proceedings have only qualified privilege. As the case in question involved a British

188

subject who had confessed during the Swiss trial that he had committed a murder of which he had been previously acquitted in an English court, it was held that there was a "legitimate interest" and that the report had qualified privilege. This decision is not, of course, authoritative in Scots law but the possibility of its reasoning being applied by a Scottish court and the possibility of an action being brought under English law in respect of circulation in England would both indicate prudence with regard to reports of foreign court proceedings. One final complication with regard to foreign courts is that some reports of foreign cases are protected by statute. Under the Defamation Act of 1952 fair and accurate reports of proceedings in courts of Her Majesty's Dominions outside the U.K. have qualified privilege.

657. There is one more counsel of prudence. We have regarded the privilege enjoyed in Scotland by fair and accurate reports of proceedings in a public court as an absolute privilege, giving protection even where there is malice. In the *Cunningham* case, 1987 S.L.T. 698, only qualified privilege was claimed.

658. To sum up, a report of judicial proceedings should *always* be fair and accurate. It is advisable, in view of the English law, that it should also be contemporaneous and that care should be taken with reports of foreign judicial proceedings.

Qualified privilege

659. Qualified privilege applies generally to statements made by a person in the discharge of some public or private duty or in matters where his own interests are involved. It applies, for example, to statements made by an employer in giving his employee a reference. No action can be founded on such statements unless there is proof of malice. This type of privilege may be relevant for newspapers. If a person has a duty to make a statement and can only make it adequately in a newspaper, then it seems that qualified privilege will protect not only him but also the paper (*Brims* v. *Reid* (1885) 12 R. 1016; *Waddell* v. *B.B.C.*, 1973 S.L.T. 246).

660. Of more interest to journalists, however, is the qualified privilege conferred on certain types of reports. Fair and accurate reports of proceedings in either House of Parliament are privileged in the absence of malice (*Cook* v. *Alexander* [1974] 1 Q.B. 279). Extracts from and abstracts of Parliamentary Papers, such as the Reports of

Select Committees have also a qualified privilege, but they must not be made into a story. If meat is put on their bones they lose all privilege (*Dingle* v. *Associated Newspapers Ltd.* [1962] 3 W.L.R. 229).

661. The Defamation Act 1952 confers qualified privilege on certain types of newspaper reports, a newspaper being defined as "any paper containing public news or observations thereon, or consisting wholly or mainly of advertisements, which is printed for sale and is published in the United Kingdom either periodically or in parts or numbers at *intervals not exceeding thirty-six days*." The Act also applies to broadcasts. The reports having qualified privilege (*i.e.* privilege unless the publication is proved to be with malice) are as follows:

(1) A fair and accurate report of any proceedings in public of the legislature of any part of Her Majesty's dominions outside Great Britain.

(2) A fair and accurate report of any proceedings in public of an international organisation of which the United Kingdom or Her Majesty's Government in the United Kingdom is a member, or of any international conference to which that government sends a representative.

(3) A fair and accurate report of any proceedings in public of an international court.

(4) A fair and accurate report of any proceedings before a court exercising jurisdiction throughout any part of Her Majesty's dominions outside the United Kingdom or of any proceedings before a court-martial held outside the United Kingdom under the Naval Discipline Act, the Army Act or the Air Force Act.

(5) A fair and accurate report of any proceedings in public of a body or person appointed to hold a public inquiry by the government or legislature of any part of Her Majesty's Dominions outside the United Kingdom.

(6) A fair and accurate copy of or extract from any register kept in pursuance of any Act of Parliament which is open to inspection by the public, or of any other document which is required by the law of any part of the United Kingdom to be open to inspection by the public.

(7) A notice or advertisement published by or on the authority of any court within the United Kingdom or any judge or officer of such a court.

662. The Defamation Act also provides that certain reports will have qualified privilege "subject to explanation or contradiction." Even if published without malice, these reports are not privileged if it is proved that the defender has been requested by the pursuer to publish a reasonable letter or statement by way of explanation or contradiction and has not done so or has done so "in a manner not adequate or not reasonable having regard to all the circumstances." These last words mean in practice that the letter or statement should be inserted in the same part of the newspaper as that in which the original report appeared. It should not be inserted in small type in a part less likely to be read by the general public. The reports having this lesser degree of qualified privilege are, to quote Part II of the Schedule to the Act:

(8) A fair and accurate report of the findings or decision of any of the following associations or of any committee or governing body thereof, that is to say—

(a) an association formed in the United Kingdom for the purpose of promoting or encouraging the exercise of or interest in any art, science, religion or learning, and empowered by its constitution to exercise control over or adjudicate upon matters of interest or concern to the association, or the actions or conduct of any persons subject to such control or adjudication;

(b) an association formed in the United Kingdom for the purpose of promoting or safeguarding the interests of any trade, business, industry or profession, or of the persons carrying on or engaged in any trade, business, industry or profession and empowered by its constitution to exercise control over or adjudicate upon matters connected with the trade, business, industry or profession or the actions or conduct of those persons;

(c) an association formed in the United Kingdom for the purpose of promoting or safeguarding the interests of any game, sport or pastime to the playing or exercise of which members of the public are invited or admitted, and empowered by its constitution to exercise control over or adjudicate upon persons connected with or taking part in the game, sport or pastime;

being a finding or decision relating to a person who is a member of or is subject by virtue of any contract to the control of the association.

(9) A fair and accurate report of the proceedings at any public meeting held in the United Kingdom, that is to say a meeting *bona fide* and lawfully held for a lawful purpose and for the fur-

therance or discussion of any matter of public concern, whether the admission to the meeting is general or restricted.

(10) A fair and accurate report of the proceedings at any meeting or sitting in any part of the United Kingdom of:

(*a*) any local authority or committee (including sub-committee) of a local authority or authorities;

(*b*) any justice or justices of the peace acting otherwise than as a court exercising judicial authority;

(*c*) any commission, tribunal, committee or person appointed for the purpose of any inquiry by Act of Parliament, by Her Majesty or by a Minister of the Crown;

(*d*) any person appointed by a local authority to hold a local inquiry in pursuance of any Act of Parliament;

(*e*) any other tribunal, board, committee or body constituted by or under, and exercising functions under an Act of Parliament, not being a meeting or sitting admission to which is denied to representatives of newspapers and other members of the public.

(11) A fair and accurate report of the proceedings at a general meeting of any company or association constituted, registered or certified by or under any Act of Parliament or incorporated by Royal Charter, not being a private company within the meaning of the Companies Act 1948.

(12) A copy or fair and accurate report or summary of any notice or other matter issued for the information of the public by or on behalf of any government department, office of state, local authority or chief officer of police.

663. These provisions are complicated but they should be read, digested and understood. They form part of the journalist's Magna Carta.

664. Paragraph (8) above covers among other things the various professional disciplinary bodies and church courts. Note that it applies only to reports of *findings and decisions* and not to reports of *proceedings*. It would seem, however, that reports of public proceedings of the professional disciplinary bodies mentioned earlier in this book will have qualified privilege subject to explanation or contradiction by virtue of paragraph (10)(*e*) above. They are all constituted and exercise functions under Acts of Parliament. Similarly, reports of proceedings at licensing boards would be protected by paragraph (10)(*e*) even if not already protected by the common law privilege attaching to reports of judicial proceedings.

665. The definition of a public meeting in paragraph (9) may cause difficulty. The mere fact that admission is restricted to those who buy a ticket does not prevent a meeting being a public meeting. But a meeting restricted to members of a particular group or sect will generally not be a public meeting. A church service has been held not to be a public meeting; so a report of a sermon would not be privileged.

666. The term "local authority" includes a regional, islands or district council or any body to which the Public Bodies (Admission to Meetings) Act 1960 applies. This Act is considered later (see para.778). It is to be noted that a report of a meeting of a *private company* is not privileged under paragraph (11).

667. There is one final provision of great importance in the Defamation Act. The statutory privilege conferred on the reports set out above does not extend to the publication of any matter which it is unlawful to publish or "*of any matter which is not of public concern and the publication of which is not for the public benefit*" (s.7(3)).

Unintentional defamation

668. As we have seen, a person can recover damages for defamation even if the statement complained of was not intended to refer to him or was not intended to be defamatory. This has given rise to some hard cases.

669. In *Morrison* v. *Ritchie* (1902) 4 F. 645, *The Scotsman* printed "birth notices" in August saying that Mrs. Morrison had given birth to twins. This statement was false but was printed by the newspaper in good faith. It had no way of knowing that Mrs. Morrison had been married for only a month. The cruel joker who inserted the notice could not be traced and an action was raised against the proprietors of *The Scotsman*. They maintained that they were not liable because the notices sent to them for publication were not defamatory on their face and they had no reason to suppose that they concealed a libel. The court rejected this defence. The defenders could not escape liability by saying that the slander was unintentional.

670. The famous case of *Hulton* v. *Jones* [1910] A.C. 20, illustrates another type of unintentional defamation. The *Sunday Chronicle* published an article describing recent motor races at Dieppe. The article contained this passage: " 'There is Artemus Jones with a woman who is not his wife. Who must be—you know—the other thing!' whispered a fair neighbour of mine excitedly into her bosom-friend's ear.

671. "Really, is it not surprising how certain of our fellow countrymen behave when they come abroad? Who would suppose, by his goings-on, that he was a churchwarden at Peckham? No one, indeed, would assume that Jones in the atmosphere of London would have taken on so austere a job as the duties of a churchwarden. Here, in the atmosphere of Dieppe, he is the life and soul of a gay little band that haunts the Casino and turns night into day, besides betraying a most unholy delight in the society of female butterflies."

672. Artemus Jones was a product of the writer's imagination. He thought that nobody could have such a name. Unfortunately for his paper, he was wrong. There was a barrister known as Artemus Jones who read the article, brought a libel action and recovered £1750 damages. This was in spite of the fact that he had no connection with Peckham and was not a churchwarden.

673. In other cases of unintentional defamation, statements referring truthfully to one existing person were held to be defamatory of another existing person. As a result of all these cases, the law placed writers and journalists in an intolerable position and encouraged "gold digging" actions. Section 4 of the Defamation Act of 1952 was intended to alleviate injustice in the case of innocent publication. Its provisions are, however, limited and it is doubtful if it has achieved its aims.

674. To establish that words were published innocently the publisher must prove (a) that he did not intend them to refer to the person complaining and did not know of circumstances by virtue of which they might be understood to refer to him or (b) that the words were not defamatory on their face, and that he did not know of circumstances by virtue of which they might be understood to be defamatory of the person complaining. The publisher must also prove in all cases that he exercised reasonable care in relation to the publication and, where he is not the author, that the words were written by the author without malice.

675. If the publisher can satisfy these conditions, he can escape liability by making an "offer of amends," under the Act. This means an offer to publish a correction and apology and where documents or records containing the words complained of have been distributed, to take reasonable steps to notify the recipients that the words are alleged to be defamatory of the person concerned. There are technical rules as to the form of the offer. These are the concern of the lawyer and as the offer must be made as soon as practicable, it is important that he should be informed as soon as it is known that the words give rise to complaint.

676. The effect of these provisions is that if a case like Artemus Jones's arose today the newspaper could escape liability by making an offer of amends under the statute. The position is not so clear with regard to the birth notices case. The newspaper might find it difficult to prove that it had exercised all reasonable care and impossible to prove that the words were written by the author without malice.

Lapse of time

677. Under the Prescription and Limitation (Scotland) Act 1973, as amended in 1985, no action for defamation may be brought unless it is begun within three years from the date when the publication or communication first came to the notice of the pursuer. The court has, however, power to extend this period if it seems to it equitable to do so.

Other defences

678. There are several defences which are applicable to other actions as well as to defamation but these are the concern of the lawyer rather than the journalist. They include a plea that the question has already been decided in a previous action between the same parties, and a plea that the pursuer consented to publication of the words complained of.

CHAPTER 17

DAMAGES

679. Having considered defences to an action for defamation, we now turn to the position where there is no defence. Here there will be either a settlement or an award of damages. The question of settlement will usually be in the hands of the newspaper's legal advisers but prompt action by the journalist or editor in publishing an apology may facilitate their task.

680. Scots law, as we have seen (para. 616), allows damages for injury to feelings alone. Substantial awards may thus be made even although the pursuer has suffered no financial loss. In theory, the question of damages is essentially one for the jury and only in exceptional cases will its award be set aside. In practice, however, most defamation actions are raised in the sheriff courts where there is no jury in this type of case. Even in the Court of Session the right to a jury in a defamation action is qualified by a discretion on the part of the Lord Ordinary to take a proof without a jury if special cause is shown and, in fact, jury trials are now very rare in defamation cases. The judge, or the jury if there happens to be one, is entitled to take various circumstances into consideration, including certain conduct of the defender in relation to the defamation complained of. It is therefore in the power of the journalist to aggravate or mitigate damages.

Aggravation

681. The general rule is that anything which increases the loss or injury to the pursuer will aggravate damages. In *Stein* v. *Beaverbrook Newspapers Ltd.*, 1968 S.L.T. 401 it was held that if a libel were actuated by malice, this fact would not by itself entitle a pursuer to greater damages. The court stressed that damages are intended to compensate the pursuer, not punish the defender (*cf. Cunningham* v. *Duncan & Jamieson* (1889) 16 R. 383, 388; *Fielding* v. *Variety Inc.* [1967] 2 Q.B. 841, 851).

682. Persistence in, or repetition of, a defamatory allegation, will aggravate damages. If a defamation in one edition comes to light immediate steps should be taken to ensure that it is expunged from later editions.

683. The extent of publication is a relevant factor in assessing damages and a pursuer can bring evidence of a newspaper's circulation in order to aggravate damages. Boasts about big circulations may backfire.

Mitigation

684. A prompt apology or explanation will tend to mitigate damages (*Morrison* v. *Ritchie* (1902) 4 F. 645). It was formerly thought that evidence of the defender's innocence or good faith in publishing the statement would also be admissible to mitigate damages (*Cunningham* v. *Duncan & Jamieson* (1889) 16 R. 383, 387, 390), but the case of *Stein* (*supra*) throws doubt on this view and suggests that the defender's lack of fault will be relevant to damages only if and in so far as it affects the extent of the pursuer's injury.

685. It will, however, be competent to lead evidence of the pursuer's bad reputation in mitigation of damages on the theory that if the pursuer has a bad reputation already, the defamation makes little difference. Evidence of this sort must probably be limited to the particular aspect of character involved in the defamation. Where a woman was said to have had an illegitimate child it was held to be relevant to prove in mitigation of damages that she was well known in the neighbourhood as a person of loose and immoral character. Proof of specific acts of adultery was, however, not allowed. As Lord President Clyde said, "The point of such a defence is not that she *is* a bad character, but that she *has* a bad character" (*C.* v. *M.*, 1923 S.C. 1).

686. The Defamation Act 1952, s.12 provides that a defender may prove in mitigation of damages that the pursuer has already recovered damages or raised an action or settled or agreed to settle in respect of publication of words similar to those on which the action is founded. This is clearly of great importance for newspapers. It discourages "gold digging" actions against a series of papers in respect of one defamatory allegation.

Interdict

687. Instead of seeking damages the person complaining of defamation may seek an interdict or interim interdict to prevent publication of the defamatory matter. These are perfectly competent remedies in relation to defamation. There is no absolute "right of unrestrained publication" in Scots law (see *Boyd* v. *B.B.C.*, 1969 S.L.T. (Sh.Ct.) 17; *Waddell* v. *B.B.C.*, 1973 S.L.T. 246). Nevertheless in deciding whether the balance of convenience lies in favour of granting an interim interdict the court will take into account the fact that the pursuer has the right to seek damages for defamation in a later action and that to this extent any harm resulting from the publication would not be irreparable (*Waddell* v. *B.B.C., supra*).

CHAPTER 18

LETTERS, ARTICLES AND ADVERTISEMENTS

688. A defamation can be contained in any part of a newspaper. It can lurk in a news item or editorial or it can be blazoned forth in a headline or even on a bill board. In these last two cases, however, the words in the headline or on the poster are regarded as simply drawing attention to a specific article and they will not usually be held to be defamatory if not so when read fairly along with the article (*Leon* v. *Edinburgh Evening News*, 1909 S.C. 1014; *Archer* v. *Ritchie & Co.* (1891) 18 R. 719). It is clear and just that a newspaper should be responsible for material produced in its own offices. It may seem less clear and less just that it should be responsible for material such as letters, articles or advertisements contributed by outsiders. This chapter deals with these matters. It is largely an application of the principles already explained.

Letters to the editor

689. A newspaper is liable for a defamation contained in letters to the editor and the person defamed can sue both it and the writer. In the case of a hidden libel, the newspaper may well be able to rely on the defence of innocent publication and an offer of amends but as we have seen it must be able to prove that the words were not written with malice.

690. Anonymous letters give rise to further difficulties. The general rule is that a paper will not be forced to disclose the name of the writer but this is a rule of practice not of law, and if the court orders disclosure, the newspaper must comply. Disclosure has been ordered when the pursuer alleged that a series of letters to the editor were in fact written by the newspaper itself as part of a systematic plan to ruin his reputation (*Cunningham* v. *Duncan & Jamieson* (1889) 16 R. 383), and a disclosure has also been ordered when a newspaper put forward a defence which the pursuer could only meet by finding out the names of the writers of the letters in question (*Ogston & Tennant* v. *Daily Record, Glasgow*, 1909 S.C. 1000). While the courts are unwilling to compel disclosure there are strong reasons why a newspaper should reveal the names of contributors of defamatory articles. If it does not, it may find itself cut off from a number of important defences.

691. It may, for example, lose the defence of qualified privilege. If the name of the writer is not disclosed it cannot be known whether he had a duty to make the statement complained of or whether he was actuated by malice (*Brims* v. *Reid* (1885) 12 R. 1016; *McKerchar* v. *Cameron* (1892) 19 R. 383); contrast *Egger* v. *Viscount Chelmsford* [1965] 1 Q.B. 248).

692. Although the law on the point is neither clear nor entirely satisfactory it seems that a newspaper may also in some circumstances lose the defence of fair comment if it will not or cannot disclose the name of the writer of a letter. This has been discussed in the previous chapter. And a newspaper will probably be cut off from the defence of innocent publication and an offer of amends if it does not disclose the author's name. It would obviously be very difficult or impossible in this case to supply the necessary proof that the words complained of were written without malice.

693. To sum up, the newspaper is in a much stronger position if it can reveal the name of the writer of letters appearing anonymously in its columns but it will not normally be compelled to make a disclosure.

694. Forged letters are a particularly insidious danger as so little can be done to guard against them. In 1963 the editor and proprietors of the *Daily Express* were sued for libel by the Orchestral Director of the Royal Opera House. The letter was a forgery. The defendants admitted that it was defamatory in that it suggested that the plaintiff was disloyal to his employers. They published a full explanation and apology, paid an agreed sum in damages and indemnified the plaintiff against his legal costs (*Smith* v. *Wood & Another, The Times*, April 10, 1963).

695. Exactly the same considerations apply to articles contributed by a correspondent and published anonymously.

Advertisements

696. In the case of advertisements and notices of births, marriages and deaths, the newspaper will again be in a weak position if it cannot disclose the name of the contributor and the rules discussed above apply. As advertisements are not usually associated with defamation it may be of value to mention two cases where they did lead to litigation.

697. In the first case a newspaper published an advertisement which read:

> "A criminal information for conspiracy to defraud is being prepared *re* the estate of B. Malyon (deceased) 74 Argyle Street. All persons having made payments at the above address since Sep-

tember . . . should send immediate information to T.Bernstein, private detective, 84 St. John Street.''

698.   The pursuer was B. Malyon's trustee and executor and had succeeded to his business which he carried on at 74 Argyle Street. He was allowed to bring an action against the newspaper as well as the private detective on the ground that the advertisement represented that he had been engaged in a fraudulent conspiracy in regard to B. Malyon's estate (*McLean* v. *Bernstein & Others* (1900) 8 S.L.T. 42).

699.   In the second case a herbalist inserted an advertisement in a newspaper disclaiming any connection with another herbalist's business and stating that he would not be responsible for any medicines sold at its address "or by any so-called herbalist." The pursuer was the herbalist at the address mentioned, and raised an action against the newspaper, claiming that the advertisement represented that her medicines were dangerous, that she was not a competent herbalist and that she falsely represented herself to be a herbalist. Her action was dismissed on the ground that the advertisement would not reasonably bear this meaning in the circumstances of the case (*Thompson* v. *Fifeshire Advertiser*, 1936 S.N. 56).

700.   Advertisements are sometimes seen which state that somebody will no longer be responsible for another's debts or which warn the public against imitation goods. Such advertisements can be dangerous (see, *e.g. Grainger* v. *Stirling* (1898) 5 S.L.T. 272; *Webster* v. *Paterson & Sons*, 1910 S.C. 459) and should be accepted with caution. Care should be taken to ensure that they are genuine and phrased so as to avoid unnecessary aspersions. In the second type of case, for example, statements which would identify particular traders should be excluded.

CHAPTER 19

ACTIONABLE NON-DEFAMATORY STATEMENTS

701. We have been considering statements which are defamatory. There are cases, however, where a person may be liable for statements which are not defamatory, in that they do not disparage a man's reputation, solvency or capacity but which nevertheless cause loss or injury. The term "verbal injury" is sometimes used to describe this type of statement but as it is used in a number of different senses it is a term which is better avoided.

702. One type of statement which has been held to be actionable is a statement holding someone up to public hatred and contempt, as by ascribing to him the expression of unpopular sentiments or the doing of unpopular acts, even although no imputation of dishonourable or immoral conduct is involved. One wartime case, for example, concerned allegations that a man had scoffed at the soldiers at the front and said that they had an easy time (*Andrew* v. *Macara*, 1917 S.C. 247; see also *Paterson* v. *Welsh* (1893) 20 R. 744). In this type of action the pursuer must prove that the statement was false (which is presumed in defamation proper), that it was made with the intention of injuring him and that it did in fact injure him by holding him up to public hatred and contempt (*Steele* v. *Scottish Daily Record and Sunday Mail Ltd.*, 1970 S.L.T. 53).

703. Another type of actionable but non-defamatory statement is that known as slander of property. If a newspaper, for example, says that a man's houses rest on insecure foundations it may not be casting aspersions on his character or solvency but it will be causing him damage if he hopes to sell (*Bruce* v. *Smith* (1898) 1 F. 327). Similar considerations apply to the type of statement known as slander of title. Here the words falsely state or suggest that the pursuer has no title, or a defective title, to his property. It is easy to imagine yet other types of false but non-defamatory statement about a person which might cause him pecuniary damage. To say that a man has gone out of business, for example, is not by itself defamatory but may cause him to lose custom (*cf. Craig* v. *Inveresk Paper Merchants Ltd.*, 1970 S.L.T. (Notes) 50). Similarly, to say that typhoid has broken out in a dairy is not necessarily defamatory but may cause ruin to the dairyman (*cf. McLean* v. *Adam* (1888) 16 R. 175). In general, statements of the kind mentioned

202

in this paragraph will be actionable if (a) they are false (the burden being on the pursuer to prove this), (b) they are made with malice or intention to injure and (c) they caused, or were calculated to cause (Defamation Act 1952, s.14), pecuniary damage to the pursuer.

704. Attempts have been made by some eminent authors (see Walker, *Delict*, pp. 736–740 (1981); Smith, *A Short Commentary on the Law of Scotland*, p. 733 (1962); the Hon. Lord Kilbrandon, "The Law of Privacy in Scotland," (1971) 2 Cambrian Law Review 39) and in a few court cases (*obiter dicta* in *Murray* v. *Beaverbrook Newspapers*, unreported, June 18, 1957 (referred to in Smith, *loc. cit. supra*); *Steele* v. *Scottish Daily Record and Sunday Mail Ltd.*, 1970 S.L.T. 53 (at sheriff court stage)) to revive the ancient doctrine of *convicium*. The essence of *convicium* is deliberate injury to a person's feelings by hurtful words. The words need not be defamatory and, on one view, it does not matter whether they are true or false. *Veritas* is no defence. Borthwick, writing in 1826, stated that "Our law holds that one may be sensibly hurt in his feelings, or in his fortune, by reproachful imputations, by sarcastical nicknames and epithets, and even by taunting allusions to the deformity of his person, or other natural defects, when these are accompanied by any ill-natured expression that may place him in a ridiculous light. All such disparagement, though it may have no effect in blackening a man's moral character, is, by our law, accounted injurious and actionable" (Borthwick, *Law of Libel and Slander in Scotland* (1826)). There are similar statements in other writers of the same period. It must be remembered, however, that the law of defamation was then in an under-developed state. As late as 1859 it was still being argued, for example, that *veritas* was not a defence to defamation (*Mackellar* v. *Duke of Sutherland* (1859) 21 D. 222). In fact, *convicium* was largely forgotten from the mid-19th to the mid-20th centuries. Instead, the law on the type of actionable non-defamatory statement referred to in paragraph 702 was developed in a whole series of cases without any mention of the word *convicium* and with the clear recognition that the pursuer had to prove falsehood. Nevertheless Professor Walker has submitted that an action of damages for *convicium* still lies "where the defender has (a) maliciously, (b) communicated of and concerning the pursuer an idea, which may be either true or false (the falsity not being an essential of the action and the truth no defence), (c) calculated to bring him into public hatred, contempt or ridicule, and has thereby caused him loss, injury or damage. The requisite malice . . . may be inferred from the idea communicated and the circumstances, and no proof of express or

203

actual malice (malevolence, spite or ill will) need be adduced" (*Delict*, p. 738; but see *McLaughlan* v. *Orr, Pollock & Co.* (1894) 22 R. 38). Fortunately for satirical magazines and children in school playgrounds there is little modern authority on *convicium* and it can hardly be regarded as a flourishing branch of the law. It is to be hoped that it will not be resuscitated. If truth is a defence, *convicium* adds little to the law on holding people up to public hatred and contempt (see para. 702 above; this branch of the law rests on a solid foundation of Inner House cases, however doubtful its origins), except the possibility of an action based on making someone look merely ridiculous, which does not in itself seem a desirable development. If truth is not a defence, a reactivated law of *convicium* would place horrifying restrictions on the freedom to tell the truth.

705. So far we have been talking of statements made *about* a person or his property. Statements made *to* a person may also be actionable if they are deliberately or negligently misleading and cause loss. Deliberately false statements causing loss would usually amount to fraud and need not concern us further. Negligently false statements are of more importance in journalism. Many newspapers have financial columns which give information about various companies and offer advice to investors. Carelessness in the preparation of these columns obviously cannot be ruled out of account. A simple misprint could result in a representation that an unsound company was perfectly sound. An error in reading a company's accounts could result in a completely misleading report. The consequences of such slips could be serious. Although the law on this point is in a state of flux, it seems probable that if a newspaper negligently gives false information or misleading advice which results in a loss to the reader relying on it, it will be liable to the reader in damages. Until the case of *Hedley Byrne & Co. Ltd.* v. *Heller & Partners Ltd.* [1964] A.C. 465 it was generally thought that no action would lie in such circumstances unless the reader could prove that he had a contract with the newspaper. This was sometimes possible. In one English case (*De La Bere* v. *Pearson Ltd.* [1908] 1 K.B. 280) a newspaper had advertised that it would deal with readers' investment queries. A reader asked for the name of a reliable stockbroker in his district and the newspaper negligently gave him the name of an unreliable, and bankrupt, stockbroker. The reader suffered loss as a result and sued the newspaper for damages. He succeeded on the ground that there was a contract between him and the newspaper, his agreement being that his query could be published and the newspaper's being that they would answer it. The spelling out of such contracts was a slightly artificial process, which was possible only where there had been some form of communication between the reader and the newspaper. There was no *general* liability on newspapers, or anybody else, for loss caused by negligent misrepresentations. The position has now changed. In the *Hedley Byrne* case (*supra*) the House of Lords held that in certain circumstances there would be a general liability for such loss, quite apart from contract. It is not entirely clear, however, what circumstances will give rise to the liability. To assess the newspaper's position in these legal quicksands necessitates a close consideration of the opinions handed down by the House of Lords. It may be noted first that *Hedley Byrne* was an English case, but Scottish cases were cited and considered in it and the principles laid down were in accordance with much legal opinion in Scotland. It has since been cited in Scottish courts and will undoubtedly be regarded as a highly persuasive authority. The facts in *Hedley Byrne* were as follows. The plaintiffs were advertising agents. They were concluding advertising contracts for a company on terms which made them personally liable. To check that the company could reimburse them they asked their bankers to find out if the company was financially sound. Their bankers asked the company's bankers and the company's bankers gave favourable reports but expressly said that these were given "without responsibility." It turned out that the company was not financially sound and the plaintiffs lost a great deal of money. They claimed damages from the company's bankers for the loss caused by their negligent misrepresentation. The House of Lords held that in this case the bankers had disclaimed responsibility and were accordingly not liable. However, the importance of the case lies as much in the statements of general principle as in the actual decision. Lord Reid said (at page 486) that there would be liability for negligent statements "where it is plain that the party seeking information or advice was trusting the other to exercise such a degree of care as the circumstances required, where it was reasonable for him to do that, and where the other gave the information or advice when he knew or ought to have known that the inquirer was relying on him." Lord Morris of Borth-y-Gest stated the principle more widely and in his statement Lord Hodson concurred. "It should now be regarded as settled," he said (at page 502), "that if someone possessed of a special skill undertakes, quite irrespective of contract, to apply that skill for the assistance of another person who relies upon such skill, a duty of care will arise. The fact that the service is given by means of or by the instrumentality of words can make no difference. Furthermore, if in a sphere in which a person is so placed that others

205

could reasonably rely upon his judgment or his skill or upon his ability to make careful inquiry, a person takes it upon himself to give information or advice to, or allows his information or advice to be passed on to, another person who, as he knows or should know, will place reliance on it, then a duty of care will arise." It need hardly be pointed out that a breach of this duty of care which caused loss would give rise to a claim for damages. Lord Devlin had the Press expressly in mind. After referring to the case of the newspaper which recommended the bankrupt stockbroker, (above), he said that such cases would now normally be decided on broad principles of negligence and not on contract. It seems to be an irresistible conclusion that the newspaper which tenders advice or information in response to readers' queries on any matter, financial or otherwise, will be liable for loss caused by reliance on negligent misrepresentations in its answers. The position in relation to statements not made in response to readers' queries is more obscure but it seems probable that even this sort of statement would fall within the *Hedley Byrne* principle if it purported to be the product of special skill, or judgment or ability to make careful inquiry and if it were the sort of statement on which readers might reasonably be expected to rely. The practical motto may well be to insert, in a suitable place, a short sentence like "No responsibility is accepted for advice or information given in these columns." As we have seen, such a disclaimer of responsibility was sufficient to protect the defendants in the *Hedley Byrne* case from a substantial claim for damages.

CHAPTER 20

DIFFERENCES IN ENGLISH LAW

706. The broad principles of the law of defamation are the same in England as in Scotland but there are several differences on particular points. The more important of these will now be briefly considered.

Distinction between libel and slander

707. Roughly speaking a defamation which is written, or expressed in permanent form is a libel in English law, while a defamation which is spoken or communicated in some other transitory form is slander. Under the Defamation Act 1952, however, a statement which is broadcast by wireless telegraphy is treated as libel.

708. The importance of the distinction is that, with some exceptions, no action will lie for slander unless the plaintiff proves that the words complained of have caused him actual pecuniary damage. The exceptional cases where an action for slander will be allowed without such proof are those involving imputations (a) of a crime punishable by death or imprisonment, (b) of having a contagious or infectious disease, (c) of unchastity in a woman or (d) calculated to disparage the plaintiff in any office, profession, calling, trade or business held or carried on by him at the time of publication.

Criminal libel

709. In English law, libel is a crime punishable by fine or imprisonment as well as a civil wrong giving rise to a claim for damages. A criminal prosecution is rare, however, and tends to be discouraged if the civil remedy is available. It should be noted that while in England there must be publication to a third party before a civil action will lie, this does not apply to a criminal prosecution. It can be brought if the statement has been made to the defamed person alone and is of a type calculated to provoke a breach of the peace.

Defences

710. Justification is the English term for *veritas*. The same principles apply as in Scotland.

711. As we saw, only contemporaneous reports of judicial proceedings have absolute privilege in English law. Non-contemporaneous reports, however, have qualified privilege provided they are fair and accurate. Reports of foreign proceedings (not coming under the Defamation Act) do not even have qualified privilege under English law unless they are of legitimate interest to the British public.

712. In England a litigant has absolute privilege with regard to statements he makes in written pleadings or instructs his counsel to make in court. In Scotland he has only qualified privilege (*M*. v. *H*., 1908 S.C. 1130).

713. Formerly the period within which an action for defamation had to be brought was six years in England. It is now three years.

Injurious falsehoods

714. The statements referred to in Chapter 19 as actionable non-defamatory statements are generally known in English law as injurious falsehoods. Before 1952 the plaintiff had to prove falsity, malice and actual financial damage in each case. Since the Defamation Act of that year he need not prove actual financial damage in many cases where the words are calculated to cause him financial damage.

Frequency of actions

715. Defamation cases are comparatively rare in Scotland but common in England. So it is now, was and apparently ever has been. Stair, writing in 1681, said "Such actions upon injurious words . . . are frequent and curious among the English: but with us there is little of it accustomed to be pursued" (I.9.4.).

Part IV

COPYRIGHT

CHAPTER 21

NATURE AND DURATION

716. The law of copyright is the same throughout the United Kingdom. It is a big subject and we can deal only with particular aspects of it here. We shall confine ourselves to United Kingdom law but it should be noted that under various international agreements many foreign works are protected in this country and British works are protected in many foreign countries. Britain has entered into such agreements with most countries except China and Russia. To obtain protection in some foreign countries such as the U.S.A. a work must have marked on it the symbol © along with the date of first publication and the name of the first copyright owner.

717. We shall also confine ourselves to those aspects of copyright law which primarily concern the journalist, that is, copyright in words, photographs and drawings, but copyright, of course, is of much wider scope and covers such things as films, ballets, sculptures, architectural works, music, gramophone records and radio and television broadcasts.

718. It also covers photocopies of text of which the original is protected by copyright. The increasing use of photocopying machines calls for the exercise of caution by journalists to ensure that the matter they copy is not so protected. No problem need arise in the copying for publication, for example, of judgments of the courts or official reports of Press notices issued for publication; but it may be necessary sometimes to exclude from a photocopy original interpretative work such as the rubric (descriptive heading or summary) preceding the actual text of a judgment. Even a public document such as a judgment which has been condensed to form a report in a book or journal may be protected by copyright since it is the product of skill and work other than that of the judge who wrote the original. Similarly, an article quoting passages from a judgment but also explaining its effect or meaning is entitled to protection. But these observations are subject to the time-limit rule explained later.

719. The present law alone is set out. This depends on the Copyright Act of 1956. In rare cases different rules may apply to works made before 1956 but in practice such cases are not likely to be of frequent occurrence. Within these limits we shall consider the nature and duration of copyright, the general rules as to ownership of copyright, the journalist's rights in his own work and finally infringement or his general lack of rights in other people's work.

720. The idea behind copyright is that a man should be able to enjoy the fruits of his own original work, secure in the knowledge that it will not be pirated by others. Copyright is thus in essence a right to prevent copying. It does not give a monopoly. If two men by some remarkable coincidence write two identical books and it can be proved that they were in fact completely independent, the one who gets into print first could not prevent the other from publishing his book. There would be no copying.

721. It is a man's work that is protected, not his ideas (*Harpers* v. *Barry Henry & Co.* (1892) 20 R. 133 at 142). This is an important distinction. Whatever may be the ethical considerations involved it is no infringement of copyright to lift the idea of another man's story and use it in a story of your own expressed in your own words.

722. Copyright protects only original works but here again it is the form rather than the content which is important. The ideas need not be original provided the form in which they appear is. And this form will be original if it involves the use of some independent knowledge, skill, judgment or labour. Thus there can be copyright in a mere compilation such as a list of football fixtures or Stock Exchange prices if skill was required in the selection or arrangement. On the same principle there can be copyright in *verbatim* newspaper reports of public speeches. Neither the ideas nor the way of expressing them would be commonly regarded as the original work of the reporter but nevertheless the conversion of the spoken word into a written report involves the use of independent skill and labour on his part and the report is regarded as an original work for copyright purposes. If, however, the speaker hands the reporter a written copy of his speech and this is published *verbatim* by the newspaper then there would be no separate copyright in the report. There would be no conversion of the spoken to the written word and no exercise of independent skill or labour.

723. Another example will help to bring out the meaning of "originality" in copyright law. A translation is an "original" work for copyright purposes. The ideas and their arrangement are not original in the ordinary sense but the translation does involve independent knowledge and hard work on the part of the translator. It is therefore protected.

724. The type of copyright which is of most importance for journalists is that subsisting in "literary works." This term is much wider than might be thought. It certainly does not mean that a work must have literary merit in order to be protected. The Copyright Act of 1956 makes this clear by including in the definition of literary work "any written table or compilation." An examination paper has been held to be a literary work for copyright purposes, the judge remarking, "In my view, the words, 'literary work' cover work which is expressed in print or writing irrespective of the question whether the quality or style is high. The word 'literary' seems to be used in a sense somewhat similar to the use of the word 'literature' in political or electioneering literature, and refers to written or printed matter." (*University of London Press Ltd.* v. *University Tutorial Press Ltd.* [1916] 2 Ch. 601 at 608).

725. In the case of "artistic works" too, paintings, drawings, engravings and photographs are protected irrespective of artistic quality. A tie-on business label has been held to be an artistic work for copyright purposes (*Walker* v. *British Picker Co.* [1961] R.P.C. 57).

726. It is clear that a "work" need not be very substantial, but a line must be drawn somewhere and in some instances protection has been refused on the ground that there was no "work." Advertising slogans consisting of a few words have been refused protection on this ground.

727. It is probably for the same reason that titles of newspapers, books and periodicals are denied copyright. An established newspaper can, however, prevent another paper being sold under the same or a similar title by means of an action for "passing-off." It must be proved that the other paper is so similar that it would be likely to deceive the public. The owners of the magazine *Punch* failed for this reason to prevent the publication of a much cheaper magazine called *Punch and Judy*. "Could anyone," asked the judge, "be misled into buying this other paper instead, which has the words 'Punch and Judy' printed on it in distinct letters with a different frontispiece, and its price a penny? I am clearly of opinion that the mass of mankind would not be so misled." (*per* Malins V.C. in *Bradbury* v. *Beeton* (1896) 18 W.R. 33; see also the old Scottish case of the *Edinburgh Correspondent Newspaper* (1822) 1 S. (N.E.) 407n.).

728. The same considerations apply to a *nom de plume*. There is no copyright, but if the name has become well known the author can bring a passing-off action to prevent its use in ways likely to deceive the public.

729. There can be more than one copyright in a particular work. Thus in the case of a newspaper, contributors may own the copyright in various articles but the newspaper will have a copyright in their lay-out on the page. Again advertisers or their agents will usually have the copyright in particular advertisements but the newspaper may have a copyright in their arrangement.

730. To sum up what has been said so far, copyright is a right to prevent copying, not a monopoly. It protects works, not ideas; form, not content. The works must be original, but need not be very original. In most cases, originality means the use of some independent skill, knowledge or labour. Merit is usually unimportant. Works can be small, but not too small. If, like newspaper titles, they are too small, they may nevertheless be protected by the law of passing-off. There can be more than one copyright in a particular work.

731. Copyright in a work comes into existence automatically with the work. There is no need for registration or other formalities. It lasts for a very long time. In the case of literary works, copyright normally lasts during the author's lifetime and for fifty years after the end of the year in which he dies. If, however, the work has not been published or otherwise exploited during the author's lifetime, there is an even longer period of protection—for fifty years after the end of the year of first publication or exploitation.

732. Copyright in artistic works is of the same duration, but special rules apply to photographs. In their case copyright continues for fifty years from the end of the year in which they are first published. This gives unpublished photographs a perpetual copyright. Publication means the issue of reproductions to the public, and not merely, for example, display of the original at an exhibition.

733. After the expiry of copyright the work becomes public property and can be freely copied.

CHAPTER 22

OWNERSHIP

734. Generally speaking the author of a work is the first owner of the copyright in it. This gave rise to difficulty in a famous case where the true author was alleged to be a spirit who had been dead for many hundreds of years and who communicated with this world through a medium. The messages were translated by the medium into suitably archaic language and the judge was thus able to hold that she had a translator's copyright in the work. He said, "I am not impugning the honesty of persons who believe and of the parties to this action who say that they believe, that this long departed being is the true source from which the contents of these documents emanate: but I think I have stated enough with regard to the antiquity of the source and the language in which the communications are written to indicate that they could not have reached us in this form without the active co-operation of some agent competent to translate them from the language in which they were communicated to her into something more intelligible to persons of the present day" (*Cummins* v. *Bond* [1927] Ch. 167).

735. Difficulties of a more terrestrial kind may arise as to the authorship of a work. If X sends an account of an incident to a newspaper and the editor alters it, who is the author of the published report? The answer will depend on the extent of the alterations. If they are slight, X will be the author; if they are more substantial, X and the editor may be joint authors; and if they are very substantial, the editor may be the sole author (see *Springfield* v. *Thame* (1903) 89 L.T. 242).

736. The author of a photograph is the person who is at the time when the photograph is taken, the owner of the material on which it is taken. Do not take your best photographs on borrowed film.

Commissioned photographs, portraits or engravings

737. Where a photograph, portrait or engraving is commissioned by someone who pays or agrees to pay for it then, in the absence of agreement to the contrary, the copyright belongs to the person who gives the commission. This gives rise to an interesting question with regard to occasions like weddings where a photographer is invited to come and take pictures but there is no payment or agreement to pay, the understanding being simply that the photographer will make his profit by

213

selling what he can. Who owns the copyright in such wedding photographs? Is a newspaper infringing copyright if it publishes pictures sent in by the photographer?

738. The answer will depend on the terms of the photographer's agreement. In the usual case, where there is no payment or agreement to pay, he will own the copyright. Even if he does not, the agreement may make provision for the sending of photographs to the Press. But newspapers can never be entirely sure of the position. Fortunately, few people object to publication of their wedding photographs in the normal way.

739. An exceptional case where a man did object, understandably, to the publication of his wedding photograph was *Williams* v. *Settle* in 1960 ([1960] 2 All E.R. 806). The plaintiff's father-in-law was found murdered. Two national newspapers procured from the photographer concerned, and published, a photograph of a group at the plaintiff's wedding which included the murdered man. The plaintiff owned the copyright in the photograph in this case and recovered damages and costs from one newspaper and an apology and undertakings from the other. He also recovered substantial damages from the photographer.

Works made by employees, other than journalists

740. Where a work is made by the author in the course of his employment under a contract of service or apprenticeship, the copyright belongs to the employer. This rule is subject to an important qualification in the case of employees of newspapers, magazines and similar periodicals. Their position is discussed in the following paragraphs.

Special rules for journalists

741. A free-lance journalist, not working under a contract of service or apprenticeship, will own the copyright in his work. This will apply even if he is commissioned to write an article or series of articles. The rules on commissioned works considered above do not apply to literary works.

742. The journalist working for a paper "under a contract of service or apprenticeship" is in a different position. The copyright in work produced *in the course of his employment* for the purpose of publication in a newspaper, magazine or similar periodical will belong to his employer "*in so far as the copyright relates to publication of the work in any newspaper, magazine or similar periodical.*" In all other respects the journalist owns the copyright in his work. This means that he can publish it in book form or use it for broadcasting or making a film. These rules are laid down in s.4(2) of the Copyright Act 1956 which reads as follows:

"Where a literary, dramatic or artistic work is made by the author in the course of his employment by the proprietor of a newspaper, magazine or similar periodical under a contract of service or apprenticeship, and is so made for the purpose of publication in a newspaper, magazine or similar periodical, the said proprietor shall be entitled to the copyright in the work in so far as the copyright relates to publication of the work in any newspaper, magazine or similar periodical or to reproduction of the work for the purpose of its being so published; but in all other respects, the author shall be entitled to any copyright subsisting in the work . . . ."

These rules can, however, be varied by agreement. In practice, although not in law, they will often be varied by the custom within newspaper offices. Neither employers nor employees will necessarily always insist on their legal rights.

Assignees

743. So far we have been considering who is the first owner of copyright but copyright is assignable. It may be transferred by assignation ("assignment" in England) during life or may transmit to a deceased person's representatives by will or under the laws of intestate succession. This means that it is often very difficult to find out who is the owner of the copyright in a particular work.

744. Assignations of copyright must be in writing. They are to be distinguished from licences. An assignation actually transfers copyright: a licence merely gives permission to do something in spite of the copyright, which remains in the hands of the person granting the licence. An assignation of copyright can be limited in various ways. It might transfer the film rights alone, for example, or the copyright in one country but not in others.

CHAPTER 23

INFRINGEMENT

745. Copyright in a work will be infringed if the work is copied, without permission, or if certain other acts reserved by law for the copyright owner are done without permission. These other acts, in the type of work we are considering, include publishing, broadcasting or making an adaptation of the work. Adaptation for copyright purposes means conversion of a non-dramatic work into a dramatic work and vice versa, translation of a work or conversion into a strip-cartoon. It follows from this general rule that there is a clear case of infringement if an article is "lifted" verbatim from another magazine or newspaper. In practice, of course, there is a great deal of tolerance and give and take among newspapers in this respect but this does not affect the legal position. Judges have remarked that a plea of custom of copying is of no more legal effect than the highwayman's plea of the custom of Hounslow Heath (*Walker* v. *Steinkopff* [1892] 3 Ch. 489).

746. How much can be copied with impunity? The Copyright Act says it is an infringement to reproduce the work, or a substantial part of it, in a material form. It is impossible to lay down a hard and fast rule as to what is a substantial part. The answer will vary with the circumstances. The quality and value of the part reproduced are very important factors. A small but vital part of a book might be held substantial while a longer but less important part might not. Four lines of a short poem by Kipling were held to be substantial enough for the copyright in them to be infringed when they were reproduced in an advertisement.

747. We have seen that copyright protects works. It does not protect ideas or information or news. It is therefore not an infringement of copyright to write an article on the basis of news or information gleaned from another newspaper. This applies clearly if a story really is rewritten in a new form, but difficult questions arise where it bears obvious similarities to the original story, even if the actual arrangement of the words is different. Again it is a question of drawing a line and it will be drawn differently in different circumstances and probably by different judges. If the second story is so like the first that the average reader of both would think on reading it that he had seen the same thing before, then there would probably be infringement. If the stories are so different that he would feel he was reading something new then there would probably not be infringement.

748. Similar rules apply to parodies. In 1960 the *Sunday Pictorial* published an article about the Duke of Edinburgh. This contained the words of a song called "Rock-a-Philip" which was an admitted parody of a popular song called "Rock-a-Billy." The owners of the copyright in the latter song brought an action for infringement but it was held that the parody was produced by sufficient independent new work to be not a reproduction but an original work.

749. It is not, of course, an infringement of copyright for a newspaper to print and publish letters or manuscripts sent to the editor. The fact that the author sends them implies a licence to publish. An interesting legal situation arises when a letter or article is sent to a newspaper for publication. In the absence of agreement, the position is that the author retains the copyright and the newspaper gets the property in the actual paper on which the words are written and, in addition, implied permission to publish for the usual fee. It is doubtful how far, if at all, the newspaper has implied permission to alter the letter or article. The view of the English courts is that in the absence of express or implied prohibition it has the right, as licensee, to make alterations (*Frisby* v. *B.B.C.* [1967] 1 Ch. 932). Moreover, a prohibition of reasonable alteration is probably not to be implied in the case of ordinary letters and unsigned articles. In the case of signed articles, however, where the author's reputation is at stake, it will be much easier to imply a term prohibiting substantial alterations without the author's consent (*Joseph* v. *National Magazine Co.* [1958] 3 All E.R. 52).

Reporting current events

750. Fair dealing with a literary, dramatic or musical work for the purpose of reporting current events in a newspaper, magazine or similar periodical is not an infringement of copyright if it is accompanied by a sufficient acknowledgment. This involves giving the name of the work and, unless it is anonymous or the author has agreed otherwise, the name of the author.

751. The most interesting questions arise with regard to reports of speeches, lectures or addresses. If no notes have been made and the speech is completely extempore, the speaker will have no copyright in his words. There is no "work" to which copyright can attach. Copyright will come into existence only when the words are taken down by a reporter and it will belong either to the reporter or his employer. If, however, the speech or lecture is made from notes, the making of a verbatim report would probably infringe the author's copyright in his notes, unless he has given consent or the report comes within one of the exceptions we are now considering. Consent may be express— "Reporters can use this"—or it may be implied if, for example, reporters are specially invited to attend a meeting or handed copies of the speech. Even if there is no consent, the report will not be an infringement of copyright if it is fair dealing for the purpose of reporting current events. What amounts to fair dealing is again a question of circumstances. To publish a few excerpts from a speech or lecture would in most cases be fair but circumstances can be imagined where it would not. To publish, for example, the whole of an unpublished poem read by a famous poet in the course of a lecture would probably be going too far as it would prejudice his chances of enjoying the fruits of subsequent publication. For copyright purposes there is no distinction between a public and a private meeting but if admission to a private meeting is on condition that there will be no publication, the reporter will be in breach of contract if he ignores the condition. Publication may then be prevented for this reason, quite apart from copyright.

752. Fair dealing for the purpose of reporting current events in a broadcast or newsreel is also allowed. The position is similar to that outlined above but in this case there need be no acknowledgment.

Reporting judicial proceedings

753. The copyright in a literary, dramatic, musical or artistic work is not infringed by reproducing it for the purposes of a report of judicial proceedings.

Criticism or review

754. The Copyright Act provides that no fair dealing with a literary, dramatic, artistic or musical work shall constitute an infringement of the copyright in the work if it is for the purposes of criticism or review, whether of that work or of another work, and is accompanied by a sufficient acknowledgment. This is an important privilege. It means that a reviewer of a book, for example, can include excerpts from the book in his review. He can also include excerpts from other works for purposes such as comparison. But the use of excerpts must be fair. It will probably cease to be so if the excerpts are published not as a basis for comment but to enable the reader to enjoy the best parts of the book without buying it.

Photographs and drawings

755. It is not an infringement of copyright to make and publish a photograph, drawing or painting of a building, sculpture or similar work which is permanently placed in a public place or in premises open to the public. This exception will protect the tourist who photographs a city's statues.

Miscellaneous

756. There are various other exceptions to the general rules on infringement but they are not of direct concern to journalists. For example, fair dealing with a work for purposes of research or private study is not as a general rule an infringement of copyright and special provisions are made for certain uses by libraries and for educational purposes.

Remedies for infringement

757. The normal remedies for infringement are an interdict to prevent continuance or an award of damages. In particularly flagrant cases a "penal" element may be added to damages by way of punishment of the infringer. Certain dealings with infringing copies in the knowledge that they do infringe can be punished by fine.

Part V

THE PUBLIC AND THE PRIVATE

Chapter 24

THE PUBLIC

758. There has been much discussion on the rights and duties of the media with regard to the invasion of privacy. From the legal point of view the position is quite clear. With one or two minor exceptions such as the right of admission to children's hearings, the journalist is in exactly the same legal position as any other member of the public. He can go to public places and public meetings. He cannot go to private places and private meetings. In many cases, of course, reporters are given special privileges such as reserved seats and free admission but these are accorded at the discretion of those who grant them and can be withdrawn at will. Privileges of this nature are not to be confused with legal rights.

759. It is obviously important for the journalist to know what is public and what is private. Certain meetings must be held in public; certain places, such as streets and various open spaces in towns, are public places; certain places are private places to which the public are invited and most places are private places to which the public are not invited. We shall consider the law applicable in these various cases.

760. Meetings and proceedings which must be held in public include court proceedings and certain local government meetings. Surprisingly, perhaps, they do not include proceedings in Parliament.

Court proceedings

761. The general rule is that proceedings in a court of law must be in public, unless justice demands otherwise. The principal applications of and exceptions to this rule have been considered elsewhere (paras. 239–252).

Quasi-judicial proceedings

762. Most inquiries, tribunals and other quasi-judicial bodies must, as a general rule, meet in public but there are numerous exceptions.

These have been mentioned earlier when discussing the various bodies concerned (Part I, paras. 178–220).

Parliament

763. Both Houses of Parliament normally admit public and Press to their meetings but this is merely practice and there is no legal right of admission. Both Lords and Commons have full power to regulate their own procedure and can hold secret sessions when they deem it expedient. Many such sessions were held during the last war. It is a breach of parliamentary privilege to publish any report of, or purport to describe the proceedings at, a secret session.

764. The question of parliamentary privilege may be mentioned briefly here, although it is incidental to the main discussion. Each House has power to punish for breaches of privilege. These have been summarised as follows:

> "disrespect to any member of the House, as such, by a person not being a member; disrespect to the House collectively, whether committed by a member or any other; disobedience to the orders of the House or interference with its procedure, with its officers in the execution of their duty or with witnesses in respect of evidence given before the House or a Committee of the House" (Anson, *Law and Custom of Parliament*, 5th ed., vol. 1, p. 187).

765. Clearly, breach of privilege could be a real danger for newspapers. "Disrespect" is a word of wide meaning. And indeed a leading newspaperman has said that the law of parliamentary privilege curbs unduly the publication of certain matters which the public should know about. "With good reason the Press steers clear of any comment on the conduct of parliamentary business or such matters as sloppy attendance or incomprehensible behaviour during late-night sessions (Mr. Cecil King in the annual report of the General Council of the Press for 1962). It should not be thought, however, that the powers to punish for breach of privilege are exercised despotically. It is not the policy of Parliament to exact a punishment for every disrespectful remark made about a Member of Parliament. It recognises the need for the expression of opinion or criticism and its policy is to take proceedings chiefly in the case of statements tending to bring Parliament itself into disrespect or contempt.

766. Technically, to publish reports of debates in Parliament at all is a breach of privilege and in the eighteenth century attempts were actually made to punish those who infringed. These led to such a public

SCOTS LAW FOR JOURNALISTS

outcry that publication of reports has been allowed ever since. But false or perverted reports are regarded as punishable in practice as well as in theory.

767. To publish information derived from the reports of select committees before they have been laid before the House is a breach of privilege. The committee is reporting to the House in the first place and only indirectly to the public. To reveal the contents of a report before Members of Parliament have had a chance of reading it is thus undesirable and dangerous. The same does not apply to White Papers. They are addressed to the public in the first instance and, while the Government in practice communicates important matters to Parliament before publication, this is a matter of courtesy alone.

768. Complaints of breach of privilege are raised in the House by a member and are then usually referred to the Committee of Privileges for a report. The Commons can imprison an offender, although this is rare. The imprisonment can be during the pleasure of the House (*i.e.* for an indefinite period) but in this event the offender must be released at the end of the Session. The House of Lords can imprison for a fixed term or impose a fine. Normally an offender is merely admonished or reprimanded (see paras. 275–276).

769. An instructive example of breach of parliamentary privilege can be drawn from South Africa, although, of course, the legislature there is especially touchy on some matters. With reference to racial disturbances in the U.S.A. and South Africa the *Pretoria News* published a cartoon with the caption: "Yes there is a difference—in Mississippi the thugs are breaking the laws, in South Africa they are making them." The editor was summoned by the Speaker and required to apologise for a breach of privilege (*The Times*, June 4, 1963).

Local authorities

770. The Local Government (Access to Information) Act 1985 by s.2 gives the public and duly accredited reporters of newspapers (which include any organisation "systematically engaged in collecting news for radio or television or for cable programme service") certain rights to attend meetings of regional, district and islands councils and their committees and sub-committees, with certain prescribed exceptions. These rights do not, however, extend to the taking of photographs at meetings or the recording of proceedings for later communication to anyone not attending—the meeting retaining a discretion to decide whether to permit such activities.

771. Press and public may be excluded for either of two reasons—

that it is likely *confidential* information will be disclosed at the meeting or that the subject-matter of discussion is *exempt* from public access.

772. Confidential information is defined as that which has been furnished by a Government department on terms forbidding its disclosure or which is prohibited to be disclosed by any enactment or court order.

773. Exempt information is defined under a list of specific subjects, including such matters as adoption or fostering of particular children, financial affairs of named individuals, details of council contracts for acquisition or supply of goods or services, details of tenders for contracts and information about counsel's advice. The list also includes "any protected informant" which means any person giving the local authority information about a crime or offence. Exclusion of press and public on the ground of exemption can take place only where a resolution to that end has been passed identifying the particular subject on the list. The Act provides a right to challenge such a decision by application to the Court of Session for judicial review. The Secretary of State for Scotland has power to extend or curtail the exemption list.

774. A meeting has power to exclude anyone to suppress disorder or other misbehaviour.

775. Press and public have a right to see copies of agendas, reports and other papers relating to meetings (but not those relating to confidential or exempt items). Such papers must be supplied on request to the media and made open for public inspection for three days before a meeting, but if it has been called at short notice, from the time it is convened. The papers are to remain open for public inspection for six years after a meeting; but where confidential or exempt matters are concerned, an official of the local authority must provide instead a written summary indicating the nature of the matters considered in private without actually disclosing the confidential or exempt information. The authority is entitled to charge for the provision of these services and also for the supply of photocopies of extracts of documents.

776. Anything contained in any document supplied to the media which is defamatory is privileged under the Act unless published maliciously.

777. Parallel provisions for England and Wales are made by s.1 of the Act.

778. The Act leaves intact the rights of access by the media in Scotland to meetings authorised by earlier enactments. It does not, however, apply to community councils. Admission to certain other stipulated bodies is covered by the Public Bodies (Admission to Meetings) Act 1960, amended by s.44 of the Local Government (Scotland) Act 1973. The only bodies left in the 1960 Act so far as Scotland is concerned are health boards set up under the National Health Service (Scotland) Act 1972 (so far as their executive functions are concerned). Joint committees of two or more local authorities, and their subcommittees, are covered by the 1985 Act.

779. The Act does not cover Scotland's five new town authorities, but in November 1986 Glenrothes set a precedent by deciding to hold its monthly board meeting in public (though with certain confidential matters withheld from disclosure).

780. The Water Act 1983, which reorganised water authorities, withdrew the right of media representatives and members of the public to attend meetings of such authorities, provided instead for news conferences to be held following meetings and set up consumer consultative committees for the water industry, which are to meet in public.

Other public meetings

781. In the case of meetings held in public places the journalist has the same right to be present as any other member of the public—a right which may be limited by bye-laws as well as by the law on such matters as breach of the peace. He cannot be singled out for exclusion by the organisers of the meeting. He has, by hypothesis, as much right to be in a public place as they have.

782. In the case of meetings or other proceedings, such as most sports meetings, to which the public are invited but which are held on private property, the journalist's rights depend on the terms of the invitation. It is open to the organisers of such meetings to exclude the media. It is open to them to impose conditions on admittance, such as a prohibition of cameras. The whole question is really one of contract between those granting and those seeking admission. The terms of the contract may be express or implied. There may, for example, be an implied term that a person may be excluded if he does not behave in a proper manner. The Court of Session has upheld a right to exclude a known criminal from an enclosure at a race meeting. One of the judges observed that "there was an implied condition attaching to the right of entry that his character was such as warranted his presence in the enclosure (*Wallace* v. *Mooney* (1885) 12 R. 710 at 713).

CHAPTER 25

THE PRIVATE

Property

783. As a general rule no one is entitled to enter a man's private property without his consent. There are exceptions. Statutes give certain inspectors and others rights of entry. Police officers with proper search warrants can enter. And generally entry is allowed if it is necessary in the public interest—to put out a fire, for example, or continue the hot pursuit of a criminal. These exceptions will not normally benefit the journalist—and so for him the normal rule applies. He is infringing the owner's legal rights if he enters his property, whether it is enclosed or not, without permission.

784. Trespass is an infringement of rights, but it is not a criminal offence. Trespassers can *not* be prosecuted and, as has been often observed, the familiar board proclaiming that they will be is a wooden lie.

785. This does not mean, however, that the property owner has no remedies. He can order an intruder to leave. If met by a refusal, he can probably remove him by the use of reasonable force (*Wood* v. *N.B. Ry. Co.*) (1899) 2 F. 1), although there is some doubt about this in the case of property other than private houses (Rankine on *Landownership*, 4th ed., 140). If the intrusion is likely to be repeated he can apply to the court for an interdict, which it is contempt of court to ignore. If the intruder has caused actual injury to the property, the owner can also sue for damages.

786. In the normal case, then, where a trespasser is unlikely to repeat the trespass and has caused no damage, all that the owner can lawfully do is ask him to leave and, if he refuses, remove him by reasonable force. If too much force is used the trespasser can sue for assault, but he starts with the scales weighted against him. In the case of private houses the courts tolerate a certain amount of violence on the part of the houseowner (Rankine on *Landownership*, 4th ed., 140) who, after all, is entitled to suspect the worst if he finds a stranger on his premises.

Person

787. Unlawful interference with the person is assault. This may result in a criminal prosecution or a civil action for damages. The law on assault should not be of concern to the journalist but there have been instances of mobbing and manhandling by reporters eager to obtain a story. To photograph a person is not by itself assault, even if he does not consent, but to force him to submit to being photographed in a certain place or in a certain pose probably would be assault (*Adamson* v. *Martin*, 1916 S.C. 319; see also paras. 466–468).

Privacy

788. The mere invasion of privacy is not in itself actionable (see *Murray* v. *Beaverbrook Newspapers Ltd.*, June 18, 1957 (unreported) referred to in T. B. Smith, *Short Commentary on the Laws of Scotland*, p. 655). It is not unlawful to photograph a person and expose his features to the public gaze even if the photograph is a bad one. Nor is it unlawful to expose a person's private life to the glare of publicity. But the courts do not look favourably on such conduct and if there is any actionable wrong involved, such as defamation or infringement of copyright or breach of confidence (*cf. Argyll* v. *Argyll* [1967] Ch. 302 in which the Duke of Argyll and *The People* were restrained from publishing certain intimate matters communicated to the Duke in confidence by his former wife during the subsistence of their marriage), they are quite likely to take the invasion of privacy into account in assessing damages (see "Privacy and The Press," 24 Modern Law Review 185). Thus in a case we have already considered, where a man's wedding photograph was published because it included a picture of his subsequently murdered father-in-law, it was said with reference to the amount of damages awarded against the photographer who had sold the picture, "it is the flagrancy of the infringement which calls for heavy damages because this was a scandalous matter in the circumstances, which I do not propose to elaborate and about which I do not propose to express a view. It is sufficient to say that it was a flagrant infringement of the right of the plaintiff, and it was scandalous conduct and in total disregard not only of the plaintiff's legal rights of copyright but of his feelings and his sense of family dignity and pride. It was an intrusion into his life, deeper and graver than an intrusion into a man's property" (*Williams* v. *Settle* [1960] 2 All E.R. 806 at 812). We have seen too that the defence of fair comment in a defamation action may not be available if the comment is on a man's private life. The position can be summed up by saying that the courts at present give no redress for invasion of privacy by itself but they do not like it and are apt to take it into account if it is an element in a case before them.

789. It has been suggested that the common law both in England (by

226

Lord Denning; see Hansard, Lords Debate 1960–1, vol. 299, col. 639) and in Scotland (T. B. Smith, *Short Commentary on the Laws of Scotland*, 653–656; Walker, *Delict*, 703) could be extended to provide a remedy for invasion of privacy. Legislation to the same end has also been discussed. The Royal Commission on the Press in 1949 considered the possibility but concluded that it would be difficult to devise legislation which would be both effective and enforceable (Cmd. 7700, paras. 642–643). In 1961 a Right to Privacy Bill was introduced in the House of Lords but, after receiving much support, it was withdrawn because of the difficulty of reconciling an effective right of privacy with the legitimate freedom of the Press (Hansard *loc. cit.* vol. 232, col. 289–299). Further Bills were presented to Parliament in 1967 and 1969, but did not reach the statute book (the history of these Bills is traced in Chapter 22 of the Younger Committee's Report). In 1972, the whole question was thoroughly reviewed by the Committee on Privacy under the chairmanship of the Rt. Hon. Kenneth Younger. In relation to invasion of privacy by the Press, the committee concluded that it was "impossible to devise any satisfactory yardstick by which to judge, in cases of doubt, whether the importance of a public story should override the privacy of the people and personal information involved" and that decisions on this point could be made "only in the light of the circumstances of each case." They did not think that such decisions should be the responsibility of the courts and were, therefore, opposed to the introduction of legislation conferring a right to privacy in relation to Press activities. Instead they recommended a strengthening of the role of the Press Council (a) by increasing its lay component and (b) by making it obligatory for a newspaper, found by the council to be at fault, to publish the critical adjudication with similar prominence, if possible, to that given to the original item of news. The committee also commended to the council the possibility of producing, and keeping up to date, "a codification of its adjudications on privacy, in a form which would give rather readier guidance to busy practising journalists, and to the interested public." The committee took a similar view of privacy in relation to broadcasting. It recommended, not legislation, but rather reliance on the B.B.C.'s Programmes Complaints Commission and the I.T.A.'s Complaints Review Board.

790. One of the matters considered by the Younger Committee was the publication in the Press of the content of wills. The committee considered that it was beyond its terms of reference to consider whether there should be public access to wills. Given that such access was provided for by the existing law, the committee saw no good reason for imposing restrictions on dissemination by the Press of this publicly available information. In 1975, however, a Private Member's Bill called the Publication of Wills Bill was introduced which, if it had become law, would have prohibited newspapers from publishing reports disclosing the size of estates of deceased persons or individual bequests made by them while leaving them free to publish the deceased's name, address and date of death, with a reference to a source such as a solicitor's office from which further information could be obtained. A similar Private Member's Bill was introduced in 1983 but failed to receive sufficient support.

Part VI

MISCELLANEOUS STATUTORY PROVISIONS

CHAPTER 26

THE REHABILITATION OF OFFENDERS ACT 1974

Purpose of Act

791. The purpose of this Act is to enable people convicted of criminal offences to wipe certain old offences off their records and continue their lives free from the constant threat of disclosure. The Act achieves its purpose by prohibiting the telling of the truth and legalising lying. It uses two key concepts, the "rehabilitated person" and the "spent conviction," the definition of which will be discussed later, after an account of the main consequences of the Act.

Restriction of information about spent convictions

792. From the journalist's point of view one of the main effects of the Act is that it restricts the availability of information about the spent convictions of a rehabilitated person. A rehabilitated person is, in general, to be treated for all purposes in law as if he had not committed the offence in question or been charged, prosecuted, convicted or sentenced as a result. Evidence of spent convictions is not normally admissible in any judicial proceedings in Great Britain and a person is not, in such proceedings, liable to be asked or bound to answer any question relating to his past which cannot be answered without acknowledging or referring to a spent conviction (s.4(1)). However, there are important exceptions to these rules. The Act does *not* affect the admission of evidence as to a person's previous convictions (a) in any *criminal* proceedings before a court in Great Britain, (b) in service disciplinary proceedings, (c) in most proceedings (such as children's hearings, or adoption, guardianship or custody proceedings) relating to children under 18 (s.7(2)). Moreover a party or witness in any proceedings can waive the protection of the Act and consent to the admission of evidence as to his spent convictions or the determination of an issue involving such evidence (s.7(2)(*f*)). In most non-judicial contexts too,

229

such as applying for a job or filling in a proposal form for an insurance policy, a person is not bound to disclose spent convictions in answer to any question about his past and is not to be subjected to any legal liability or prejudice for his non-disclosure (s.4(2) and (3); the Secretary of State has power to make orders excluding or modifying the application of these provisions in particular circumstances). Moreover, it is an offence for a person, such as a court official, police officer, or civil servant, who in the course of his official duties has access to official records or the information contained therein to disclose, "otherwise than in the course of those duties," information about spent convictions (s.9; there is a defence in s.9(3) which covers disclosure to, or at the express request of, the rehabilitated person). The phrase "otherwise than in the course of those duties" probably relates to disclosure by one official to another, and is probably not intended to cover, for example, disclosure by a Press officer to the Press. If such disclosure to the Press were regarded as covered by the phrase, the further question would arise whether the journalist receiving the information was a "person who, in the course of his official duties . . . had custody of or access to any official record of the information contained there." It would be difficult to argue that he was. He would receive the information in the course of his duties, but he would not have custody of or access to it in the course of his *official* duties. On a proper reading of the Act the obligation would seem to be on court officials, police officers and other officials to hold back the relevant information and not on the Press. This view is supported by s.9(4) which makes it an offence to obtain information about spent convictions from any official record by means of any fraud, dishonesty or bribe. The purpose of s.9 of the Act, in short, is to keep information on spent convictions within the confines of official records and the effect of ss.4 and 9 is to restrict the information available to the Press and public.

Effects on law of defamation

793. The other main effect of the Act from the point of view of Press law is that it limits the availability of certain defences to an action of defamation. First, a defender in such an action cannot rely on the defence of *veritas* in relation to a spent conviction if the publication is proved to have been made with malice (s.8(5)). It is not clear exactly what is meant by "malice" in this connection. It cannot include, as it does in some other contexts, the lack of any honest belief in the truth of the statement made. On the other hand it probably includes an intention to injure wholly or mainly for the gratification of personal spite or ill will. A newspaper which published details of a rehabilitated person's spent convictions because it was annoyed by his unco-operative attitude in some other context would, if its malice could be proved, be unable to rely on the defence of *veritas*. Secondly, a defender in an action for defamation cannot rely on the privilege attaching to a fair and accurate report of judicial proceedings if it is proved that the report contained a reference to evidence which was ruled to be inadmissible in the proceedings because it related to a spent conviction (s.8(6)). This provision does not apply to *bona fide* law reports and reports or accounts of judicial proceedings "published for *bona fide* educational, scientific or professional purposes, or given in the course of any lecture, class or discussion given or held for any of these purposes" (s.8(7)). These are the only two respects in which the law of defamation is altered by the Act, which expressly provides that spent convictions can be referred to in other respects to enable a defender to rely on any defence of *veritas* or fair comment or of absolute or qualified privilege which is available to him (s.8(3) and (4)). Moreover, the law of defamation is not in any way altered by the Act if the publication complained of took place before the conviction was spent (s.8(2)).

Sentences subject to rehabilitation

794. Some sentences are excluded from rehabilitation under the Act. The convictions to which these sentences relate accordingly never become spent convictions and the person on whom they are imposed never becomes a rehabilitated person in relation to them. These sentences excluded from rehabilitation are as follows:

(a) a sentence of imprisonment for life
(b) a sentence of imprisonment or corrective training for a term exceeding 30 months
(c) a sentence of preventive detention and
(d) a sentence of detention during Her Majesty's pleasure or for life, or for a term exceeding 30 months, passed under s.53 of the Children and Young Persons Act 1933 or under s.57 of the Children and Young Persons (Scotland) Act 1937 (s.5).

All other sentences are subject to rehabilitation.

Effect of subsequent conviction

795. A subsequent conviction after the rehabilitation period does not revive the earlier conviction: it remains spent (s.1(1)). The effect of a

231

subsequent conviction during the rehabilitation period depends on its nature. If it is a conviction for a minor offence (in Scotland, an offence within the jurisdiction of the district courts) it has no effect on rehabilitation (s.6(6)). If it is a more serious offence but does not involve a sentence excluded from rehabilitation (*i.e.* heavier than 30 months' imprisonment or detention) it delays the expiry of the rehabilitated period until the end of the rehabilitation period applicable to the new offence or the old offence whichever ends later (s.6(4)). If the subsequent conviction involves a sentence excluded from rehabilitation then it precludes rehabilitation altogether and the old offence never becomes spent (s.1(1)).

Rehabilitation periods

796. The Act provides for different rehabilitation periods depending on the gravity of the sentence and the age of the offender. In the case of adult offenders the scale is as follows (s.5(2) Table A).

Table A

Sentence	Rehabilitation Period
Imprisonment or corrective training for 6–30 months	10 years
Imprisonment for a term not exceeding 6 months	7 years
Fine or other sentence subject to rehabilitation	5 years

In the case of persons under 17 these periods are reduced by half and there is a special scale for certain sentences confined to young offenders. This is as shown on page 233 (s.5(2) Table B).

The rehabilitation period applicable to an order discharging a person absolutely for an offence is six months from the date of the conviction (s.5(3); the same period applies to a discharge by a children's hearing under s.43(2) of the Social Work (Scotland) Act 1968). If a person is put on probation the rehabilitation period ends one year after the date of the conviction or when the probation order ceases to have effect, whichever is the later (s.5(4); the same rule applies if a person is conditionally discharged, or bound over to keep the peace or be of good behaviour). A similar rule—one year or the duration of a period of care, residential training or supervision, whichever is the longer—applies in relation to various orders dealing with children and young persons, including a supervision requirement under the Social Work

Table B

Sentence	Rehabilitation Period
Borstal training	7 years
Detention for 6–30 months under s.53 of the Children and Young Persons Act 1933 or s.57 of the Children and Young Persons (Scotland) Act 1937	5 years
Detention for not more than 6 months under either of the above provisions	3 years
Detention in a detention centre under s.4 of the Criminal Justice (Scotland) Act 1963	3 years

(Scotland) Act 1968 (s.5(5)). If a convicted person is made the subject of a hospital order (under Pt. V of the Mental Health Act 1959 or Pt. III of the Mental Health (Scotland) Act 1983 or Pt. VI of the Mental Health (Scotland) Act 1984) (with or without an order restricting discharge) the rehabilitation period ends five years after the date of the conviction or two years after the hospital order ceases to have effect, whichever is later (s.5(7)). Finally, if a convicted person has any disqualification imposed on him (such as a disqualification from driving) the rehabilitation period ends when the disqualification ceases to have effect (s.5(8); the same rule applies to a "disability, prohibition or other penalty"). These are the main rules on rehabilitation periods but the Act contains other provisions and also empowers the Secretary of State to make orders varying the above periods. The result is a complex piece of legislation. It will often be difficult to know whether a conviction is spent. Fortunately, as we have seen, the main sanction of the Act lies in the law of defamation and, so long as there is no malice, and no reference in a report of judicial proceedings to evidence *actually ruled to be inadmissible* under the Act, the journalist has the protection of the usual defences and privileges and has nothing to fear from the Act.

"Rehabilitated person" and "spent conviction"

797.   On the expiry of the rehabilitated period applicable to a conviction which is subject to rehabilitation the person concerned becomes a rehabilitated person and the conviction becomes a spent conviction (s.1(1)). This is subject to the rules on subsequent conviction considered above: rehabilitation under the Act is designed for those who do not commit other serious offences during the rehabilitation period.

It is also subject to the sentence being served, at least in the case of imprisonment and other custodial sentences (s.1(2); non-payment of a fine does not prevent rehabilitation; nor does failure to comply with any requirement of a probation order, suspended sentence or supervision order). The escaped convict does not become a rehabilitated person.

Application to service disciplinary proceedings

798. Findings of guilt by army, navy or air force courts-martial or other competent authorities are treated as convictions for purposes of the Act but only if (a) the offence is also a civil offence or comes within a specified list of service offences or (b) the punishment is imprisonment; cashiering, discharge with ignominy or dismissal with disgrace from Her Majesty's service; dismissal from Her Majesty's service; or detention for a term of three months or more (s.2). The rehabilitation period for cashiering, discharge with ignominy or dismissal with disgrace from Her Majesty's service is 10 years; for dismissal from Her Majesty's service, seven years; and for a sentence of detention, five years: these periods are halved if the person sentenced was under 17 years of age when found guilty (s.5(2)).

Application to children's hearings

799. Children's hearings do not convict or sentence the children who come before them. Their approach is intended to be therapeutic rather than punitive. Nevertheless it was thought to be desirable that people brought before them on an offence ground should have the chance of becoming rehabilitated persons under the Act. If it were otherwise a boy sent to a residential school for stealing lead from a roof would be denied the opportunity of living down his offence. Accordingly, the Act provides that if a child is referred to a children's hearing on an offence ground and that ground is either accepted by the child (and, where necessary, his parent) or established to the satisfaction of the sheriff on a referral to him, then the acceptance of establishment of the ground shall be treated for the purposes of the Act as a conviction and any disposal of the case thereafter by a children's hearing as a sentence (s.3).

Application to foreign courts

800. The Act applies to convictions by or before courts outside Great Britain (s.1(4)). In calculating rehabilitation periods in relation to such convictions a sentence is treated as if it were the nearest British equivalent (s.5(9)). But a conviction by a court outside Great Britain does not delay or preclude rehabilitation in relation to a previous conviction (s.6(6)).

CHAPTER 27

PRINTER AND PUBLISHER

801. There are various statutory provisions which apply primarily to the editorial or managerial side of the newspaper business but which journalists should nonetheless know. These provisions apply to both Scotland and England unless otherwise stated.

Name of printer

802. The name and address of the printer must be printed on the first or last page of every newspaper and periodical (and most other printed matter—the Newspapers, Printers and Reading Rooms Repeal Act 1869; the Printers Imprint Act 1961) printed in Scotland or England. If this is not done, printers, publishers and distributors can be fined up to £25 for each offending copy. Prosecutions must be brought in the name of the Lord Advocate in Scotland and the Attorney-General or Solicitor-General in England.

Registration

803. Newspapers must register annually with the General Post Office in London in order to get the benefit of reduced rates of postage.

804. English newspapers not belonging to an incorporated joint stock company must register annually with the Registrar of Newspaper Returns (the Newspaper Libel and Registration Act 1881). There is no such obligation on Scottish newspapers.

Keeping copies

805. The printer of a paper (if it is printed for hire, reward, gain or profit—which covers most cases) must keep at least one copy, showing on it the name and address of the person for whom it was printed. He must preserve it for six months and show it to any justice of the peace requiring to see it within that period. There is a £20 fine for failure in any of these respects (Newspapers, Printers and Reading Rooms Repeal Act 1869).

236

Delivering copies to museums and libraries (Copyright Act 1911, s.15)

806.   The publisher of every newspaper, periodical or book published in the United Kingdom must within a month of publication deliver a copy to the British Library, at his own expense.

807.   On demand, he must also deliver a copy to the Bodleian Library, Oxford; the University Library, Cambridge; the National Library, Scotland; the Library of Trinity College, Dublin and in certain cases the National Library of Wales. A separate demand need not be made for each copy of a newspaper. One demand can cover all numbers subsequently published.

808.   There is a fine of up to £25 and the value of the paper, book or magazine for failure to comply with these provisions.

Obscene matter

809.   Section 51 of the Civic Government (Scotland) Act 1982 makes it an offence to display any obscene material (any book, magazine, bill, paper, print, film, tape, disc or other kind of recording, photograph, drawing or painting) in a public place, which means a place to which the public are allowed access, whether on payment or otherwise. It prohibits the publication, reproduction, sale, distribution, printing and keeping of obscene material. The penalty for contravention is, on summary conviction, a fine not exceeding £2,000 or imprisonment for up to three months, or, on indictment, a fine of no stated limit or imprisonment for up to two years, or both in each case. There is a defence where it can be proved all due diligence was used to avoid an offence. The section does not apply to television, sound broadcasts or plays.

CHAPTER 28

ADVERTISEMENTS

810. The publication of certain advertisements is illegal and can result in a fairly heavy fine or imprisonment or both. Except where otherwise stated all the offences mentioned carry maximum fines of from £50 to £1000. For racial discrimination legislation as it affects advertising see paras 850–851.

Medical advertisements

811. It is an offence to take part in the publication of an advertisement containing an offer to treat any person for cancer, or to prescribe a remedy or give advice on the treatment of that disease (Cancer Act 1939, s.4).

812. The Medicines Act 1968 repealed certain earlier statutes dealing with advertisements of treatments for particular diseases and instead introduced a set of offences in connection with medical advertisements generally. Under s.93 of the Act it is an offence to issue, at the request or with the consent of "a commercially interested party" (a term which includes most manufacturers and suppliers of medicines), a false or misleading advertisement relating to medicinal products. An advertisement is false or misleading for this purpose if it falsely describes the medicinal products or if it is likely to mislead as to their nature, quality, uses or effects. In the case of certain medicinal products which are subject to a licence it is also an offence, under the same section, to issue an advertisement containing recommendations other than those authorised by the licence. In both cases, however, it is a defence for an accused person to prove that he did not know, and could not with reasonable diligence have discovered, that the advertisement was false or misleading or contained unauthorised recommendations.

813. Where a product licence is in force for medicinal products of a particular description only the holder of the licence can authorise advertisements relating to such products. Accordingly, it is an offence under s.94 of the Medicines Act 1968 to issue any such advertisement at the request or with the consent of any other commercially interested party. It is, however, a defence for an accused person to prove (a) that he exercised all due diligence to secure that the section would not be

238

contravened, and (b) that the contravention was due to the act or default of another person.

814. The Medicines Act 1968 also empowers the appropriate Ministers to make regulations prohibiting, or regulating, particular types of advertisements in relation to medicinal products. The regulations may, for example, prohibit the advertising of treatments for particular diseases, or prohibit advertisements containing particular misleading words or phrases, or require medical advertisements to take a certain form and contain specified particulars. The defence mentioned in paragraph 813 above is available in relation to a contravention of these regulations.

Food advertisements

815. It is an offence to be a party to the publication of an advertisement giving a false or misleading description of any food or drug (Food and Drugs (Scotland) Act 1956, s.6(2)). There are special provisions for margarine advertisements designed, it seems, to prevent all possibility of confusion with butter (Labelling of Food (Amendment) Regulations 1955, Sched. 2). However, it is a defence to prove that the advertisement was published in the ordinary course of business by a person whose business it is to publish or arrange for the publication of advertisements. This will normally protect newspapers.

Experiments on animals

816. It is an offence to publish an advertisement of a public exhibition of an experimental or scientific procedure on an animal which may have the effect of causing the animal pain, suffering, distress or lasting harm (Animals (Scientific Procedures) Act 1986, s.16).

Fraudulent advertisements

817. It is a serious offence to distribute circulars which to one's knowledge fraudulently induce or attempt to induce people to invest money. This will not involve a newspaper proprietor, publisher or distributor in liability unless he knows of or is a party to the fraud (Prevention of Fraud Investments Act 1958, s.14(1), (4)).

Consumer credit advertisements

818. The Consumer Credit Act 1974 contains provisions on consumer credit advertisements, such as most advertisements of hire-purchase facilities and most moneylenders' advertisements (ss.43 to 47 and s.151). Regulations provide for the form and content of such advertisements so as to ensure, among other things, that they give a fair indication of the credit or hire facilities offered and of their true cost. The Act itself makes it an offence to publish a consumer credit advertisement which conveys information which is misleading in a material respect. It also prohibits certain advertisements of credit facilities in relation to goods or services which are not available for cash. There are similar restrictions on advertisements by credit brokers, debt adjusters and debt counsellors. All these provisions apply expressly to the publisher of an advertisement as well as to the advertiser but newspapers and others are protected by a provision that it is a defence for a person charged to prove (a) that the advertisement was published in the course of a business carried on by him and (b) that he received the advertisement in the course of that business, and did not know and had no reason to suspect that its publication would be an offence.

Adoption and care of children

819. It is an offence to publish knowingly an advertisement indicating that a parent or guardian wants a child adopted, or that a person wants to adopt a child or that any person other than a registered adoption society or local authority is willing to make arrangements for the adoption of a child (Adoption (Scotland) Act 1978, s.52).

820. A provision aimed at the fiendish practice of baby farming makes it an offence to publish knowingly an advertisement that a person will undertake or will arrange for the care and maintenance of a child, unless the advertisement truly states the person's name and address (Children Act 1958, s.37).

Licensed betting office advertisements

821. It is an offence to publish or permit to be published an advertisement of a particular licensed betting office or of licensed betting offices in general. But it is a defence for a person to prove that he did not know and had no reasonable cause to suspect the nature of the advertisement and that he had taken all reasonable steps to ascertain that it did not infringe the Betting, Gaming and Lotteries Act 1963 (s.10(5)). It should be noted that an advertisement contravenes the statutory requirements if it indicates where a licensed betting office can be found, even although it does not state that it is a licensed betting office. Thus to publish an advertisement in the form "A. Smith, Commission

Agent, 12 High Street, Greentown" would be an offence if the premises were in fact a licensed betting office (*Farrell* v. *Caledonian Publicity Services Ltd.*, 1963 S.L.T. 306).

Lotteries

822. A lottery is a scheme for distributing prizes by lot or chance. With certain exceptions considered later, all lotteries are unlawful. It is an offence to print or advertise lottery tickets; to print, publish or distribute any advertisement of a lottery, or any list of lottery winners, or any such matter relating to a lottery as is calculated to induce people to participate in it or in other lotteries (Lotteries and Amusements Act 1976, s.2). It is, however, a defence to prove that the lottery in question was one of the few types of lawful lotteries mentioned below and that the person charged believed, and had reasonable ground for believing, that none of the statutory conditions applying to the lottery had been broken.

823. The four types of lawful lottery mentioned above are as follows:

(1) Small lotteries incidental to certain entertainments such as bazaars, sales of work, fetes, dinners, dances and sporting or athletic events (*id.* s.3). There must be no money prizes and tickets must be sold and the result declared only at and during the entertainment in question. The lottery must not be the only, or the only substantial, inducement to persons to attend the entertainment. The whole proceeds of the entertainment (including the proceeds of the lottery), less expenses and a small sum for the purchase of prizes, must be devoted to purposes other than private gain. This exception would cover, for example, an announcement in an advertisement of a football match that a bottle of whisky would be raffled.

(2) Private lotteries (*id.* s.4). These are lotteries held by and for people belonging to the same society, working on the same premises or living on the same premises. The main conditions applying to this kind of lottery are that the sale of tickets must be restricted to the people mentioned, the net proceeds must be devoted only to the provision of prizes or the purposes of the society holding the lottery and there must be no outside advertisement. The tickets must contain certain information and must all be the same price. This exception would cover, for example, an announcement in a newspaper that So-and-so had won the local golf club's sweepstake on the Derby.

(3) Lotteries promoted by societies established and conducted wholly or mainly for charitable, sporting, cultural or other purposes which are not purposes of private gain nor purposes of any commercial undertaking (*id.* s.5). A society must register with the appropriate district or islands council if it wishes to promote lawful lotteries, and it must keep within certain financial and other limits.

(4) Local lotteries promoted by local authorities in accordance with an approved scheme.

(5) Art union lotteries (*id.* s.25(6), Art Unions Act 1846). Art unions are societies which purchase works of art or raise money for their purchase and distribute works of art or money among their members by lot or otherwise.

Amusements with prizes

824. None of the restrictions relating to lotteries apply to amusements with prizes provided as an incident to entertainments such as a bazaar, sale of work, fete, dinner, dance or sporting or athletic event. The proceeds must be devoted to purposes other than private gain and the opportunity to win prizes must not be the only substantial inducement to attend the entertainment. The restrictions on lotteries do not apply to amusements with prizes provided on premises authorised by the local authorities or at fun fairs held by travelling showmen (*id.* s.16). Certain conditions must be observed.

825. A newspaper will generally be quite safe in advertising fetes, bazaars, fun fairs, etc. even if the advertisement states that certain amusements with prizes will be provided.

Prize competitions

826. It is an offence to conduct in or through any newspaper, magazine or other periodical (a) any competition in which prizes are offered for forecasts of the result of a future event or of a past event the result of which is not yet ascertained or not yet generally known or (b) any other competition, in which success does not depend to a *substantial degree* on the exercise of skill (*id.* s.14). In *News of the World Ltd.* v. *Friend* [1973] 1 W.L.R. 248 the House of Lords held that the newspaper's "Spot-the-ball" competitions did not infringe this provision. The paper published a photograph of an actual incident in a football game but with the ball eliminated. Competitors were asked to mark-with a cross the position where the ball was most likely to be. The winning entry was that which corresponded most closely with the opinion of a panel of experts as to the logical position of the ball in the circumstances (which might not be the same as the true position of the ball in the original photograph). The court took the view that competitors were being asked to use their skill and judgment and not just to forecast a future event (the decision of the panel of experts).

Advertisements of foreign betting

827. With a view to protecting the country's revenue from general betting duty and pool betting duty it has been made an offence, subject to certain limited exceptions, to advertise foreign pool betting or coupon betting or betting with a bookmaker outside Great Britain (Betting and Gaming Duties Act 1972, s.9).

Gaming advertisements

828. The Gaming Act 1968 defines gaming as "the playing of a game of chance for winnings in money or money's worth, whether any person playing the game is at risk of losing any money or money's worth or not." The term is wide enough to include shove halfpenny and bingo as well as the more sophisticated games normally played in casinos.

829. The Act (s.42) makes it an offence to publish any advertisement informing the public that any premises in Great Britain are premises on which gaming takes place or inviting the public to take part in such gaming. It is also an offence to publish advertisements inviting the public (a) to apply for information about taking part in any gaming in Great Britain or (b) to subscribe money or money's worth to be used in gaming anywhere or (c) to apply for information about facilities for such subscriptions. There are, however, exceptions for advertisements of certain kinds of gaming. The first relates to gaming as an incident of a bazaar, sale of work, fete, dinner, dance, sporting or athletic event or other entertainment of a similar character. The second relates to games played at an entertainment promoted otherwise than for purposes of private gain and complying with certain stringent conditions. This exception could cover, for example, advertisements of a bingo session held to raise funds for a football supporters' club. The third exception relates to gaming at amusement arcades or similar premises which are used wholly or mainly to provide amusements by means of gaming machines and which have a permit from the local authority to do so. The fourth exception covers gaming at any travelling showmen's pleasure fair.

830. The Gaming Act 1968 provides for the licensing of certain gaming premises including bingo club premises. The mere fact that premises are licensed to carry on gaming does not mean that they can be advertised (other than by a sign or notice displayed on the premises themselves). However, there is a specific provision allowing the publication in any newspaper of a notice stating that a licence under the Gaming Act has been granted, provided that the notice is published not later than 14 days from the date when the licence was granted or from such later date as the licensing court may specify and provided it is in a form approved by the licensing court. The Act also *requires* applications for licences to be advertised in a newspaper: so there can clearly be no objection to publishing these.

831. The provisions restricting gaming advertisements do not apply to the publication of an advertisement in a newspaper which circulates wholly or mainly outside Great Britain.

832. Finally, it is a defence to a prosecution under these provisions for the accused to prove that he is a person whose business it is to publish or arrange for the publication of advertisements and that he received the offending advertisement for publication in the ordinary course of business and did not know and had no reason to suspect that its publication would amount to an offence.

False trade descriptions

833. The Trade Descriptions Act 1968 prohibits false trade descriptions (as defined in the Act) and various other misstatements, such as false indications that goods are being offered at a cut price. The Act also gives the Department of Trade power to require certain advertisements to include certain particulars if they think this is necessary or expedient in the interests of consumers. Although the Act is aimed primarily at misstatements by those supplying goods and services, certain of its provisions apply to those publishing advertisements. If a newspaper knew that an advertisement contained a false trade description (*e.g.* that goods advertised as new were in fact second-hand or reconditioned) it would be guilty of an offence under the Act if it published it. Obviously, however, newspapers cannot be expected to investigate the accuracy of every statement made in their advertising columns. Accordingly s.25 of the Act provides that it shall be a defence for the publisher of an advertisement to prove that he is a person whose business it is to publish or arrange for the publication of advertisements and that he received the advertisement for publication in the ordinary course of business and did not know and had no reason to suspect that its publication would amount to an offence under the Act.

Pirate radio stations

834. Under the Marine etc. Broadcasting (Offences) Act 1967 it is an offence to publish the times or other details of broadcasts to be made from pirate radio stations or to publish advertisements calculated to promote their interests.

Cars

835. An advertisement for new cars which contains any statement about fuel consumption must include information about results of relevant official tests.

Surrogacy arrangements

836. The Surrogacy Arrangements Act 1985 makes it an offence to publish any advertisement containing an indication (a) that any person is or may be willing to enter into a surrogacy arrangement or to negotiate or facilitate the making of a surrogacy arrangement or (b) that any person is looking for a woman willing to become a surrogate mother or is looking for persons wanting to carry a child as surrogate mother.

Obscene publications

837. Obscenity is an offence at common law in Scotland (but see para 809). The broad test is whether the publication complained of is calculated to deprave and corrupt those who are likely to read it. In England the law is contained mainly in the Obscene Publications Act 1959, which lays down a similar test. The Indecent Advertisements Act 1889 deals mainly with the affixing or inscribing of indecent advertisements on walls and similar places and the distribution or exhibition of indecent matter in the streets. Section 52(1)(*d*) of the Civic Government (Scotland) Act 1982 makes it an offence to publish any advertisement conveying that the advertiser distributes or intends to distribute an indecent photograph of a child under 16.

Harmful publications

838. It is a statutory offence to print, publish, sell or hire "horror comics" (Children and Young Persons (Harmful Publications) Act

1955). This will not affect the average newspaper as the statute applies only to works which consist wholly or mainly of picture stories portraying the commission of crimes or acts of violence or cruelty or incidents of a repulsive or horrible nature in such a way that the work as a whole would tend to corrupt a child or young person into whose hands it might fall; but would apply, *e.g.* to "video nasties."

Election matter

839. It is an offence to incur expense without the written authority of the election agent in issuing advertisements, circulars or publications with a view to promoting or procuring the election of a candidate at an election (Representation of the People Act 1983, s.75(1)(*b*)). This does not prevent newspapers commenting on an election with complete freedom and presenting a candidate or his views or disparaging another candidate (*id.* s.75(1)(*c*) and proviso). It has been held that there was an offence when a publication advised electors to vote against a candidate but did not advise them to vote for his opponent. It nevertheless tended to promote the opponent's election. But to offend, the publication must tend to promote or procure the election of a *particular* candidate and not merely a political party as a whole. This was decided in a case in which the proprietors of *The Times* and others were prosecuted in respect of an advertisement condemning the financial policy of the Labour Party and saying that the election would give an opportunity of saving the country from being reduced to bankruptcy through the policies of a Socialist Government. The judge observed that no reasonable jury could find that this advertisement presented to the electors of any particular constituency any particular candidate (*R. v. Tronoh Mines Ltd. and Others* [1952] 1 All E.R. 697).

840. It is also an offence to print, publish, post or distribute any bill, placard or poster having reference to an election unless the name and address of the printer and publisher appear on its face (Representation of the People Act 1983). This provision might apply, for example; to newspaper posters proclaiming "Vote for Blogg."

Accommodation agencies

841. It is an offence under the Accommodation Agencies Act 1953, to issue any advertisement describing any house as being to let without the authority of the owner of the house or his agent. It is also an offence under the Act to demand or accept certain illegal commissions for registering people seeking tenancies or for supplying particulars of houses to let. However, the Act expressly provides that "a person shall not be guilty of an offence under this section by reason of his demanding or accepting any payment in consideration of . . . the publication in a newspaper, of any advertisement or notice, or by reason of the . . . publication . . . of an advertisement or notice received for the purpose in the ordinary course of business."

Sex Discrimination

842.   Under s.38 of the Sex Discrimination Act 1975 it is unlawful to publish or cause to be published an advertisement which indicates, or might reasonably be understood as indicating, an intention by a person to do any act which is or might be unlawful discrimination on grounds of sex in the employment field or in other fields. This provision does not apply to an advertisement if the intended act would not in fact be unlawful. For example, the 1975 Act does not apply to employment for the purposes of a private household or where the number of persons employed by the employer does not exceed five. A private householder or, say, a solicitor employing only three people could therefore lawfully advertise for a male gardener or a female secretary respectively even though such advertisements are in general unlawful. The section provides that for its purposes the use of a job description with a sexual connotation (such as "waiter," "salesgirl," "postman" or "stewardess") shall be taken to indicate an intention to discriminate, unless the advertisement contains an indication to the contrary. It would obviously be impossible for newspapers and others in a similar position to check the lawfulness of each advertisement submitted to them. They could not be expected, for example, to carry out independent inquiries into the number of people employed by a particular advertiser. The section therefore provides a defence for the publisher of an advertisement if he proves (a) that the advertisement was published in reliance on a statement made to him by the person who caused it to be published to the effect that the intended act would not in fact be unlawful and (b) that it was reasonable for him to rely on the statement.

Equal opportunities

843.   In 1981 the Equal Opportunities Commission issued guidance notes on the advertising provisions of the Act which included points for the guidance of advertisers. These included the following: "Watch out for words like salesman, storeman/woman. If these are used, make sure the ad clearly offers the job to both sexes. Make sure that

247

advertisements for jobs which have in the past been done mainly by men or women only (*e.g.* mechanic, typist) could not be understood to indicate a preference for one sex. If the ad contains words like he, she, or him, make sure that they are used as alternatives, *e.g.* he or she, or him/her, and are consistent throughout the advertisement. In one way or another the ad must make it clear that the vacancy is open to both men and women. Pictures can give a biased impression too. If they are used, ensure that men and women are shown fairly, in both numbers and prominence. Otherwise a bold disclaimer should be placed as close to the illustration as possible."

Advertising standards

844. Publishers are well advised to be familiar with the British Code of Advertising Practice, administered by the Advertising Standards Authority. Although the code is not statutory, the Authority has power, where an advertisement is found to have contravened the code, to order the advertiser to amend or withdraw it from publication. The aim of the code is to protect consumers from unacceptable or misleading advertising, its philosophy, in brief, being that "if an advertiser can't prove it, he can't say it"; and the Authority summarises its message thus: "All advertisements should be legal, decent, honest and truthful." The code, which is under constant review, makes special provision for political and religious advertising, to avoid undue suppression of freedom of speech. Publishers of newspapers and periodicals are entitled to withdraw any advertisement they think is contrary to the code, which is available from the Authority at Brook House, Torrington Place, London, WC1E 7HN. Separate codes regulating television, radio, cable and satellite broadcast advertisements are administered by the Independent Broadcasting Authority, 70 Brompton Road, London, SW3 1EY.

845. In relation to children the British Code of Advertising Practice says advertisements should contain nothing which might cause them physical, mental or moral harm, or which exploits their credulity, lack of experience or sense of loyalty, and should not encourage them to make themselves a nuisance to their parents or anyone else with the aim of persuading them to buy an advertised product.

In 1986 the Independent Broadcasting Authority had regard to a case of juvenile credulity when it upheld a complaint by a telephone subscriber who was faced with a £400 telephone bill after his daughter, aged 15, had made numerous calls in response to British Telecom's TV advertisement promoting its "Talkabout line." He first complained to

B.T., maintaining that his daughter was led to believe the service was free, and when B.T. denied responsibility he took his complaint to the Authority, which upheld it, and B.T. then agreed to revise its advertisement to make it clear to children that they had to ask their parents before using the "Talkabout" service.

CHAPTER 29

RACE RELATIONS

846. It is an offence under s.70 of the Race Relations Act 1976 to publish or distribute written matter which is threatening, abusive or insulting and is likely to stir up hatred against any racial group in Great Britain. The Act, in amending the Public Order Act 1936 and repealing earlier Race Relations Acts, removed the need to prove *intention* to stir up such hatred in order to obtain a conviction.

847. It has to be appreciated it is not an offence under the Act to give vent to racial hatred; freedom to do so has survived; the offence is in acting in a way that is *likely* to stir it up. John Kingsley Read was acquitted of a charge of incitement to racial hatred when—with reference to the death of an Asian student by stabbing in 1976—he exclaimed, "One down and one million to go," but he had been charged under the Race Relations Act 1965, which required proof of intent. Would Read's remark have been "likely" to stir up racial hatred as conceived in the 1976 Act? We shall probably never know, but whether any particular comment or outburst exceeds the bounds of lawful free expression of opinion must be a matter of degree in all the circumstances in which it is made, and it may be too much to expect that courts' decisions will be entirely consistent in the matter. Indeed, since cases brought to trial tend to give publicity to those who least deserve it, or to the causes they seek to promote, encourage greater polarity of public opinion on racial issues, and thus discourage prosecution even in cases where the Act might indicate it is well justified, it may be arguable that the statutory position now threatens more harm than good.

848. The journalist—as well as the publisher and distributor—does well to be familiar, however, with the general import of a provision which carries, on summary conviction, imprisonment for up to six months or a fine not exceeding £1,000, or both, or, on indictment, imprisonment for up to two years or a fine without specified limit, or both.

849. The s.70 prohibition does not apply to fair and accurate reports of public hearings before any court or tribunal exercising judicial authority, or to reports of proceedings in Parliament. It is a defence to a charge under the section to prove that the accused was not aware of the

250

content of the written matter in question and neither suspected nor had reason to suspect it of being threatening, abusive or insulting. "Racial group," as used in the section, means a group of persons defined by reference to colour, race, nationality (which includes citizenship) or national origins. In a test case in 1983, the House of Lords, overruling the English Court of Appeal, decided that Sikhs qualify for protection under the Act as a racial group. The Court of Appeal had held that they were a religious community and did not enjoy such protection. The Lords ruled that a Birmingham headmaster unlawfully discriminated against a Sikh pupil in refusing to allow him to wear a turban in school. Lord Fraser of Tullybelton (a Scottish Lord of Appeal), giving the leading judgment, said the Sikhs were a group defined by reference to ethnic origins for the purposes of the Act.

850. Section 29 makes it unlawful to publish or cause to be published through any of the media an advertisement which indicates an intention to discriminate racially, but certain exceptions are made, *e.g.* in relation to advertisements regarding employment where being of a particular racial group is a genuine occupational qualification for the job, and in relation to provisions which may be contained in charitable deeds. Special exceptions are also made (s.39) to permit discrimination on the basis of nationality or place of birth if this is for the purpose of selecting competitors for sporting events. And there is no offence in publishing a discriminatory advertisement if the publisher relied on information from the person inserting it to the effect that publication would not be unlawful and if the publisher could reasonably rely on that assurance.

851. The Act does not restrict publication of rules or advertisements dealing with rules about employment in the service of the Crown or by any public body under regulations made by the Minister for the Civil Service in relation to persons of particular birth, nationality, descent or residence.

852. Section 43 set up the Commission for Racial Equality, to work towards the elimination of discrimination, promote equality of opportunity, and good relations, between persons of different racial groups, to keep the working of the Act under review and, where appropriate, to propose changes in the law. It issues codes of practice and can conduct formal investigations into cases of alleged breach under the Act, at which it can require the attendance of witnesses and production of documents. It can apply to the courts for enforcement of these requirements. Its reports may be made public, but information supplied to it must not be disclosed unless required by a court or with the informant's

251

consent. Complaints of alleged offences under the Act in the employ-ment field are heard by industrial tribunals, which have power to make compensation orders or other directions to minimise any adverse effect of an act of proven discrimination, but there is also provision for dis-puted matters to be settled by conciliation officers.

"Adjectival racism"

853. The Press Council during 1986 dealt with a series of complaints about a practice of some newspapers specifying the skin colour or race of the offender or defendant in reports of cases of violence or serious crime—dubbed by some writers "adjectival racism." Its adjudications have no legal force, but they at least offer editors a basis on which to focus the issues involved in considering how to proceed in this sensitive area. One of the grounds of complaint was that where reports some-times described offenders as black, no mention was made of the fact, in other similar kinds of case, that the offenders were white.

854. On April 10 the council upheld a complaint against the *Daily Telegraph* in respect of its description of a rape gang as black, and held that this was an irrelevant prejudicial description which tended to exacerbate hostility against minority groups. The then editor, William Deedes, maintained there would always be differences on what was or was not relevant in a particular case. The council ruled that reference to race or colour was objectionable where it was both irrelevant to the report and in a prejudicial context. There might be cases where it would be relevant to refer to race or colour without substantial risk of prejudice. Where, however, the reference was to a person convicted or accused of violent crime as black, this was both irrelevant and prejudi-cial. It tended to exacerbate hostility against minority groups, who were at risk of serious prejudice within the community. Accepting that there were different views on the matter, the council believed its view served the interests of better community race relations and should be respected.

855. In a case in May it heard a complaint that the same paper reported that a 16-year-old white girl told the Old Bailey she was raped "about 30 times" by a gang of black youths. The council held that no evidence was reported that the crimes had been racially motivated and the paper should not have introduced the defendants' colour or race into the story. But it held it was not improper that the paper failed to identify the colour or race of defendants or victims in other reports cited.

856. The council in July, however, rejected a complaint against the paper that in reporting the Tottenham riots it specified that alleged offenders later brought before the court in connection with the disturbances were black. The editor, Max Hastings, said he was determined to preserve editorial discretion as to whether or not it was appropriate to mention the colour of a person named in news items. The council took the view that the colour of those involved in the Tottenham riots was relevant to the reports of the court cases covered by the paper. The *Daily Telegraph*, it may be noted, in other reports of violent crimes during the year, specified the colour of assailants where this was not black.

857. In another case in December the council found it was not improper or irrelevant for the *Daily Telegraph* to refer to the colour of two armed burglars in a report of their trial. It said counsel's description of one of the accused as black was relevant to the trial. It was the way in which a principal witness distinguished between the two in her evidence of what they did and said. The complaint in this case also was rejected.

858. The question of *relevance* is necessarily central to many such cases, but what is relevant in a particular case must depend on a wide range of circumstances, including the degree to which the colour or race specified represents a minority in the local community, whether the colour of the individual's skin is actually mentioned in the court hearing being reported (when there would be a legal right in the paper reporting it, under s.4 of the Contempt of Court Act 1981), whether in the context specification of colour is necessary for completeness of the report for the readers' purposes, prevalence of violent crimes at a particular time among persons of a particular colour, and the extent to which editorial policy is conceived to include the right to publish such facts as seem necessary to inform the public about the risks to which people may be exposed in modern society, and especially in certain areas. The editor's attitude may justifiably be swayed by what in his judgment is *relevant* in terms of news value; and it should not be forgotten that newspapers have some duty to their readers to keep them informed of matters of public safety, in general and in particular instances. (See also para. 220).

CHAPTER 30

OFFICIAL SECRETS

859. The journalist may in the pursuit of news come up against the barrier of the Official Secrets Acts. Under these Acts it is an offence to be in or around a prohibited place for any purpose prejudicial to the safety or interests of the State (Official Secrets Act 1911, s.1). Prohibited places also include (s.3 as amended by Official Secrets Act 1920, s.10) Her Majesty's arsenals, naval or air force establishments, factories, stations, dockyards, camps, ships and aircraft. They also include places where the Crown has munitions or models or papers relating to munitions. Various other places may be specifically declared to be prohibited. A person can be convicted if his conduct or the circumstances of the case indicate that his purpose was prejudicial to the interests of the State. This purpose need not be expressly proved by the prosecution (s.1(2)).

860. It is also an offence under the Act to make such things as sketches, photographs or notes which might be useful to an enemy. The same applies to obtaining communicating or publishing documents or information which might be useful to an enemy. In these cases a purpose prejudicial to the safety or interests of the State is usually presumed unless the contrary is proved (Official Secrets Act 1911, s.1).

861. It is an offence for those having access to official secrets to communicate them to unauthorised persons. Of more interest to journalists is the provision that a person who knowingly and willingly receives such a communication is also guilty of an offence (s.2).

862. In certain cases a police officer above the rank of inspector can require a person to give information relating to an offence or suspected offence under the Official Secrets Acts. It is an offence to fail to comply with such a requirement or knowingly to give false information. But the officer must have the authority of the chief officer of police and, except in emergencies, a Secretary of State must have given his express permission (Official Secrets Act 1939, s.1).

863. The system of "D notices" deserves mention in connection with official secrets, although it is a matter of practice, not law. The system is administered by the Services, Press and Broadcasting Committee which has both media and civil service representatives. The service

254

departments bring matters before the committee and make known their wishes with regard to publication or otherwise. The committee considers and decides the matter and then sends "D notices" to the participating sections of the media. The notices indicate what information should not be published. Doubts about the interpretation or application of D notices are generally resolved by consulting the secretary of the committee. The whole system is a voluntary one, based on mutual trust: there are no legal sanctions for breach of a D notice. The system is generally said to have worked extremely well, apart from one or two isolated incidents. The most notable of these was the "D notice affair" of 1967 which arose out of the disclosure by the *Daily Express* that cables sent out of Britain were regularly made available to the security authorities for scrutiny. The Government said this was a breach of D notices: the *Express* maintained it was not. A committee of inquiry found for the *Express*, but the Government purported to "reject" this finding. The D notice system was subjected to careful examination but survived. It was revised in 1982 after a lengthy examination, and four subjects were dropped—advice on Royal Navy warship construction and equipment; aircraft and aero-engines; prisoners of war and evaders; and the whereabouts of the former K.G.B. chief in Canberra, Vladimir Petrov, and his spy wife, who defected to Australia in 1954. Terrorism figures in the revised list. In the introduction to the up-dated set of notices, presented in simpler and more general terms than formerly, it is stated, "Dissemination of sensitive information . . . can also be of value to terrorist groups who lack the resources to obtain it through their own efforts." The system now covers:– 1. Defence plans, operational capability, state of readiness and training; 2. Defence equipment; 3. Nuclear weapons (this item bears the warning that publication of design information could assist nuclear weapon states to improve their nuclear capability and non-nuclear states to acquire one or sub-national groups to produce explosive nuclear devices); 4. Radio and radar transmissions; 5. Cyphers and communications (with the request that extreme discretion should be used in reporting ostensible disclosures of information published at home or overseas about British codes and cyphers and that such information should not be elaborated upon without reference to the secretary of the committee); 6. British security and intelligence services (the names "security service" (MI5) and "secret service" (MI6) have been dropped); 7. War precautions and civil defence; 8. Photographs of defence establishments, installations, dockyards and factories.

SCOTS LAW AND *SPYCATCHER*

864. Ban a book and make it a best-seller: that was the bitter lesson facing the British Government as it pursued its relentless efforts through the English civil courts, and elsewhere including New South Wales and Hongkong, in 1987 to stop publication of extracts from the book *Spycatcher* written in retirement in Australia by Peter Wright, a former MI5 officer. A more pointed lesson for Scottish journalists was the impotence of the English interim injunctions north of the Border. (See also paras. 870–871) While the English proceedings were going through all stages to the House of Lords the book was published in the U.S.A. and copies entered Britain and were put on sale unhindered.

865. The understandable object of the Government, through the Attorney-General, was to stop Wright's breach of a life-long obligation of confidence which he owed it. The legal mechanisms available to it proved, however, unequal to the task outside the jurisdiction of the English courts.

866. Scottish editors were alive to the fact that orders made by English courts did not rule in Scotland. Some of them, having taken legal advice, published extracts from the book and reports of the court proceedings in Sydney, all prohibited to English editors by interim injunctions.

867. The House of Lords decision was intended to preserve the ban in the interests of national security, pending a full hearing of the case, and to prevent future repetition of Wright's breach of duty by other members of the British secret service.

868. Although the Lord Advocate issued a warning that he would take proceedings in the Court of Session against any Scottish publication which breached the House of Lords ban, no action was in fact taken in the Scottish courts—tacit confirmation that the legal advice on which Scottish editors decided to publish was well founded, and a tribute to the special care taken to ensure that nothing they printed or broadcast reached across the Border.

869. Nothing could have better illustrated the special place of Scottish editors under their separate and independent legal system. The alleged revelations made by Wright about the internal workings of MI5, and the issues raised by the efforts to have him silenced, were of undoubted public interest—having been already published in the U.S.A. and also circulating in other countries. Had he been living in the U.K. he could have been prosecuted under the Official Secrets Acts.

870. The ineffectiveness of an English injunction in Scotland was also underlined when the *Glasgow Herald* published the contents of a confidential despatch from H.M. Ambassador to Saudi Arabia in 1986. An injunction had been granted by the English courts to prohibit publication of the despatch by the *New Statesman*, but the editor of the *Herald* took the view that the order had no application north of the Border.

871. In that case the Government did seek an interim interdict in the Court of Session against the *Herald*. However, by the time an interdict was granted by Lord Davidson at his home in the early hours of the morning, the paper was already on the streets with the despatch reproduced in full.

CHAPTER 31

REPORTS OF ENGLISH COMMITTAL PROCEEDINGS

872. Scots lawyers have often in the past been critical of the English system of holding a preliminary public inquiry before examining justices to decide whether or not someone should be committed for trial on an indictable offence. It was pointed out that this could result in publicity which might prejudice potential jurors against the accused. The system was contrasted with the Scottish system of private preliminary proceedings.

873. The Criminal Justice Act 1967 introduced special rules designed to prevent prejudicial pre-trial publicity in relation to English committal proceedings. The proceedings are still generally held in public but the rules make it unlawful to publish *anywhere in Great Britain* a report of any committal proceedings in England and Wales if the report contains any matter other than certain permitted particulars. The prohibition ceases to apply, however, after the conclusion of the defendant's actual trial. If there are two or more defendants the prohibition normally lasts until the conclusion of the trial of the last one to be tried. However, if the magistrates proceed, during the inquiry, to try one or more of the defendants summarily (as they are entitled to do under certain statutory provisions) while committing the other defendants or any of them for trial, it is permissible to publish a report of the summary trial which includes material from the preceding committal proceedings. The purpose of this last concession is no doubt to enable newspapers to publish enough to make a report of the summary trial intelligible.

874. Should the magistrates decide not to commit the defendant(s) for trial the prohibition then flies off. As the object of the prohibition is to protect the defendant, it is provided that he can ask magistrates to order that it shall not apply in relation to particular proceedings. The permitted particulars, which may be included in a report even though it is published before the trial, are as follows:

(a) the identity of the court and the names of the examining justices;

(b) the names, addresses and occupations of the parties and witnesses and the ages of the defendant or defendants and witnesses;

258

(c) the offence or offences, or a summary of them, with which the defendant or defendants is or are charged;
(d) the names of counsel and solicitors engaged in the proceedings;
(e) any decision of the court to commit the defendant or any of the defendants for trial, and any decision of the court on the disposal of the case of any defendants not committed;
(f) where the court commits the defendant for trial, the charge or charges, or a summary of them, on which he is committed and the court to which he is committed;
(g) where the committal proceedings are adjourned, the date and place to which they are adjourned;
(h) any arrangements as to bail on committal or adjournment;
(i) whether legal aid was granted to the defendant or any of the defendants.

875. It will be noted that the prohibition is on *publishing* a report, not on making a report. It would, therefore, be possible for a Scottish newspaper to obtain a report of committal proceedings quite legitimately from an English correspondent. In such a case the newspaper would have to be careful not to publish anything other than the permitted particulars until it was lawful to do so. In the normal case this would be after the conclusion of the trial.

876. One effect of the Criminal Justice (Amendment) Act 1981 is that reporting restrictions are no longer automatically lifted at the request of one of several defendants. If one or more defendants object to the restrictions being lifted the court can lift them only if satisfied this is "in the interests of justice." The kind of consideration the court may have to have in mind is whether one defendant wants publicity in the hope of encouraging an important witness for his defence to come forward.

877. The coverage of committal proceedings can be further affected by the operation of s.4(2) of the Contempt of Court Act 1981, which gives courts power to postpone publication of reports of proceedings to avoid prejudicing other proceedings which are pending or imminent. In an appeal against an order made by Horsham Magistrates under the section in 1981 the English High Court ruled that magistrates must not make an order that is wider than necessary to secure the desired end, namely to prevent prejudice to the administration of justice. Holding the magistrates' order was too wide the court said it should have been limited to sensitive matters disclosed during the committal hearing.

259

APPENDIX

CONTEMPT OF COURT ACT 1981

STRICT LIABILITY

1. In this Act "the strict liability rule" means the rule of law whereby conduct may be treated as a contempt of court as tending to interfere with the course of justice in particular legal proceedings regardless of intent to do so.

2. —(1) The strict liability rule applies only in relation to publications, and for this purpose "publication" includes any speech, writing, broadcast or other communication in whatever form, which is addressed to the public at large or any section of the public.

(2) The strict liability rule applies only to a publication which creates a substantial risk that the course of justice in the proceedings in question will be seriously impeded or prejudiced.

(3) The strict liability rule applies to a publication only if the proceedings in question are active within the meaning of this section at the time of the publication.

(4) Schedule 1 applies for determining the times at which proceedings are to be treated as active within the meaning of this section.

3. —(1) A person is not guilty of contempt of court under the strict liability rule as the publisher of any matter to which that rule applies if at the time of publication (having taken all reasonable care) he does not know and has no reason to suspect that relevant proceedings are active.

(2) A person is not guilty of contempt of court under the strict liability rule as the distributor of a publication containing any such matter if at the time of distribution (having taken all reasonable care) he does not know that it contains such matter and has no reason to suspect that it is likely to do so.

(3) The burden of proof of any fact tending to establish a defence afforded by this section to any person lies upon that person.

(4) Section 11 of the Administration of Justice Act 1960 is repealed.

4. —(1) Subject to this section a person is not guilty of contempt of court under the strict liability rule in respect of a fair and accurate

report of legal proceedings held in public, published contemporaneously and in good faith.

(2) In any such proceedings the court may, where it appears to be
necessary for avoiding a substantial risk of prejudice to the administration of justice in those proceedings, or in any other proceedings pending or imminent, order that the publication of any report of the
proceedings, or any part of the proceedings, be postponed for such
period as the court thinks necessary for that purpose.

(3) For the purposes of subsection (1) of this section and of section 3 of
the Law of Libel Amendment Act 1888 (privilege) a report of proceedings shall be treated as published contemporaneously—

> (a) in the case of a report of which publication is postponed pur-
> suant to an order under subsection (2) of this section, if pub-
> lished as soon as practicable after that order expires;
> (b) in the case of a report of committal proceedings of which publi-
> cation is permitted by virtue only of subsection (3) of section 8
> of the Magistrates' Courts Act 1980, if published as soon as
> practicable after publication is so permitted.

(4) Subsection (9) of the said section 8 is repealed.

5. A publication made as or as part of a discussion in good faith of
public affairs or other matters of general public interest is not to be
treated as a contempt of court under the strict liability rule if the risk of
impediment or prejudice to particular legal proceedings is merely
incidental to the discussion.

6. Nothing in the foregoing provisions of this Act—

> (a) prejudices any defence available at common law to a charge of
> contempt of court under the strict liability rule;
> (b) implies that any publication is punishable as contempt of court
> under that rule which would not be so punishable apart from
> those provisions;
> (c) restricts liability for contempt of court in respect of conduct
> intended to impede or prejudice the administration of justice.

. . . . .

OTHER ASPECTS OF LAW AND PROCEDURE

8. —(1) Subject to subsection (2) below, it is a contempt of court to obtain, disclose or solicit any particulars of statements made, opinions expressed, arguments advanced or votes cast by members of a jury in the course of their deliberations in any legal proceedings.

(2) This section does not apply to any disclosure of any particulars—

(*a*) in the proceedings in question for the purpose of enabling the jury to arrive at their verdict, or in connection with the delivery of that verdict, or

(*b*) in evidence in any subsequent proceedings for an offence alleged to have been committed in relation to the jury in the first mentioned proceedings,

or to the publication of any particulars so disclosed.

. . . . .

9. —(1) Subject to subsection (4) below, it is a contempt of court—

(*a*) to use in court, or bring into court for use, any tape recorder or other instrument for recording sound, except with the leave of the court;

(*b*) to publish a recording of legal proceedings made by means of any such instrument, or any recording derived directly or indirectly from it, by playing it in the hearing of the public or any section of the public, or to dispose of it or any recording so derived, with a view to such publication;

(*c*) to use any such recording in contravention of any conditions of leave granted under paragraph (*a*).

(2) Leave under paragraph (*a*) of subsection (1) may be granted or refused at the discretion of the court, and if granted may be granted subject to such conditions as the court thinks proper with respect to the use of any recording made pursuant to the leave; and where leave has been granted the court may at the like discretion withdraw or amend it either generally or in relation to any particular part of the proceedings.

(3) Without prejudice to any other power to deal with an act of contempt under paragraph (*a*) of subsection (1), the court may order the instrument, or any recording made with it, or both, to be forfeited; and any object so forfeited shall (unless the court otherwise determines on application by a person appearing to be the owner) be sold or otherwise disposed of in such manner as the court may direct.

(4) This section does not apply to the making or use of sound recordings for purposes of official transcripts of proceedings.

10. No court may require a person to disclose, nor is any person guilty of contempt of court for refusing to disclose, the source of information contained in a publication for which he is responsible, unless it be established to the satisfaction of the court that disclosure is necessary in the interests of justice or national security or for the prevention of disorder or crime.

11. In any case where a court (having power to do so) allows a name or other matter to be withheld from the public in proceedings before the court, the court may give such directions prohibiting the publication of that name or matter in connection with the proceedings as appear to the court to be necessary for the purpose for which it was so withheld.

. . . . .

13. —(4) In any case where a person is liable to be dealt with for contempt of court during the course of or in connection with Scottish proceedings he may be given legal aid, and the Legal Aid (Scotland) Act 1967 shall have effect subject to the amendments set out in Part II of Schedule 2.

(5) This section is without prejudice to any other enactment by virtue of which legal aid may be granted in or for purposes of civil or criminal proceedings.

PENALTIES FOR CONTEMPT AND KINDRED OFFENCES

. . . . .

15. —(1) In Scottish proceedings, when a person is committed to prison for contempt of court the committal shall (without prejudice to the power of the court to order his earlier discharge) be for a fixed term.

(2) The maximum penalty which may be imposed by way of imprisonment or fine for contempt of court in Scottish proceedings shall be two years' imprisonment or a fine or both, except that—

(*a*) where the contempt is dealt with by the sheriff in the course of or in connection with proceedings other than criminal proceedings on indictment, such penalty shall not exceed three months' imprisonment or a fine of level 4 on the standard scale or both; and

(*b*) where the contempt is dealt with by the district court, such

263

penalty shall not exceed sixty days' imprisonment or a fine of level 3 on the standard scale or both.

(3) Section 207 (restriction on detention of young offenders) and sections 175 to 178 (persons suffering from mental disorder) of the Criminal Procedure (Scotland) Act 1975 shall apply in relation to persons found guilty of contempt of court in Scottish proceedings as they apply in relation to persons convicted of offences, except—

- (a) where subsection (2)(a) above applies, when sections 415 and 376 to 379 of the said Act shall so apply; and
- (b) where subsection (2)(b) above applies, when section 415 of the said Act and subsection (5) below shall apply.

(4) Until the commencement of section 45 of the Criminal Justice (Scotland) Act 1980, in subsection (3) above for the references to section 207 and section 415 of the Criminal Procedure (Scotland) Act 1975 there shall be substituted respectively references to sections 207 and 208 and sections 415 and 416 of that Act.

(5) Where a person is found guilty by a district court of contempt of court and it appears to the court that he may be suffering from mental disorder, it shall remit him to the sheriff in the manner provided by section 286 of the Criminal Procedure (Scotland) Act 1975 and the sheriff shall, on such remit being made, have the like power to make an order under section 376(1) of the said Act in respect of him as if he had been convicted by the sheriff of an offence, or in dealing with him may exercise the like powers as the court making the remit.

. . . . .

SUPPLEMENTAL

. . . . .

19.   In this Act—

"court" includes any tribunal or body exercising the judicial power of the State, and "legal proceedings" shall be construed accordingly;

"publication" has the meaning assigned by subsection (1) of section 2, and "publish" (except in section 9) shall be construed accordingly;

"Scottish proceedings" means proceedings before any court, including the Courts-Martial Appeal Court, the Restrictive Practices Court and the Employment Appeal Tribunal, sitting in Scotland, and includes proceedings before the House of Lords in the exercise of any appellate jurisdiction over proceedings in such a court;

"the strict liability rule" has the meaning assigned by section 1;

"superior court" means the Court of Appeal, the High Court, the Crown Court, the Courts-Martial Appeal Court, the Restrictive Practices Court, the Employment Appeal Tribunal and any other court exercising in relation to its proceedings powers equivalent to those of the High Court, and includes the House of Lords in the exercise of its appellate jurisdiction.

20. —(1) In relation to any tribunal to which the Tribunals of Inquiry (Evidence) Act 1921 applies, and the proceedings of such a tribunal, the provisions of this Act (except subsection (3) of section 9) apply as they apply in relation to courts and legal proceedings; and references to the course of justice or the administration of justice in legal proceedings shall be construed accordingly.

(2) The proceedings of a tribunal established under the said Act shall be treated as active within the meaning of section 2 from the time when the tribunal is appointed until its report is presented to Parliament.

. . . . .

SCHEDULE 1

1. In this Schedule "criminal proceedings" means proceedings against a person in respect of an offence, not being appellate proceedings . . . ; and "appellate proceedings" means proceedings on appeal from or for the review of the decision of a court in any proceedings.

2. Criminal, appellate and other proceedings are active within the meaning of section 2 at the times respectively prescribed by the following paragraphs of this Schedule; and in relation to proceedings in which more than one of the steps described in any of those paragraphs is taken, the reference in that paragraph is a reference to the first of those steps.

CRIMINAL PROCEEDINGS

3. Subject to the following provisions of this Schedule, criminal proceedings are active from the relevant initial step specified in paragraph 4 until concluded as described in paragraph 5.

4. The initial steps of criminal proceedings are—

(*a*) arrest without warrant;

(*b*) the issue, or in Scotland the grant, of a warrant for arrest;

(*c*) the issue of a summons to appear, or in Scotland the grant of a warrant to cite;

(*d*) the service of an indictment or other document specifying the charge;

.   .   .   .   .

5. Criminal proceedings are concluded—

(*a*) by acquittal or, as the case may be, by sentence;

(*b*) by any other verdict, finding, order or decision which puts an end to the proceedings;

(*c*) by discontinuance or by operation of law.

6. The reference in paragraph 5(*a*) to sentence includes any order or decision consequent on conviction or finding of guilt which disposes of the case, either absolutely or subject to future events, and a deferment of sentence under section . . . 219 or 432 of the Criminal Procedure (Scotland) Act 1975 . . .

7. Proceedings are discontinued within the meaning of paragraph 5(*c*)—

.   .   .   .   .

(*b*) in Scotland if the proceedings are expressly abandoned by the prosecutor or are deserted *simpliciter*;

.   .   .   .   .

8. Criminal proceedings before a court-martial or standing civilian court are not concluded until the completion of any review of finding or sentence.

.   .   .   .   .

10. Without prejudice to paragraph 5(*b*) above, criminal proceedings against a person cease to be active—

(*a*) if the accused is found to be under a disability such as to render him unfit to be tried or unfit to plead or, in Scotland, is found to be insane in bar of trial; or

    (*b*) . . . , in Scotland where a transfer order ceases to have effect by virtue of section 73(1) of the Mental Health (Scotland) Act 1984,
but become active again if they are later resumed.

11.   Criminal proceedings against a person which become active on the issue or the grant of a warrant for his arrest cease to be active at the end of the period of twelve months beginning with the date of the warrant unless he has been arrested within that period, but become active again if he is subsequently arrested.

OTHER PROCEEDINGS AT FIRST INSTANCE

12.   Proceedings other than criminal proceedings and appellate proceedings are active from the time when arrangements for the hearing are made or, if no such arrangements are previously made, from the time the hearing begins, until the proceedings are disposed of or discontinued or withdrawn; and for the purposes of this paragraph any motion or application made in or for the purposes of any proceedings, and any pre-trial review in the county court, is to be treated as a distinct proceeding.

. . . . .

14.   In Scotland arrangements for the hearing of proceedings to which paragraph 12 applies are made within the meaning of that paragraph—

    (*a*) in the case of an ordinary action in the Court of Session or in the sheriff court, when the Record is closed;
    (*b*) in the case of a motion or application, when it is enrolled or made;
    (*c*) in any other case, when the date for a hearing is fixed or a hearing is allowed.

APPELLATE PROCEEDINGS

15.   Appellate proceedings are active from the time when they are commenced—

    (*a*) by application for leave to appeal or apply for review, or by notice of such an application;

(*b*) by notice of appeal or of application for review;

(*c*) by other originating process,

until disposed of or abandoned, discontinued or withdrawn.

16.   Where, in appellate proceedings relating to criminal proceedings, the court—

(*a*) remits the case to the court below; or

(*b*) orders a new trial or a *venire de novo*, or in Scotland grants authority to bring a new prosecution,

any further or new proceedings which result shall be treated as active from the conclusion of the appellate proceedings.

GLOSSARY

Ab ante — before, previously

ab initio — from the beginning

absolvitor — decree absolving defender

actus Dei — act of God

ad factum praestandum — obligation to perform an act other than payment of money

adhere — (court) affirm; (spouse) live with

ad hoc — for this purpose

ad interim — in the interval; meantime

Adjournal,Acts of — procedural rules made by High Court

ad litem — as regards the action

adminicle — piece of supporting evidence

ad valorem — according to value

advise — give judgment

advocation — form of criminal appeal usually by prosecution at preliminary stage

a fortiori — all the more

agnate — related through father

alibi — elsewhere (special defence plea)

aliment — maintenance enforceable by law

aliquot — integral factor

aliunde — from a different source

a mensa et thoro — from bed and table (separation)

ante omnia — first of all

apparent insolvency — insolvency which has become public

a posteriori — reasoning from effect to cause

appoint — to order, direct

a priori — reasoning from cause to effect

arbiter — one chosen by parties to settle difference (in England)—arbitrator)

as accords (of law) — in conformity with the law

assize — jury

assoilzie (z silent) — absolve

aver — to state in written pleadings

a verbis legis non est recedendum — the words of a statute must be strictly adhered to

avizandum — to be considered (reserved judgment)

Back letter — document qualifying another which purports to give an absolute right

bairns' part of gear — (see legitim)

barratry — acceptance of bribes by a judge

before answer (allowance of proof) — before the law of the case is determined

269

bill of suspension	form of appeal to Justiciary Appeal Court
bona fide	in good faith
brevi manu	short cut; summarily
brutum fulmen	harmless thunderbolt; vain attack
Calling	first step in civil action
calumny, oath of	formerly oath (in divorce cases) that facts pleaded are believed to be true
Candlemas	February 2, quarter-day
casual homicide	blameless killing
caution (pronounced "cay-shun")	security
caveat	"let him take care"; legal document lodged by party to ensure no order passes against him in his absence
certiorate	give formal notice of a fact
champerty	offence of assisting a party in a suit without having an interest except to share in any pecuniary outcome
circumvention	dishonest taking advantage of a facile person for gain
cite	to summon to court
cognate	related through mother
commit	consign to prison to await further procedure
compear	to appear and participate in an action
compos mentis	of sound mind
conclusion	relief sought in an action
condescendence	statement of averred facts or contentions
conditio si testator sine liberis decesserit	principle by which a will not dealing with children is revoked by birth of a child
consanguinean	relationship between brothers or sisters who have the same father but different mothers
consistorial	relating to questions of status, such as matrimonial proceedings
continue	adjourn (case) to later date
contra bonos mores	in breach of moral law
contumacy	failure to obey court order
courtesy	widower's liferent of his wife's heritage (now obsolete)
crave	formally ask court (as in petition)
curator ad litem	officer appointed by court to assume responsibility for interests of litigant
curator bonis	officer appointed by court to manage a person's estate
cy-près	as near as possible (applied to necessary variation of terms of trust, will, etc.)

Damnum	harm, loss
damnum fatale	loss due to act of God
data	statements acknowledged as true
decern	give formal, final decree
declarator	binding statement of rights of a party issued by court
declinature	refusal of judge to take jurisdiction because of his interest or relationship
de die in diem	from day to day
de facto	in point of fact; actual
deforcement	offence of resisting officer of law to prevent him carrying out his duties
de futuro	in the future
de jure	in point of law; legal (as opposed to actual)
delectus personae	choice of person who is thereby excluded from delegating his duty
delict	a wrong
de minimis (non curat lex)	the law ignores trifles
de novo	of new; afresh
de plano	summarily; simply; without further procedure
de presenti	now
desert	to abandon (diet)
design	to set forth person's occupation and address
dies non	a non-legal day
diet	date fixed for hearing of a case
diligence	execution against a debtor; procedure for recovery of document
disentail	release from entail (q.v.)
dispone	to convey (land)
D-notice	D=defence (see Chapter 30)
dominus litis	person controlling lawsuit who is not actually a party to it
Edictal citation	method of citing persons who are furth of Scotland or sheriffdom
effeir	to correspond, appertain
embracery	attempt to corrupt a jury, or acceptance of bribe by juror
entail	restriction of heritage to prescribed line of heirs (incompetent since 1914)
eo ipso	by the thing itself
ergo	therefore
error calculi	error in calculation
escheat	forfeiture of a person's estate
esto	assuming; let it be assumed
ex adverso	opposite to; adjacent
ex animo	willingly; intentionally

271

excambion	contract for exchange of one piece of land for another
ex concesso	from what has been admitted
executor-dative	executor appointed by court
executor-nominate	executor appointed by testator
ex facie	on the face of it
ex hypothesi	by the hypothesis
ex justa causa	for just cause or sufficient reason
ex officio	by virtue of office
ex parte	in absence of a party; one-sided; partisan
expenses	payment for legal services (in England—costs)
expose	put up for sale
ex post facto	after the event; retrospectively
ex proprio motu	on (the court's) own initiative
ex re	arising in the circumstances
ex tempore	without premeditation
extract	authenticated copy of decree, etc.
Facsimile	exact copy
fee	full right of property (as opposed to liferent, *q.v.*)
fiar	owner of a fee
fiars (prices)	average prices of grain fixed annually to determine ministers' stipends
filiation	determination by court of paternity
force and fear	duress vitiating a contract
force majeure	something beyond the control of man; that cannot be prevented
forisfamiliation	departure of child from family on becoming independent
forum (or fora)	platform; court; tribunal
fugitation	outlawry
fulmen brutum	vain threat
fund in medio	amount under dispute in action of multiplepoinding (*q.v.*)
furtum grave	theft which formerly merited death penalty
furth	outside (*e.g.* the country)
Garnishment	order not to pay creditor(s) before first settling debt to third party holding judgment against his creditors
gift	bequest
glebe	land in parish to which minister has right apart from stipend
grassum	single payment made in addition to periodic one, such as rent
Habeas corpus	writ releasing person from prison (English law)

habile	apt
habit and repute	reputation of being married without formal ceremony, entitling parties to declarator of marriage
hamesucken	assault upon man in his own home
haver	person holding documents he is required to produce in court
heritage	land and buildings passing to an heir on owner's death
holograph	wholly handwritten and signed by the author
homologate	approve and thereby validate
horning	ancient procedure for public denunciation of a debtor
hypothec	security for debt, such as right of landlord over tenant's goods in premises let to him
Impeachment	special defence accusing another of the crime charged (known also as incrimination)
impetrate	procure, to another's prejudice
in camera	behind closed doors
in causa	in the case (of)
incompetent	in conflict with the law applicable
indictment	accusation of a crime made in name of Lord Advocate
induciae	time limit
in extenso	in full
in faciendo	in doing
in favorem	in favour
infeft	having a feudal title to heritage
in forma pauperis	in the character of a pauper
in foro	in court
in futuro	in the future
in gremio	in the body (of a deed etc.)
in hoc statu	at this stage; in the present state of affairs
in initio litis	at the outset of the action
in jure	in right
in limine	at the outset (threshold)
in litem	in the case
in loco parentis	in the place of a parent (e.g. guardian)
in mala fides	in bad faith
Inner House	appellate department of Court of Session comprising First and Second Divisions
in re	in the case of
in rem suam	in one's own affairs
in rem versum	to one's own account
in retentis	kept for the record
in solidum	for the whole sum

instruct	to vouch or support
inter alia	among other things
inter alios	among other persons
interdict	judicial prohibition (in England—injunction)
interlocutor	formal minute of court decision
interpone authority to joint minute	give court's approval to agreement between parties
interrogatories	written questions put to witness excused from attending court
in toto	totally
inter vivos	between living persons (with reference to deeds)
intromit	to handle, deal with, funds, property, etc.
ipse dixit	bare assertion
ipso facto	by the fact itself
ipso jure	by the force of law alone
irritancy	forfeiture of a right due to neglect or contravention (*e.g.* lease)
irrelevant	even if proved, would not justify remedy sought
ish	termination, usually of lease
Judicial factor	person appointed by court to manage affairs of another
jus mariti	right of husband to part of wife's moveable property (now abolished)
jus quaesitum tertio	contractual right of a person arising out of a contract between two others to which he is not a party
jus relictae	widow's right to share of husband's moveable property
jus relicti	widower's right to share of wife's moveable property
jus tertii	right of a third party
Justiciar	ancient term for Lord Justice-General
justifiable homicide	killing in exercise of public duty
justo tempore	in due time
Lammas	August 1, quarter-day
lawburrows	ancient process for security against apprehended molestation
legitim	children's right to share of parent's moveable property at death
legitimation per subsequens matrimonium	rendering child legitimate by subsequent marriage of parents
lenocinium	procuring by husband of his wife's adultery

274

lesion	detriment, loss, injury
lex loci contractus	law of the place where contract was made
lex patriae	law of one's own country
lien	right to retain property of a debtor until he pays
liferent	right entitling a person for life to use of another's property
light	property owner's obligation not to obstruct neighbour's light
liquid (sum)	of ascertained amount
List D	category of school which replaced "special" school
loco parentis, in	in the place of a parent (*e.g.* guardian)
locus	place
locus standi	right to be heard in court
Mala fides	bad faith
mala in se	bad in itself
Martinmas	November 11 or 28, quarter-day
medio tempore	in the meantime
medium concludendi	ground of action
medium filum	centre line of river
minor	person aged between 12 and 18 if female, and 14 and 18 if male
minute	document by which party defines his position to the court
misfeasance	doing of an act in an unlawful manner
missives	writings exchanged by parties negotiating for a contract
modus	mode, manner
Moorov doctrine	the principle that, where an accused is charged with a series of similar offences closely linked in time and circumstances, the evidence of one witness as to each offence will be taken as mutually corroborative
mora	delay in making claim
mortis causa	to take effect after death
muirburn	seasonal burning of heather
multiplepoinding	action raised nominally by one party but in which a number of conflicting claims are made to a fund in medio
murmur (a judge)	to slander him
Necessitas juris	by necessity of law
nemo	no one
next-of-kin	relatives entitled to succeed to moveable property under common law
nihil novit	he knows nothing

275

nobile officium	equitable jurisdiction of High Court of Justiciary or Inner House of Court of Session by which strictness of common law may be mitigated, or a remedy given where not otherwise available
nolle prosequi	decision by prosecutor to stop proceedings
nomine damni	in name of damages
nominal raiser	holder of fund in a multiplepoinding when another initiates proceedings
nonage	minority and pupillarity (under 18)
non compos mentis	not of sound mind
non constat	it is not evident, not agreed
nonfeasance	omission to do a legal duty
notour bankruptcy	insolvency which has become public, a prerequisite in most cases of sequestration now, apparent insolvency
Obiter dictum	judge's expression of an opinion not forming part of court's decision
obtemper	obey (court order)
onerous	granted for value
onus	burden (*e.g.* of proving case)
oppression	use of office or process of law to commit injustice
Outer House	department of Court of Session exercising jurisdiction of first instance
outputter	one who passes counterfeit coins
Pactum illicitum	unlawful contract
panel, pannel	prisoner at bar
paraphernalia	woman's clothes and adornments which remained her own on marriage (obsolete)
pari passu	share and share alike; side by side
parole (evidence)	oral (term borrowed from England)
particeps criminis	accomplice
patrimonial	pertaining to property; pecuniary
party-minuter	party entering proceedings by lodging a minute
penal action	one in which not only damages are sought, but also a sum as penalty
per capita	divided equally among persons
per incuriam	by mistake
per se	of itself; by himself
per stirpes	division among children of the shares that would have been their parents' (as opposed to per capita)
plagium	child-stealing
poind (pronounced "pind")	to take debtor's moveable property by way of execution

276

praepositura	wife's implied agency to purchase household supplies on husband's credit (obsolete)
precognition	statement from witness of evidence he is prepared to give
prescription	restriction of a right owing to passage of a specific period of time
prima facie	at first sight
primo loco	in the first place
probable cause	case satisfactory on the face of it
probative document	one which by its nature appears to afford proof of its contents
process	documentary course of an action from first step to final judgment
pro confesso	as if conceded
pro forma	as a mere formality
pro hac vice	for this occasion
pro indiviso	undivided
pro loco et tempore	for the place and time
proof	hearing of evidence by a judge
pro rata	proportionately
prorogate	extend time allowed; or submit to court's jurisdiction
pro tanto	to that extent
pro tempore	for the time being
protestation	procedure whereby defender compels pursuer to proceed with his case or end it
prout de jure	by all the means known to the law
pro veritate	as if true
punctum temporis	point of time
pupillarity	state of being child up to age of 12 (girl), 14 (boy)
Quantum lucratus	as much as he has profited
quantum meruit	as much as he has earned; what is due
quantum valeat	for what it is worth
Queen's and Lord Treasurer's Remembrancer	administrator of Crown revenues in Scotland
quid pro quo	exchange of equivalents
quoad ultra	otherwise; with regard to other matters
Rank	to admit a claimant to his rightful place (*e.g.* in multiplepoinding)
ratio decidendi	line of reasoning; basis of judgment
real raiser	party who, holding fund in medio, initiates action of multiplepoinding
reclaim	to appeal to Inner House of Court of Session against Outer House judgment

record	statement by parties to an action of their claims and answers; document containing these
reduce	annul; rescind; set aside (by action of reduction)
regalia majora	Crown rights, *e.g.* to hold seashore in trust for public (inalienable)
regalia minora	Crown rights, such as salmon fishing, which may be subject of grant
rei interventus	rule barring a party, who knowingly permits another to depart from form, to challenge the resulting contract
relevant	applied to case where, if facts stated are proved, pursuer would be entitled to remedy he seeks
relocation	re-letting
repel	reject (a plea or objection)
repone	to restore a party as a litigant
res gestae	things done
res judicata	matter already judicially decided
res noviter	information newly discovered
res publicae	things owned by the state
resting-owing	unpaid (debt)
respondentia	money lent on ship's cargo subject to certain conditions
review	revision by appeal court
rider	addition by jury to its verdict; claim lodged in multiplepoinding
rolls	list of cases to be heard in court
roup	auction
rubric	head-note; summary given at head of law report
Saevitia	legal cruelty (obsolete)
sanctuary	protection against claims once enjoyed by debtor (*e.g.* by taking refuge in Holyrood Abbey)
sasine	a putting into possession of land
scienter	knowledge of animal's dangerous tendency
Sederunt, Acts of	procedural rules made by Court of Session
separatim	separately
sequestrate	render bankrupt (strictly it is the estate which is sequestrated)
seriatim	singly, in regular order
serve	to deliver (a court document)
servitude	burden or obligation on a piece of land
simpliciter	simply, absolutely, without qualification
sine die	without a date being fixed

sine qua non	indispensable condition
Single Bill	motion in the Inner House of the Court of Session
singular successor	person obtaining property otherwise than as heir
sist	to stay or stop a process; to summon or call a party
sleep	a civil action may fall asleep after a year without any step of procedure being taken; it may be revived by a minute of wakening
socius criminis	accomplice in a crime
solatium	damages for injured feelings, grief, pain
solum	ground, foundation, bed of river
special case	method of obtaining legal opinion of Inner House of Court of Session where facts are agreed
spei emptio	purchase of a chance (*e.g.* succession)
spes successionis	hope of succession (as heir apparent)
status	standing, rank
status quo	existing situation
subjects	property, usually heritable
subpoena	under penalty
sui generis	of its own kind
summons	court writ bearing royal mandate; document served on defender by which pursuer initiates civil action
superior	grantor of a feu
supersede	postpone
superinduction	unwarranted alteration of a deed
supra	above
suspension	stay of diligence
Tacit relocation	implied re-letting
taciturnity	keeping silent about a debt leading to inference of payment
tailzie (z silent)	entail (*q.v.*)
teind	tithe, tenth part of annual produce of land
tender	offer in settlement made by defender to pursuer
tenor, proving the	establishing the effect of a document (*e.g.* will) the principal copy of which has been lost
terce	widow's liferent of one-third of husband's heritage (abolished)
thole an assize	undergo trial, after which no further trial on same charge may take place
tinsel of feu	forfeiture for non-payment of feu duty

title to sue	legal right to bring an action
tocher	dowry
trespass	temporary intrusion on land without owner's consent or permission
trial	hearing of a case before a jury
Truck Acts	legislation limiting payment of wages in kind (now repealed)
tutor	guardian of pupil child
Ultimus haeres	last heir (the Crown), to whom estate falls when all other claims fail
ultra valorem	beyond the value
ultra vires	beyond (one's legal) powers
unum quid	one thing; single unit
upset price	price at which property is exposed for sale by auction
uterine	born of same mother but different father
utter	to put false writing or currency into circulation
Veritas	truth (defence to action of slander)
vice versa	conversely
vis et metus	force and fear (*q.v.*)
viva voce	orally
volenti non fit injuria	no injustice is done to a party by an act to which he consents (defence to action for damages)
Wakening	step taken to revive action which has gone to sleep (*q.v.*)
warrandice	guarantee of a right contained in a deed, usually disponing heritage
white-bonnet	one who bids at auction to enhance price
Whitsunday	May 15 or 28, quarter day
writ	a writing possessing legal significance
writer	old name for solicitor

ABBREVIATIONS

The following abbreviations are among those most frequently found in the Court of Session rolls:

AG	Against (between names of parties in Calling List)
Alit	Aliment
(a.p.)	Assisted person (under the Legal Aid Scheme)
C.B.	Curator bonis
C.R.& P.	Count, reckoning and payment
cy-pres	"As near as possible" (see Glossary)
Decl. of Null.	Declarator of nullity
Diss.of Marr.	Dissolution of marriage
Eosd.(eosdem); eund.(eundem)	"Same as in case above" (with reference to names of counsel)
I.P.D.	*In praesenti Dominorum* (in their Lordships' presence)
J.F.	Judicial factor
Min.	Minute
MP	Multiplepoinding (see Glossary)
N.P.	Notary-public
p(per)	"Represented by" (with reference to counsel after name of party)
Pet.	Petition
R.M.	Reclaiming motion (see Glossary)
Sep. & Alit	Separation and aliment
S.& I.	Suspension and interdict
S.M.&A.	Summons, minute and answers
Trs.	Trustees
* (asterisk)	Preceding name of case in the motion roll, indicates counsel will appear (the absence of an asterisk indicates there will be no appearance).

INDEX

(Numbers refer to paragraphs)

283

Representation of the People Act
1983, 615
Restrictive Practices Court, 154–156
Richardson v. *Wilson*, 253, 289–292,
400–401
rixa, 640
Roman law, 1
Royal Commission, 192–193
Royle v. *Grey*, 462

Safeguarder, 566
Scottish Land Court, 161
Scottish Law Commission, 2, 604
search, police powers of, 58
Second Division, 115
separation, 522
sheriff, fitness for office, 217–218
sheriff court,
civil, 110–112
criminal, 40–42, 605
divorce, 519, 524
jurisdiction, 30–31, 41, 110–112
shipping inquiries, 197–200
slander, 616
Smith v. *Ritchie*, 460
Social Work (Scotland) Act 1968,
561–565
society, loss of, 587
solatium, 581, 587
solemn jurisdiction, 30–31, 51, 62
et seq.
solemn procedure, 62 *et seq.*, 78, 349
Solicitor-General, 45, 49, 607
solicitors, 20 *et seq.*, 213–215
solvent abuse, 37
sources, journalists', 360–365, 378,
395, 431 *et seq.*
sources of law, 5 *et seq.*
"special cases", 239–240
special defences, 63
spent convictions, 792 *et seq.*
sporting events, violence, 77
spot-the-ball advertisements, 826
Spycatcher case, 864–869
Standing Civilian Courts, 177

"starred motions", 343
stated case, 79–80
Stirling v. *Assoc. Newspapers*, 376,
472
strict liability, 382
Stuurman case, 448–452
summary,
causes, 112
jurisdiction, 30, 51
procedure, 53 *et seq.*, 78
trial, 246–248
summons, 120–121, 254, 287 *et seq.*,
399–401
supersede extract, 347
Supreme Court of Judicature, 143
synod, 165
Sweeney case, 488–492
Sweet v. *Parsley*, 248

Tape recorders, 366, 428–430
television, 369, 549, 809, 859–863
tenor, proving the, 110
thalidomide, 286, 420–422
tip-off, 273, 280
trade descriptions, 833
Traffic Commissioners, 183
Transport Tribunal, 183–184
treason, 91
Treaty of Accession, 146
trespass, 784–786
trial procedure, 54
tribunals, 178 *et seq.*, 379, 395,
441–442
tribunals of inquiry, 187 *et seq.*
trust disposition, 269
trust variation, 591–593

Undefended divorce, 518 *et seq.*
unintentional defamation, 668–676
untrue report, contempt, 423

Vacation court, 245
Valuation Appeal Court, 153
vandalism, 74
variation of trust, 591–593

290